Manufacture of Snacks Food, Namkeen, Pappad & Potato Products

With Directory of Present Manufacturers, Manufacturers/Suppliers of Plant & Machineries and Raw Material Suppliers

Manufacture of Snacks Food, Namkeen, Pappad & Potato Products

With Directory of Present Manufacturers, Manufacturers/Suppliers of Plant & Machineries and Raw Material Suppliers

Written By

EIRI BOARD OF CONSULTANTS & ENGINEERS

ENGINEERS INDIA RESEARCH INSTITUTE

4444449, Nai Sarak, Main Road, Delhi - 110006 (India)
Ph: +91-11-23918117, 23916431, 45120361, 23947058
* E-Mail: eiritechnology@gmail.com & eiriprojects@gmail.com
*Website: www.eiriindia.org & www.industrialprojects.in

PRINTED & PUBLISHED BY

ENGINEERS INDIA RESEARCH INSTITUTE

4449, Nai Sarak, Main Road, Delhi - 110006 (India)
Ph: +91-11-23918117, 23916431, 45120361, 23947058
* E-Mail: eiritechnology@gmail.com & eiriprojects@gmail.com
*Website: www.eiriindia.org & www.industrialprojects.in

Distributors:

EIRI PROJECT CONSULTANTS AND PUBLISHERS
4/54 Roop Nagar, Delhi-110007
and
Industrial Technologies, India
Nai Sarak, Delhi-110006

Revised & Enlarged Edition

ISBN: 9788186732373

Printed in New Delhi (INDIA)

₹ 900/- or US$ 100

Printed & Published by Sudhir Gupta for
"Engineers India Research Institute", 4449 Nai Sarak, Main Road,
New Delhi -110006

Preface

The book '**Manufacture of Snack Food, Namkeen, Pappad & Potato Products**' covers almost all the basic and advanced details to setup own unit of Snack Food, Namkeen Plant, Potato Chips Plant, Sweets Plant, Pappad Plant & Other related various products. The Chapters covering in this book are Extruded Snacks, Potato Based Textured Snacks, Health Food Snacks, Snack Food Preservation & Packaging, Details of Plant, Machinery & Equipments for Snacks Food, Instant Noodles, Namkeen Industry, Namkeen & Sweets, Processed Products from Potato, Pappad & Barian Plant, Potato Chips/Waffers (Both Indian & Imported), Ready to Eat Processed Cooked Food, Ready to Eat Moong Halwa, Panjeeri etc., Rice Puff, Rice Flakes, Corn Flakes, & Wheat Flakes, Snack Food, Packaging of Snack Food, Cereal & Legume Based Foods - Raw Material, Preparation, Packaging etc.

Apart from the above chapters the other most important chapters viz: Present Manufacturers/Suppliers of Machinery & Raw Materials for Snacks Food, Pappad, Namkeen, Potato Chips etc. have also been included for the benefit of new entrants.

The book has been written for the benefit and to prove an asset and a handy reference guide in the hands of new entrepreneurs & well established industrialists.

Director

EIRI Board of Consultants & Engineers

4449, Nai Sarak, Main Road, Delhi - 110006 (India)

E-Mail: eiritechnology@gmail.com & eiriprojects@gmail.com

Website: www.eiriindia.org & www.industrialprojects.in

CONTENTS AND SUBJECT INDEX

CHAPTERS PAGE NO.

1

EXTRUDED SNACKS

Consumers today are demanding an ever broadening selection of snack foods. Extrusion has provided a means of manufacturing new and novel products and has revolutionized many conventional snack manufacturing processes. Extrusion equipment offers many basic design advantages that result in minimizing time, energy, and cost while at the same time introducing a degree of versatility and flexibility that was not previously available.

Many common snack foods such as fried or baked collettes (corncurls) are corn based and produced on rather simple single-screw high pressure extrusion cookers. Others snack products (for, example half products or third & generation products) may require more sophisticated twin screw extrusion equipment.

Snack producers today are faced with an increasing number of extrusion equipment styles and suppliers. In one respect this will complicate the snack producers choice of equipment but on the other hand will lead to a wider use of extrusion and increased availability in terms of lower cost.

The influx of the so-called "new technology" twin screw extruder in recent years will require the snack food manufacturer to acquire a better understanding of the mechanism of single and twin-screw extruders. This will increase ones ability to apply and use each of the processes for the applications in which they perform most efficiently. No individual extruder type whether single-or twin-screw, will be compatible with all specific processes and/or raw materials.

TERMINOLOGY

Food or snack extruders are generally divided into two major categories (1) single screw and (2) twin screw. Single screw extruders may be divided into four subcategories low shear forming, low shear cooking, medium shear cooking and high-shear cooking. Twin screw-extruders may be divided into several subcategories co-rotating intermeshing; co-rotating non-intermeshing counter-rotating intermeshing counter-rotating non-intermeshing and conical intermeshing. In the past, the most popular and successful extruders in the snack food production plant have been the single screw extruders; and there are many applications today where these extruders are ideal from an economic point of view. However, in recent years the twin screw extruder has begun to challenge the dominance of the single screw extruder for snack food production.

The food extruder must exercise a number of functions in a short time under controlled, continuous or steady state operating conditions. These functions may include heating cooling, conveying, feeding, compressing, reacting, mixing, melting, cooking, texturing and shaping.

Energy sources to provide heat for cooking texturing or melting may include.

Conversion: Mechanical energy is dissipated into the extruder in the form of heat caused by shearing or friction generated by pumping or conveying inefficiencies. For high shear extruders it is possible that 100% of the heat may be generated through shear. This type is referred to as an adiabatic extruder.

Conduction: Heat is transferred through the barrel of the extruder from a thermal fluid or other external source.

Convection: Heat is transferred to the extrudate by direct contact such as steam injection.

Each energy source has its advantages and disadvantages. In most cases, a combination of the three will be most practical.

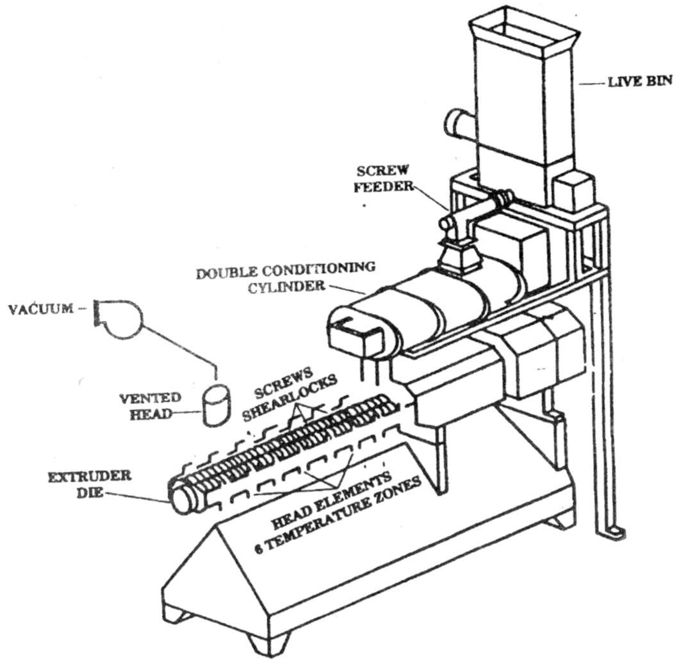

Figure 6-1 Cutaway view of twin-screw extruder.

There are several basic components having specific functions common to all extrusion systems (Fig.6.1).

1. A holding bin for mixed raw material capable of discharging raw premixed dry ingredients continuously and uniformly

2. A variable speed metering/feeding device to feed the raw dry mixed ingredients uniformly and in an uninterrupted manner at the desired flow rate.

3. A preconditioner in which liquids and/or steam, and/or other vapors may be uniformly combined with the premetered dry (or pretempered) ingredient mix

4. An extruder assembly whose configuration of barrel segments, screws and shearlocks has been preselected to properly feed, knead and cook the dry or premoistened process material

5. A final die to restrict the extruder discharge and to shape the final product.

6. A cutting device to cut the extruded profile to the desired length

EXTRUSION PROCESS

The most important criterion for extruding a wide range of raw materials to produce a wide range of finished products is the selection of a proper extruder configuration. The term extruder configuration is subdivided into three distinct categories; (1) the feeding and preconditioning configuration; (2) the screw and barrel profile of the extruder; and (3) the die configuration.

Preconditioning Configuration

Preconditioning may be defined as a prerequisite processing step of putting a substance into the proper or desired condition. Preconditioning is a very important part of the extrusion process. Mixing, hydration, cooking, pH modifications and addition of vapors, flavors, lipids, colors, etc. may all take place in a properly designed preconditioning process. The single most important aspect of the preconditioning system is the added mixing and retention time, which is imperative for all reactions, chemical or physical.

There are basically two types of continuous preconditioners available :

Pressurized conditioning chambers normally provide approximately 1-3 minutes residence time at temperatures up to 240°F (115°C). Research indicates that pressurized preconditioners have a negative effect on the nutritional quality of food and feed products. Their design and operation are more complex than those of atmospheric preconditioners.

Atmospheric conditioning chambers provide from 20 to 240 seconds retention during which time a product formulation is preheated and the moisture is allowed to penetrate the individual particles. Preconditioning is known to enhance flavour development and to aid in the final product texture. This has been most evident in the production of cereal and snack products, especially corn and oat based products. Oats, for example, have a bitter aftertaste that may be removed by preconditioning.

In addition to flavor development, preconditioning reduces extruder component wear, refines cell structure and permits increased throughput of the extruder.

The method of water addition is an important part of preconditioning a product formulation. The residence time of the raw material in the conditioning cylinder after water injection along with steam injection permits the moisture to penetrate the grain particles equally throughout each particle. This equilibration of moisture assures a more uniformly cooked and textured final product.

The conditioning cylinders typically used in the extrusion cooking processes may be equipped with either a single, dual agitators, or dual agitators with differential speed. Single-agitator mixing cylinders are used in extrusion applications of low to moderate capacity where steam and water are mixed and continuously blended with the dry raw material substrate.

Dual agitator/differential speed preconditioners provide the longest controlled residence time and therefore the best and most thorough blending of moisture into dry raw materials. This preconditioning usually pays for itself quickly through improved flavor, increased production capacity of the final product and reduced extruder component wear.

Before purchasing an extrusion system, careful consideration should be given to the effect preconditioning will have on the final product and how these changes or improvements will influence the product sales potential.

Extruder Configuration

The barrel of the extruder is made up of screws, heads,

and flow restrictors or shearlocks (Fig. 6.2). Typically a number of different segmented screw designs and configurations may be placed on an extruder shaft. Each screw is designed to perform a specific function. Some screws must convey raw material and/or preconditioned material into the extruder barrel while other screw elements must compress and degas the extrudate. Other screw elements must create backflow and shear or perform other tasks. Where kneading is required, kneading screws may have one or multiple flights. Some kneading screws may be cut flighted or have interrupted flighting in order to add turbulence increase backflow or increase mechanical energy dissipation into the extrudate. The cut flighted screw elements reduce conveying efficintly & thus add residence time to the products being conveyed through the barrel of the extruder. The screws may also various pitches to control (usually to increase) residence time within the extruder processing chamber without changing the free volume of the screw. The final cooking screws may be conical. These conical final screw elements cause a rapid pressure increase a uniform pressure distribution around the screw periphery and dampening of any pulsations that may be present in the final section of the extruder.

Screws are not the only component that effect shear energy input or mechanical energy dissipation within the barrel of the extruder. Heads or the barrel segments that surround the screws have a profound effect as well. The barrel segments may be ribbed to increase the function of each specific extruder segment. For example the ribbing may be used to increase the volume in the inlet of the extruder barrel for achieving higher throughputs.

Special attention should be give to the use of conical sections at the discharge of an extruder barrel. In a twin screw extruder conical end sections separate the product flow channel into two isolated flow channels flexibility and also minimizes screw and barrel wear which is problematic and costly in most twin screw systems. Wear is minimized because the two isolated conical flow channels distribute

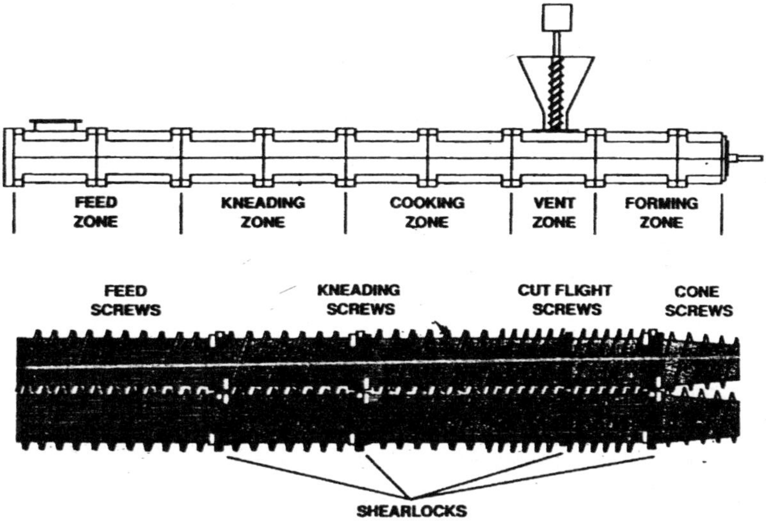

Figure 6-2 Extruder components.

the product uniformly around the periphery of each extruder shaft. This uniform product distribution centers each shaft or screw within its respective flow channel much like the function of an internal bearing.

Both single screw and corotating twin screw extruders may be subdivided into processing zones the feeding zone the kneading zone and the final cooking zone (Fig. 6.3).

The feeding zone of the extruder is that area where the low density discrete particles of raw materials are introduced into the extruder barrel inlet. This low density often preconditioned material is then transported into the interior of the extrusion processing chamber. The flow channel of the screw is typically filled with low density material in this zone. The density is low because of the air entrapped in the incoming material and because of the granular nature of the material, The incoming materials compressed slightly in this zone, with the air being expelled. Water is typically injacted the extruder barrel to facilitate textural development and viscosity development, and to enhance conductive heat transfer.

The kneading zone, of the cooking extruder continues the compression started in the feeding zone and the flow channels of the extruder achieve Within this zone of the extruder barrel the extrudate begins of lose some of its granular definition, extrudate density begins to increase, and pressure begins to develop in the extruder barrel. The mechanism of shear begins to play a dominant role in the kneading zone because of the barrel fill condition that exists here.

Within the kneading zone of the extruder barrel the discrete particles of material begin to agglomerate because of the increasing temperature resulting from conduction, direct steam injection, and viscous energy dissipation. The extruder begins to form a more integral flowing doughlike mass and as it moves through the kneading zone will typically reach its maximum compaction.

The final cooking zone of the extruder barrel is that area where homogeneity is achieved and texturizing occurs. Temperature and pressure typically increase rapidly. In this region shear rates are highest because of the extruder

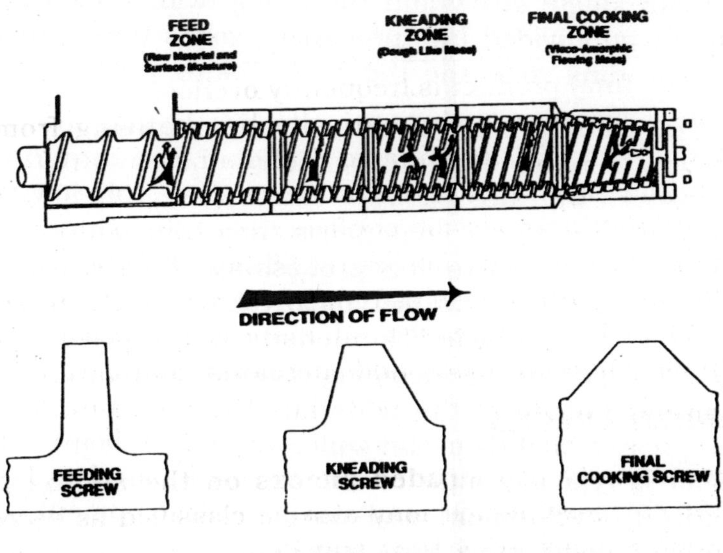

Figure 6-3 Extruder configuration design.

screw configuration and maximum compression of the extrudate. The pressure, temperature, and resulting fluid viscosity are such that the extrudate will be expelled from the extruder die to yield the desired final product texture, density, colour and functional properties.

The single screw extruder has some definite process limitations in the food processing industry. The most obvious limitation centers around the inability of the single screw extruder to transport sticky and/or gummy raw materials. From a process application and quality control point of view the single screw extruder may sometimes be limited in its ability to maintain process stability. Process instability on the single screw extruder generally manifests itself in product inconsistency i.e. nonsteady state flow at the extruder die.

In special cases venting and forming zones may be added downstream of the cooking zone (Fig. 6.2). These zones are normally used for moisture removal applications or forming of high bulk density products.

Die Configuration

Die design and its effect on functional properties and quality of a final product is frequently overlooked. Die shear rates may be altered dramatically by changing from a single die with one opening to a triple or quadruple die with multiple openings and flow channels (Fig. 6.4). When changing from a single die configuration to a multiple die configuration the degree of barrel fill is also increased. In general, dies with high shear rates cause starch, bearing products to have increased stickiness, increased water absorption characteristics and increased solubility.

EXPANDED SNACKS

The majority of extruded snacks on the market fall into this category, which may also be classified as second generation snacks. Expanded snacks may take on various marketing styles including: high fiber, lowcalorie high protein nutritional etc. They are usually "light" having low

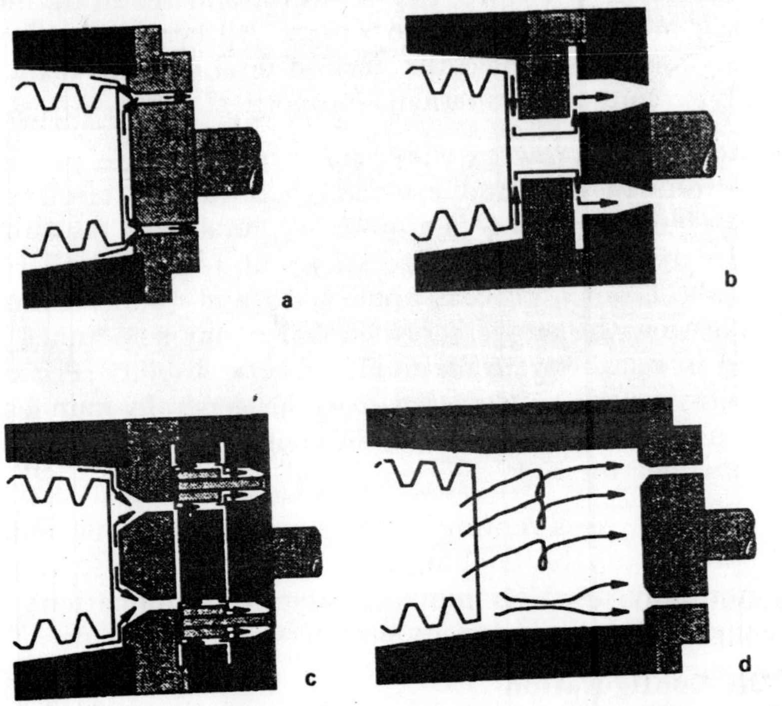

Figure 6-4 Die types: (a) single die; (b) double die; (c) triple die; (d) single die with spacer.

bulk density and are seasoned with an array of flavors, oils and salt (Fig. 6.5).

Fried Collettes

One of the most familiar expanded snacks is the so called fried collettes produced from corn meal or grits and normally coated with cheese powders and flavors.

Product Description Corn meal with a properly quantified and equilibrated moisture content is fed into an extruder. The pressure and heat generated inside. The extruder vaporizes the moisture in the corn meal. As this heated mixture is forced between two brass rotating heads the pressure of the steam vapor is released very rapidly

Figure 6-5 Typical finished expansion-extruded snacks.

causing a "popping" or "puffing" of the corn meal. This leaves a rough cylinder shaped product known as a collette. The extruded collettes are then sifted, fried in vegetable oil, and coated with a mixture of vegetable oil, cheese and salt.

Process Description A variety of equipment is used in the manufacture of fried cheese puffs. A brief description of the major pieces follows.

1. The blender moisturizes corn meal through use of a vertical auger moving the meal from bottom to top of the mixing tank with water being added in measured amounts.

2. Bucket elevators are used to transfer moisturized corn meal from the blender to the extruder holding hopper.

3. The extruder consists primarily of a screw and a set of heads called rotors and stators through which the corn meal is forced. As the corn meal passes through the extruder it is compressed. The work performed on the corn meal during the extrusion is transferred into heat. This pressure and heat causes the corn meal to become a very viscous and substantially homogeneous mass. As this material passes through the heads the superheated moisture instantaneously vaporizes, causing the "popping" or "puffing" of the corn meal.

4. A perforated tumbler that is designed to remove most small pieces and unpopped meal from the good collettes before frying.

5. The fryer is designed to remove moisture and introduce oil into the collettes, both direct, fired and heat exchanger type fryers work well. Because of the short residence time of the product in the fryer, proper sizing is critical to achieve correct oil turnover rates.

6. The coating tumbler is designed for a uniform and positive flow of product down the length of the unit. Longitudinal flights turn the bed of collettes over while liquid cheese slurry is dispensed inside the tumbler at the infeed end.

7. The cheese mix system consists of constant, temperature, hot, water, jacketed kettles equipped with mixers and recirculating pumps where cheese, oil, and salt are homogeneously mixed together. The temperature of the cheese, oil mix is held to 120 130°F (49-55°C) and must never exceed 145°F(63°C).

Formulation : Corn meal is the primary ingredient for

TABLE 6-1. TYPICAL CORN MEAL SPECIFICATIONS FOR FRIED COLLETTES

Granulation (mesh)	Percent retained on screen
16	0
20	0 – 2
25	0 – 10
30	25 – 50
40	45 – 65
50	0 – 8
60	0 – 2
Moisture	11 – 13
Fat	<1

this type of product. Typical corn meal specifications used are shown in Table 6.1.

Final Product Specifications	4.0-6.5 lb/ft^3
Bulk density (before frying)	(80-104 g/litre)
Moisture (finished product)	1.0-2.0%
Salt	1.8-2.8%
Oil (finished product)	32-38%
Cheese	5.0-6.5%

Baked Collettes or Shapes

Product Description : The other most popular example of expanded, extruded snacks is the baked collette (corn curl). There are spin, offs of the expanded snack concept utilizing other cereal grain flours, tuber flours, fibers, and proteins. Potato is commonly added to corn or rice to make potato flavored snacks. Snacks containing high levels of potato flour or granules (greater than 65%) are better suited for the twin, screw extruder because of the sensitivity of potatoes to heat. The bland flavor of rice makes it desirable for preserving more expensive flavor attributes.

Fiber, cellulose, bran and fruit-derived pectins may be blended with cereal grain or protein bleads to make healthy nutritional snacks. Fiber and proteins may each be added at 20% levels to expanded snack formulation with little effect on flavor and expansion. Higher levels may be added when more soluble fibers and proteins are utilized. Low levels of low molecular weight starches will also counter the effects of fiber and protein additions. Extrusion reacted fiber or bran yield softer textured snacks when high levels of fiber are desired.

Process Description : Properly selected ingredients are fed into an extruder at a constant rate. The ingredients are exposed to moisture, heat and pressure as they are transported through the extruder into the extruder die. As the material exits the extruder die it expands owing to pressure release and is sized to the proper length with a rotating knife to produce a collette, ball shape or multiple shape depending on the shape of the extruder die. These colettes or shapes are then dried or baked and coated with oils, flavors and/or seasoning.

There are many extruders on the market today that are capable of making good, quality expanded snacks. Single screw extruders can do an excellent job and have been well proven in this market. The twin, screw extruders, however offer some advantages in flexibility of raw ingredients and process control, but their basic functions are the same.

The extruder includes a feeder for providing a means of getting a uniform flow of material into the extrusion process. Any instability or nonuniformity in the feed flow will affect the rest of the process. For a raw ingredient such as corn meal, small vibratory feeding systems are the most commonly used.

Extruders for second generation snack products are normally short in length (less then 10:1 length:diameter (L/D) ratio). Typical processing conditions are.

Extruder	300-400 rpm
Extruder barrel temperature	250-320°F (120-160°C)
Extruder barrel pressure	70-150 atm.
Dry ingredient feed rate	205 lb/hr (450 kg/hr)
Moisture added into the extruder	5.9 lb/hr (13 kg/hr)
Moisture of extruded product	8-10% MCWB
Bulk density of extruded product	3.0-4.0 lb/ft^3 (48-64 g/litre)

It is important that the proper extruder configuration, consisting of screws, steamlocks and barrel segments be selected to properly feed, knead and cook the process material as it passes through the extruder.

The die configuration used to produce corn snack products is a critical part of the extrusion process. Single, double and even triple die plates may be used to alter or change the final product texture and mouthfuls. The speed of the rotating knife assembly regulates the length of the final product.

Moisture of the extruded product is normally between

8 and 10% moisture content on a wet basis and it requires additional drying to produce the desired product crispness. Temperatures of 300°F (150°C) and retention times of 4-6 minutes are used to lower the moisture of these products to 1-2% moisture.

Before coating the extruded products with flavors, the fines that have been produced during the conveying and drying must be separated. The fines tend to absorb the flavor and oil coatings, causing agglomerations of fines and flavors into forms that are undesirable.

The most popular flavoring for extruded corn, based snack products is cheddar cheese. Two methods of application are most common. When using the dry flovour application method, the extruded product is first sprayed with vegetable oil and then dusted with a variety of dry flavors and/or seasonings. Alternatively, the oils flavors and spices may be mixed together in a tank and applied to the extruded product as it is tumbled in a flavor application reel.

Formulations

Some typical formulations are listed in Table 6.2

The particle size of corn meal or the cereal grains used may actually influence the texture and mouthful of the final snack product. Degermed corn meal most commonly used in extrusion systems today would have particle size analysis and specifications as listed in Table 6.3

Many other grades or granulations of degermed corn meal are available. If a finer texture or cell structure or softer bite for a snack are desired, a snack producer may wish to use raw materials having particle size as listed in Table 6.4.

On the other hand, some consumers prefer extruded snacks that exhibit a more crunchy texture with a slightly larger cell structure. For this type of texture, a coarser granulation of degermed corn grits is desired (Table 6.5).

Premoistering of coarse granulation ingredients may be required to eliminate grittiness in the final product.

A larger amount of flour or fines in coarse meals is undesirable for extrusion, especially when using a single-screw extruder. Flour tends to segregate in the feeding system and in the inlet portion of the extruder barrel. When water is added in the extruder barrel, the flour will absorb the water quickly leaving less moisture available for the coarser particles.

TABLE 6.2. TYPICAL SECOND GENERATION SNACK FORMULAES

	Percent
High protein snack	
Rice flour	35
Wheat flour	35
Soy concentrate	20
Sugar	6
Cornstarch	2
Vegetable oil	2
Potato stick snack	
Potato granules	64
Degermed corn meal	35
Vegetable oil	1
Corn curls	
Degermed corn meal or grits	100

TABLE 6.3. SPECIFICATIONS FOR MOST COMMONLY USED DEGERMED YELLOW CORN MEAL

Analysis performed	Typical analysis (%)	Analysis range (%)	
		Minimum	Maximum
Moisture	12.0	11.0	13.0
Protein	7.0	6.0	8.0
Oil	0.7	0.5	1.0
Fiber	0.5	0.4	0.6
Ash	0.4	0.3	0.5

Nitrogen free extract (%)	79.4		
Bulk density loose (lb/ft^3)	39.0		
Percentage granulation sieve			
On 16	0	0	0.1
On 20	0.3	0	2
On 25	8.7	4	18
On 30	43	30	50
On 40	45	35	55
On 50	2	0	8
Thru 50	1	0	2

TABLE 6.4. SPECIFICATIONS FOR SOFTER TEXTURE DEGERMED YELLOW CORN MEAL

Analysis performed	Typical analysis (%)	Analysis range (%) Minimum	Maximum
Moisture	11.0	10.0	12.0
Protein	8.0	7.5	9.0
Oil	0.6	0.3	0.9
Fiber	0.4	0.3	0.5
Ash	0.3	0.1	0.5
Percent nitrogen free extract	79.7		
Bulk density loose (lb/ft^3)	44		
Percent granulation US sieve			
On 30	0.1	0	0.5
On 40	0.4	0	1
On 60	80	70	90
On 80	15	10	20
Thru 80	4.5	1	7

TABLE 6.5. SPECIFICATIONS FOR CRUNCHY DEGERMED YELLOW CORN GRITS

Analysis performed	Typical analysis (%)	Analysis range (%)	
		Minimum	Maximum
Moisture	11.5	11.0	12.0
Protein	7.5	6.5	8.5
Oil	0.7	0.4	1.0
Fiber	0.5	0.3	0.6
Ash	0.4	0.3	0.6
Bulk density loose (lb/ft^3)	42		
Percent granulation US sieve			
On 10	0	0	0.1
On 14	2.5	0	5
On 20	65	60	75
On 30	31	25	40
On 40	1	0	2
Thru 40	0.5	0	2

This circumstance may disrupt the product and cause fluctuations in the final product quality.

Listed in Table 6.6 are some typical cheese-oil coating formulations.

Quality Control Considerations

Always consider the functionality, organoleptic characteristics, product image and nutritional value of your product. Quality control considerations include.

Table. 6.6. TYPICAL CHEESE COATING FORMULATION

Ingredient	Formula A (%)	Formula B (%)
Extruded corn product	57.8	66.0
Coconut oil	28.0	24.0
Cheddar cheese powder	7.0	9.3
Acid whey powder	3.5	--
Cheese flavor	3.5	0.7
Salt	0.2	--
Total	100.0	100.0

1. Determination of moisture, oil and salt in the final product
2. Determination of cheese coating on final product
3. Oil absorption characteristics
4. Final product color
5. Final product bulk density

THIRD GENERATION SNACKS

Product Description

Third, generation snack products or pellets are sometimes referred to as semi or half-products. Following extrusion cooking and forming, they are dried. Once they reach their final texture, they are ready to be consumed after frying in hot oil, puffing with hot air, or by secondary expansion extrusion by the snack processor or by packers prior to packaging. They can also be sold as consumer item to be fried in the home, in restaurants, etc. for immediate consumption. After the final puffing step, the products can be salted or flavored externally. Some products have flavoring within the pellet it self. The stability during storage and the high bulk density of the packaged, nonexpanded third generation snack adds an interesting dimension to its marketing potential. New variants of the original third generation snacks can now be expanded or puffed by infrared or microwave heating.

Process Description

A typical flow diagram for the production of third generation snacks is shown in Fig 6.6.

After the dry ingredients have been uniformly blended, the liquid ingredients such as shortenings, flavors or water are applied as a spray in the batch mixer or injected into the preconditioning cylinder of the cooking extrusion system. In the extrusion cooking step, the raw materials must be completely cooked unless the formulation contains pregelled starches. Cook is defined as the combination of temperature, residence time, & moisture content during extrusion to fully gelatinize the starchy components in the formulation. The temperature profile in the extruder must be above the gelatinization temperature of the starches found in the formulation unless they have been precooked.

Typical extrusion cooking processing conditions include.

Extruder rpm	180-250 rpm
Barrel temperatures	212-300°F (100-150°C)
Moisture content (extruder)	25-35%
Residence times	
Cooking zone	15-20 seconds
Forming zone	30-45 seconds

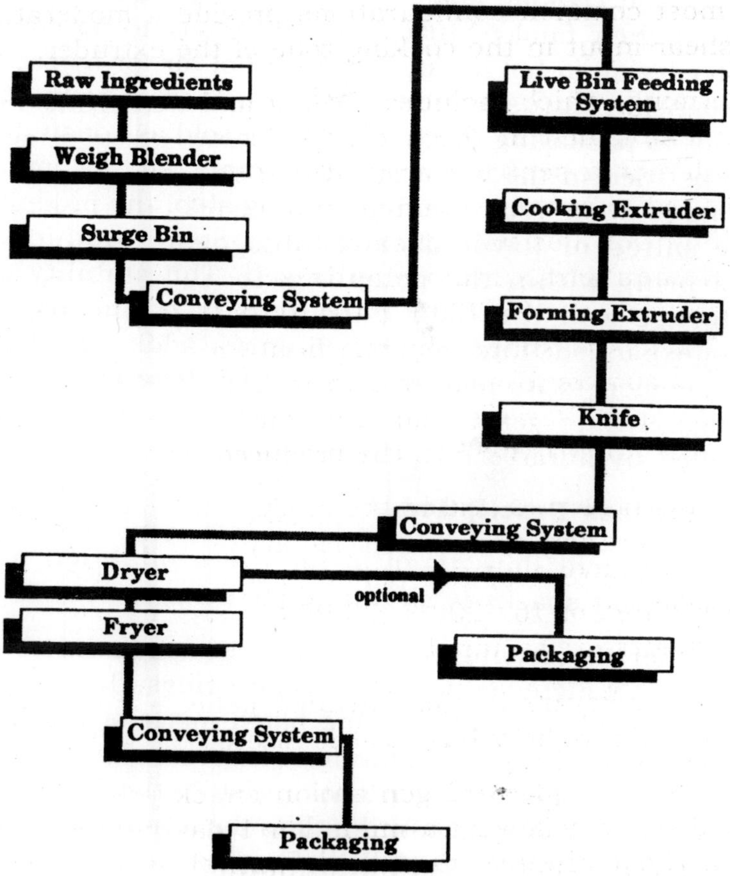

Figure 6-6 Typical flow for extrusion cooking of third-generation snacks

The specific mechanical energy input is usually quite low as the main proportion of energy required for the gelatinization of the starch is supplied from conductive or convection energy sources.

Conductive and convection energy sources include steam, hot water, or other thermal fluids circulated through the jacketed barrel to provide external heat and/or steam and hot water injected directly into the product in the mixing cylinder or extruder barrel. Various heads, screws and steamlock designs can be incorporated into the configuration to produce the desired cooking conditions. The most common configurations provide a moderate to low shear input in the cooking zone of the extruder.

Forming, which includes cooling and densifying, may be accomplished in the secondary zone of the cooking extruder or a separate extruder. The forming zone is configured to contain a minimum of restrictions except for the final die. Positive forward transport configurations complement maximum cooling to reduce product temperatures to 195-230°F (90-110°C). The cooled, visco, elastic mass is shaped by the final formings die which contains sufficient open area to proven expansion of the cooked dough. Various shapes of third, generation snacks before and after frying may be produced (Fig. 6.7).

Drying is very critical in the production of good quality third, generation snacks. Proper drying will reduce the moisture content of the pellet to approximately 12%. Temperatures of 167-208°F (70-95°C) and retention times of 1-3 hours are required.

Some moisture in the extruded pellet is distributed close to its periphery but most is located in the center.

Properly dried third generation snack pellets fry or expand better following a minimum 1 day period during which the moisture migrates eventually to reach an equilibrium.

Prior to consumption, third generation snacks are usually expanded in hot oil or air. Frying involves complete immersion of the pellets in oil at 300-350°F (150-175°C) for 30-40 seconds. The expansion of pellets in hot air is relatively new and has gained popularity owing to the low caloric content in the final product.

It must not be forgotten that these half products may also, after moistening, be used as a feedstock in the most simple form of expansion extruder to produce a variety of shapes and sizes and flavors of final product for local consumption. For geographic situations where transport of delicate, fragile and bulky product with a short shelf life makes it impossible (technically and economically) to import in and where volume of production does not warrant a complete manufacturing facility, this alternative to frying or hot air expansion of half-products to give a more locally "tailored" product has proved very helpful and has proved popular in North Africa and the Middle East.

Formulations

A wide range of raw ingredients may be selected suitable for third generation snack formulations. Combined ingredients must contain high levels of starch to maximize the expansion of the final product during exposure to hot oil or air. Levels of 60% or less of total starch in the formulation will give only slight expansion in the final processing step and will yield a final product with a crunchy, hard texture. Examples of this type of product would be those containing mainly whole ground corn, such as the traditional corn chip snack.

As the total starch level is increased above 60% the final product will expand more, resulting in a light, frothy texture.

Shortening or vegetable oils (1-3%) and emulsifiers (0.5-1.0%) are usually included in the formulation as processing aids, to reduce stickness and to impart a uniform cellular structure in the final product.

Table 6.7 contains generic formulations representing two different textures.

TABLE 6.7 TYPICAL FORMULATIONS FOR THIRD GENERATION SNACKS

Hard crunchy texture	Soft frothy texture
94.5% Ground corn	55.2% Cornstarch
5.0% Cornstarch	27.5% Wheat starch
0.5% Monoglyceride	14.0% Tapioca starch
	2.5% Liquid shortening
	0.8% Monoglyceride

Examples of a suitable monoglyceride or emulsifier are Eastman Chemical's Myvaplex 600 or Grinsteads Dimodan P.V.

Extrusion systems for the production of third generation snacks are efficient, economical to run and produce a product with built in marketing flexibility owing to long shelf life and high bulk density prior to frying, hot air expansion, or secondary expansion extrusion.

PRECOOKED MASA SNACKS

Product Description

The increased demand for precooked masa flours. Along with increased demands, manufacturers have desired more efficient and cost effective way to produce precooked masa flours. The traditional corn cooking procedures to prepare masa are consequently being replaced by more efficient, large scale operations where the corn is cooked and ground immediately with little or no steeping.

Process Description

When using bulk corn to prepare the masa, five steps are usually involved (Fig. 6.8).

Corn from bulk storage is ground through a 1.5 mm screen and transferred to a batch or continuous blending/

mixing system.

Ground corn is kneaded with water and calcium hydroxide ($CaOH_2$) to produce a moisture content of 20-25% and calcium hydroxide level of approximately 0.5-1%. Normally a 15-minute mix time allows sufficient moisture penetration. The exact moisture and calcium hydroxide levels will depend on the variety of corn and the type of calcium hydroxide used.

The extrusion process consists of several steps A feeder controls the rate of flow through the extrusion process.

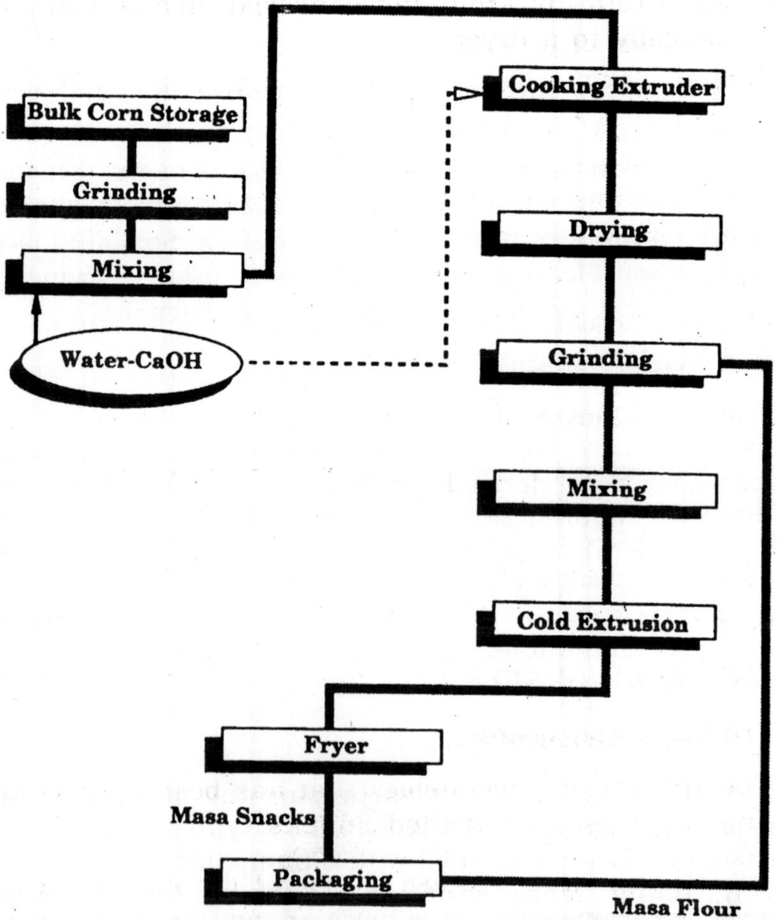

Figure 6-8 Typical flow for extrusion cooking of precooked masa snacks

This is very important for stability and a uniform final product quality. Live steam is injected into the mixing cylinder to temper the corn prior to extrusion to ensure that all particles have been fully penetrated with moisture. Temperatures of 194-203°F (90-95°C) are desirable. The preconditional corn is extruded through a 1/6-1/4 inch (6-9 mm) die orifice (number of holes is dependent on capacity of the equipment) with a minimal amount of mechanical shear energy input. Generally the temperature of the extruder barrel is approximately 250-300°F (120-150°C) and barrel pressures are between 10 and 15 atmospheres. As the extrudate exits the die orifices it is sized by a rotating knife and conveyed mechanically or pneumatically to a dryer.

The cooked moist extrudate must be dried to approximately 10-12% moisture. The drying is done rapidly to produce a nonsticky premium quality precooked masa. Temperatures of 300°F (150°C) for 15 minutes residence time are commonly used.

After drying the processed corn is ground through a 40 or 60-mesh screen and stored for packaging.

As more manufacturers convert their masa production lines to this energy efficient process new simple methods of producing corn chips, tortilla chips, and other masa base snacks have been derived. The precooked masa flour may be simply tempered with water and formed into a shape using a forming extruder. The formed snacks are then fried, flavored and packaged, ready for sale to the consumer.

COEXTRUDED SNACKS

Product Description

Coextrusion is a technology that has been in practice for many years. Coextruded snacks typically have an extrusion cooked outer shell with a pumpable, but not free flowing, filling. Many variations of this concept may be made with dies and post extrusion equipment such as rollers stampers and belt type cutters. Variations may include exotic shapes pinched ends to entrap the filling multiple shells and fillings, sandwich shapes, etc.

Few truly coextruded snacks have found success in the consumer market place. In many cases, the shelf life of these products has been short owing tc migration of moisture and/or lipids from the filling to the outer shell. However, technological advances related to this area are providing ways to increase the compatibility of products having a wide range of different moisture and lipid contents.

Process Description

The choice of the extruder type and configurations is largely dependent on the final product characteristics desired. The processing control advantage of the twin screw extruder will make it a best choice for this type of product. If a low density cereal based snack with a low density cereal based filling is the product of choice, then two extruders configured for low density snacks and sharing one common die would be used (Fig 6.10).

Die Design

Coextrusion dies may follow several different design concepts. It is extremely important to understand fully the possible design considerations and limitations. Normally simple snack extruders may be fitted with dies for filling or sandwiching techniques (Fig. 6.11).

The extrusion cooked portion of the snack will flow directly through the die parallel to the direction of flow through the extruder barrel. The filling will first be pumped into the die perpendicularly to the flow of the outer shell extrudate into the center of the extrudate flow region, then turn 90 degrees to flow with the shell extrudate. The anount of filling pumped into the outer shell may within a small range, control the outer product dimensions and the filling to shell ratio of the final product (see Fig. 6.12).

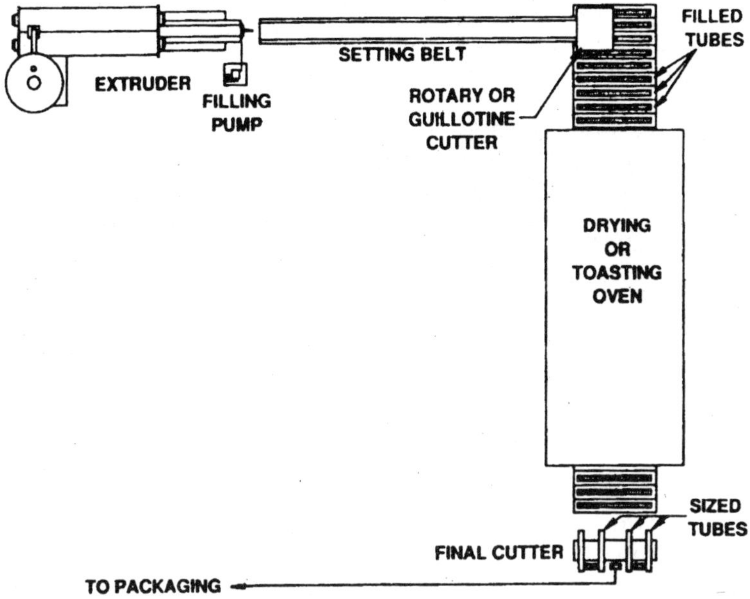

Figure 6-10 General layout for extrusion of co-extruded tubes.

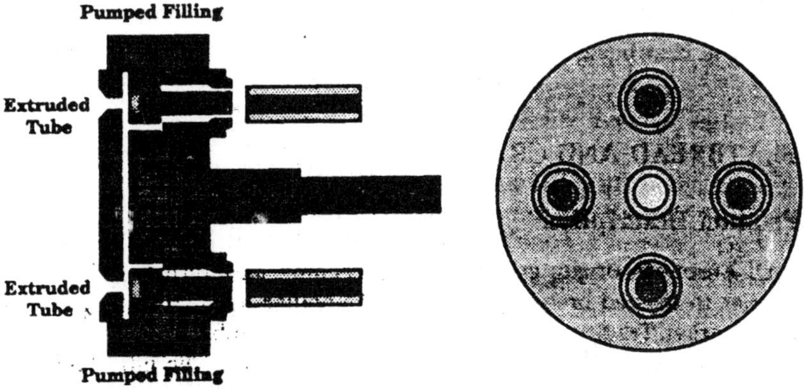

Figure 6-11 Typical filled-tube die.

$D_{sb}:D_{sa}$ = Shell Expansion Ratio
$D_{fb}:D_{fa}$ = Filling Expansion Ratio
$D_{sa}:D_{fa}$ = Shell to Filling Ratio

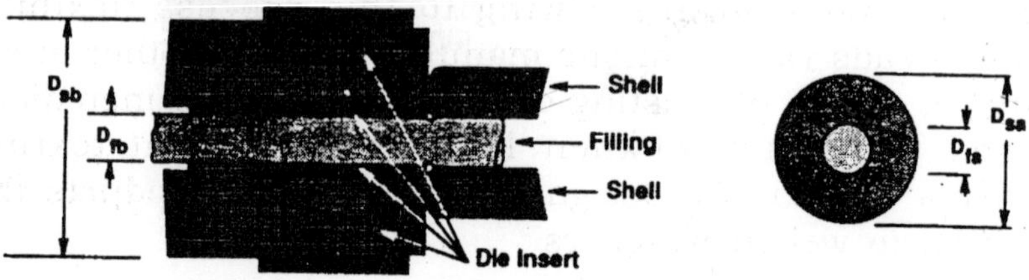

Figure 6-12 Normal expansion ratios for highly expanded co-extruded shells and filling.

Pulling or stretching of the extrudate may also be used to control the wall thickness of the outer shell, therefore affecting the filling to shell ratio. Careful consideration needs to be given to extrudate fillings that are heat sensitive or contain a high lipid content. When extruding highly expanded outer shells, temperatures may reach 285-300°F(140-150°C). Fillings injected through the die at these temperatures may see a temperature rise of 85-120°F (30-50°C) unless special insulating materials are used. The temperature rise comes not from the die alone but also from the heat being transferred from the extrudate into the filling.

FLATBREAD AND CRACKER SNACKS

Product Description

Of European origin, crispbread has become an international product. Similar to toasted bread, it has become popular in the expanding health food market. Traditional methods of producing crispbread involved rolling and sheeting of a dough followed by a baking step. The introduction of the extrusion process, with either twin screw or single screw extruders has complemented and even replaced the traditional methods of production. Extruded flatbreads, or crispbread, can be produced economically in a greater variety of forms and flavours to suit local tastes than traditional crispbread. The extruded crispbread can be processed to almost any texture, toasted and even sandwiched with various fillings to broaden the product possibilities. Owing to this process flexibility crispbreads vary from one manufacturer to another in size shape, degree of toasting color, texture, & the ingredients used. By virture of their low density & light texture, crispbreads can be designed as low calorie products that appeal to weight watchers.

Although crispbread can resemble crackers in many ways, it is generally a direct, expanded extrudate. Manufacturers of crispbread with the support of flavorists, nutritionists, and food scientists, are improving the market potential. The current market tends to favor the savory end of the flavor spectrum, but sweetened varieties of crispbread are marketed. These sweetened products may range from simple chocolate enrobed crispbreads to those sandwiched with a cheese or jam layer.

Although various shapes have been introduced, the most common is a flat, rectangular shaped portion. Large crispbread sections may have creases that allow portions to be snapped off and consumed as a finger food for consumption with savory dips.

Process Description

Raw materials including powders, whole grains and/or meals, are preblended and metered into the extrusion device. The most typical extruder utilized is the corotating twin, screw cooking extruder. Although blends of flour, milk powder, vegetable oil, sugar and salt are metered as a dry mix into the extruder, liquids such as syrups or oils may also be injected into the extruder barrel to very the formulation. The mix is cooked and formed in the extruder under low moisture (10-15%) and high temperature (250-350°F 120-175°C) conditions to yield a light, crispy product. Mechanical energy inputs are generally high and output capacities range from 90-15,500 lb/hr.

The discharge of the extruder is usually equipped with a single or multi slotted die with plastic or Teflon guides on the outboard side. The strands of extruded product are conveyed to a cutting unit and then dried or toasted to 4% final moisture content. Occasionally the strands are continuously extruded into a travelling band oven where temperatures of up to 750°F (400°C) are achieved. Baking or toasting time is very short (5-15 seconds) to achieve the desired color development and moisture content (4-6%). A cutting device at the end of the toaster chops the crispbread into the required lengths, which are then transferred by conveyors to packaging equipment. The specific density of the crispbread is very low and the final product is usually 'stacked' in the retail package to avoid breakage and allow portion selection.

Utilization of this same process flow allows one to manufacture similar products such as pretzels and breadsticks. The major modifications are the shape of the die opening (usually round) and the postextrusion enrobing steps. Pretzels and breadsticks are coated with a dilute caustic solution after extrusion but prior to toasting or baking. Salt, sesame seeds, or other particulate foods may be applied after the caustic spray.

Formulation

To improve the nutritional appeal of crispbreads, various sources of bran or fiber are added to base formulations. In Europe, different types of crispbread are produced with dietary fiber levels of about 12%. A formulation for the production of a Swedish crispbead via extrusion cooking is:

60%	cereal flour or starch
30%	wheat bran
10%	wheat gluten

This formulation contains a calculated dietary fiber of 20.4%. Increasing the fiber content of higher levels will decrease the expansion and increase the density of the final product.

A more typical crispbread formulation would be as follows.

68%	wheat flour
20%	rice flour
5%	sugar
4%	dried milk
1%	salt
2%	vegetable oil

Increasing the protein, fat or fiber levels will decrease expansion and yield a harder bite and texture. Conversely increasing the starch level will increase expansion and yield a softer bite.

Further Possibilities

The quality of extruded flatbread or crispbread can be optimized via experimental design using a systems analysis model to describe various relations calculated by polynomial regression. Through this, it is possible to influence processing conditions, extrusion configurations, and formulations to achieve desired product qualities.

As described earlier, chocolate enrobing may be applied as a final processing step. Manufacture of multicolored or multiflavored portions is possible by stratagic injection of liquids prior to the final die.

HIGH MOISTURE DOUGH SNACKS

Product Description

There are a variety of snack and snacklike products that can be produced from simple piston extruders or cold forming screw extruders. These products include fabricated French fried potatoes, onion rings, fishmeat cakes, meat balls, fruit bits, fruit, flavored, snacks etc. All of these snack products are high in moisture and doughlike in consistency. Twin screw forming extruders may be required where the doughs are sticky. The self wiping features of twin screw corotating extruders prevents product buildup in the root diameter of the screws and provides a positive conveyance for uniform product shape.

Process Description

Although the sophistication of equipment utilized in the production of high moisture dough snacks may be as simple as a conventional meat grinder, highly engineered volumetric filling machines may sometimes be employed for continuous operations. Where simple meat grinders are used as cold forming extruders, the grinding plate and rotary knife serve as the die and cutter for relatively simple shapes. More elaborate shapes require the use of single or twin screw forming extruders or piston type fillers. Ring sheped products, for example, can be produced by piston fillers or by depositing a ring shaped dough directly into deep fat frying vats. Fabricated onion rings are occasionally processed in this manner.

Formulation

There are essentially three distinct types of dough employed with the simple cold forming extruders. One relies upon starches as the primary binder and a second relies upon proteins, while the other involves the use of gums such as alginates.

The formulation containing alginates for the production of the onion rings as follows.

Wheat flour	20.0%
Corn starch	24.4%
Sugar	32.0%
Onion powder	5.0%
Propylene glycol	4.7%
Water	14.0%
Sodium alginate	0.3%

The sodium alginate contained in this formulation reacts with calcium ions from a calcium chloride solution applied to the surface of the formed product. This results in a gel like skin over the outside surface of the shaped piece, which retains the product shape.

Methylcellulose and other colloids have been incorporated successfully into doughs containing potato or vegetable solids and cereal flour or starches. The colloid is usually rehydrated in water before incorporation into the formulation causing the product to gel when heated. The strength and texture of the final product is dependent upon the viscosity and concentration of the colloid and water solution. Levels of methylcelluose, for example, may vary from 0.1 to 2%.

Other high moisture dough snack formulations contain starch as the binding agent. The starch may or may not be pregelatinized or otherwise modified. The starch is usually dry blended with the other ingredients and may be prewetted with water. The resulting dough is then extruded to the desired shape and then stamped prior to frying or baking. The production of potato snacks involves blending potato flakes with starches and water to form doughs containing 40-50% water. The dough is kneaded and cold formed before cutting and frying.

Meat snacks utilize protein and other binders to help hold these products together. Usually, a high moisture "dough" is prepared by blending raw meat, spices and small amounts of cereal and soy flours. This dough is cold formed into the desired shape and postextrusion frying or baking denatures the protein and sets the final shape. Typical snacks prepared in this manner include the beef jerky and "slim jim" products.

CONCLUDING COMMENTS

Remember that extrusion (twin screw or single screw) is a processing tool that may assist the snack food producer in the development and production of new innovative products. Reliability, maintenance and sanitation are three important features that must be given utmost consideration when evaluating food extrusion equipment. These are only surpassed by the equipment's ability economically to produce the final desired product. Twin screw extruders are not a panacea, but are an impressive, remarkebly versatile and controllable processing tool. Only by matching process and product requirements with equipment performance will the producer be able to select the type fo extruder, twin or single, best suited for this application.

2

POTATO BASED TEXTURED SNACKS

The last decade has seen the continuing growth of a sector of the food industry that supplies nibble type products sold under the general description of "savory snacks". Manufactured for eating as alternatives to patoto chips or nuts these snacks are made by a variety of methods. As the market expands and the consumer becomes more selective the manufacturer has to invest increasingly more time and money in product and process technology.

Corn in various forms is traditionally a mainstream raw material for the production of savory snacks, but a major proportion of these tonnages is accounted for by products made from potatoes, either alone or in admixture with other root crops or cereals.

The commercial success of snack products relies very heavily upon novelty or uniqueness. The technologist seeks to otbain this by combinations of shape and texture that are usually related. The functionality of the substrate is a major contributor to the texture of the product and is often the primary reason for selection. In recent years the nutritional contribution the snack may make to the total diet has started to feature and this has led to the use of a wide range of starch, containing vegetables and legumes together with fiber from tuber and cereal sources and vegetable protein.

In this chapter, the use of potato and other vegetables as the main structure forming materials is considered together with the most commonly used methods for processing them into ready to eat fabricated snacks.

RAW MATERIALS

Although the processing of potato and other sharch based ingredients to form textured snacks has been carried out for many decades, difficulties are still encountered in reproducing, within a narrow range, product textures and expansion ratios that ensure consistent quanlity and permit profitable manufacture of these items.

Chemical, biochemical and physical characteristics of the raw materials used, together with the process variables, have to be considered and controlled where possible or appropriate.

- The ingredients with which we are particularly concerned here are.
- Potato dehydrates, i.e., granules, flakes, (whole and ground), ground potato dice, potato starch, and potato fiber
- Vegetable dehydrates i.e. spinach, carrot, onion, tomato
- Legumes, i.e., green pea, beans

All of these materials are in use sometimes in admixture but usually combined with cereals notably wheat flour, rice flour, tapioca and corn in various forms.

As will be seen, these major structure forming ingredients used for snack making are all agricultural crops. They are grown, harvested, and stored (usually at the point of growing) under conditions that vary according to both geographic location and growing season.

Before being textured for snack making they have already undergone at least one primary process, usually milling. In the case of some potato dehydrates the modification to structure is very considerable. In most cases, the primary processing is not designed to produce characteristics ideally suited to say, low shear extrusion but is aimed at producing an ingredient for a completely different use such as rehydration for table use or for incorporation into soups or convenience foods. It is not surprising therefore that we sometimes have to work with ingredients with functional characteristics that are occasionally uncontrolled and often undesirable. In some instances our raw materials are low-cost by products from mainstream production.

The moisture content, protein content, oil content and the nature of the starch all have a bearing on the texture of the final snack and the way in which the ingredients behave during production. These characteristics are influenced by several factors such as genetic considerations commercial modification and environmental storage, all of which are usually outside the control of the snack technologist. Particle size, for example, influences hydration and gelation behavior during processing.

Milling, chemical modification and again genetics, can result in materials with the same agriculatural origin having significantly different processing characteristics. The work done, and its point of incidence in the extrusion process, for instance, greatly affects product texture even when using ingredients of common origin. The screw speed affecting both temperature and pressure, residence time, screw configuration, and die design (which affects shear forces) are all variables that the snack manufacturer can use to alter product textures.

A large selection of starch containing substrates can be used for making snacks. Natural crops either alone or in admixture with other unmodified ingredients can be variously processed to produce a wide selection of textures. Starches that have been heat treated or chemically modified can be added to alter expansion and mouthfeel. Cost and availability are important criteria to be applied in selection.

Given this background it can be seen that the type of potato raw materials and chemical and physical specifications for them cannot generally be established in isolation. The snack making process to be used has to be considered and the required material processing behavior established.

For the manufacture of fabricated snacks the potato ingredients used are usually supplied in dehydrated form and for this reason raw potatoes are excluded from this discussion.

Raw material characteristics which affect processing behaviour include.

Particle size
Bulk density
Nature of dehydration process
Use, level, and type of processing aids (such as emulsifiers) used during dehydration

Raw material characteristics that affect the finished product include

Flavour
Reducing-sugar level
Nature of gel structure

In order to reconcile processing requirements with finished product attributes mixtures of different types of dehydrated potato ingredients are used.

Potato Granules Potato granules are cooked peeled potatoes dehydrated by the add back granule process. In outline, potatoes are peeled, sliced, washed, blanched in hot water and cooked. After steam cooking the cooked slices are mashed and mixed with minor additives such as sulfite and emulsifier. After conditioning, the prepared mash is dried in an airlift dryer and sieved. Part of this sieved material is continuously fed back as seed material to the mashing and mixing drum where it combines with the infeed from the steam cooker. After sieving the product is finally dried in a fluid bed drying system.

A typical product made by this process and used in snack making has the following specification.

Viscosity peak (75/700)	7400-7500 B.U.
Moisture content (%)	7.0 ñ 1.0
Reducing sugars (%)	2.0 max
Sulfite (SO_2) (p.p.m)	400 ñ 100
Mono- + diglycerides (%)	0.50 max
Sodium acid pyrophosphate (%)	0.25 max
Particle size distribution	
Retained 250 μm screen	trace
Through 180 μm screen	99% min
Microbiologic assay	
Yeast and mold	10/g max
Salmonella Absent	
E. Coli	Absent
Coliform	10/g max
Total plate count	50,000/g max

The dehydrated products should by typical of mashed potato and free of excessive stickiness or pastiness. Stickiness and pastiness is a function of water absorption the ability of the granule to hold water is an important function in snack making since this determines dough cohesiveness. Many methods for measuring this have been proposed and are variously used.

In use, potato granules contribute to good potato flavour and products made from high levels of potato granules have good, lightly crisp, tender textures. When granules are used alone, however, this tenderness results in poor piece strength leading to excessive breakage during packaging and transport in the bag.

Commonly, therefore, formulations will also contain potato flake, either whole or ground and potato starch.

Potato Flakes

Cooked peeled potatoes are dehydrated into flake form which may then be ground into a granuler powder. The process is well known and documented.

Whole potatoes are peeled, sliced, washed hot, water blanched, and cooled so as to partially retrograde the amylose contained in the potatoes. After steam cooking the cooked potato is mashed with any required additives, i.e., emulsifiers. The resultant cooked mash is roller dried on drum dryers and, if required, ground to the required particle size specification.

A variation on the standard product is "LL/LP" flakes, particularly advantageous for snack making use where enhanced potato flavor is a benefit. In this process the potatoes are either unpeeled or only peeled to the minimum so as to retain as much as possible of the outer cortical layer of the potato where a high level of potato flavor is found. Peeling, of course, must be sufficient to remove surface blemishes. Additionally, the standard precooking and cooling stage is eliminated so as to retain as much as possible, of the water soluble flavor constituents.

As well as having improved flavour, this type of potato flake also has a greater water absorption and therefore its behavior in snack making formulations is very different from the standard material.

It is common practice to make potato flakes as a by product of French fries manufacture. In this case the offcuts, nibbins and slivers are used for the raw feedstock and the slicing and washing stages mentioned above form part of the mainstream French fry line.

A typical potato flake for use in potato snack making has the following specification.

Moisture content (%)	6.0-8.0
Reducing sugars (%)	3.0 max
Mono and diglycerides (%)	0.35-0.50
Bulk density (g/ml)	0.51-0.57 but will depend on degree of grinding
Particle size distribution	
Whole flakes	Minimal fragmentation of the roller dryer output to facilitate packing. Fine particles or dust minimal
Ground flakes	
Retained 125 μm screen	85%
Through 500 μm screen	100%
Microbiogic assay	
Yeast and mold	10/g max
Salmonella	Absent
E. coli	Absent in 1 g.
Coliform	10/g max
Total plate count	50,000/g max

To harden expanded potato snack textures, assist with moisture distribution between dough ingredients, and reduce raw material costs potato flour and/or potato starch is frequently used.

Potato Starch Potato starch or farina food grade is a refined white dry powder that results from washing grinding and juicing raw potato tubers. The fiber, protein, and protamylase is separated before the residual starch slurry is concentrated, refined and dried to produce an uncooked bland starch product.

Potato Flour Whole potato flour is made from grinding potato dice. For the production of potato dice, washed, peeled potato tubers are cut to the required size, washed, water blanched and sulfitted. The blanched dice are dried usually on a fluidized belt dryer. The dehydrated dice are then ground to produce potato flour.

Potato flour is an uncooked, dried whole potato ingredient low in potato flavour often used as a major structuring ingredient in snacks produced by cooking and forming extrustion.

Potato starch (Farina) conforms typically to the following specification.

Moisture (%)	19.0-21.0
Ash (%)	1.0 max
pH	6.0 - 8.0
Particle size analysis	Average particle size 40-60 μm
Microbiologic Assay	
Total plate count	1000/g max
Yeasts and molds	10/g max
E. coli	Absent
Salmonella	Absent

Potato flour is a white/cream colored powder with a mild potato flavor having the following typical characteristics.

Moisture (%)	6.0-8.0
Redusing sugars (%)	3.0 max
Particle size analysis	
Retained 180 μm screen (%)	1.0 max
through 75 μm screen (%)	40.0 max
Bulk density (g/liter)	815-855
Free starch (%)	43-48
Amylograph 150 g/211 ml water 86°F (30°C)	600 B.U.
Sulfite (SO_2)	Absent
Microbiologic Assay	
Total plate count	25,000/g max
Yeast and mold	20/g max
E. coli	Absent
Salmonella	Absent
Coliforms	10/g max

METHODS OF MANUFACTURE

Fabricated snacks can generally be classified under three main process headings forming and frying of wet dough: high shear dry extrusion and low-shear pellet extrusion.

Forming and Frying of Wet Dough

Since the time potato chips first became a commercial success, food processors have been attempting to produce a prefabricated potato based product that has both the flavor and the texture of the traditional chip which is produced by deep fat frying thin slices of fresh potato. Such a product should have the textural characteristics of the natural product and be capable of being mass produced at relatively low cost.

Early attempts to achieve this were generally unsuccessful. Methods have been described using potato flour dispersed in a binder gel, and in one process an algin based gel firmed with a calcium salt was used to make long cylinders of potato dough, which were cut into thin slices and fell directly into a bath of hot fat. A product resembling Lefsa the Scandinavian bread has been described that is produced by frying shaped pieces of dough made from dehydrated potato flakes, wheat flour and yeast.

In recent years several products have appeared, initially in the United States but latterly in the United Kingdom and Europe, that are made from potato dehydrate doughts having a moisture content of about 40-55% by weight. When rapidly heated, as with deep fat frying the structure formed results from the gelatinization of the starch components. The resultant expansion is deliberately controlled by addition of nongelatinized potato solids so as to produce a texture similar to that of a potato chip.

In this process, a dough is formed from potato dehydrates typically 15 parts by weight ground potato flakes, 15 parts by weight whole potato flakes, and 15 parts by weight potato starch. Discrete pieces of vegetable or vegetable powder such as spinach can be added to the dough if required to introduce variety of texture, taste, and appearance. Vegetable powders with high reducing sugar content such as carrot should be avoided because the finished product color may become too dark if these are used at significant levels.

The dough is fed continuously through rotating rollers that compress it into a cohesive sheet about 1/2 inch (12 mm) thick. This sheet is conveyed through a series of reduction rollers so as to reduce its thickness to about 1/16 inch (1.5 mm). It is important that this reduction occurs gradually. Excessive work at this stage causes cell damage resulting in the formation of a sticky sheet that is difficult to cut and an unevenly overexpanded finished product. The reduction rollers can be vertically mounted or horizontally as with a cracker plant.

Once the sheet has been reduced to the required thickness it is continuously passed under a suitably engraved rotary cutting roller. In the case of noninterlocking shapes the cutting scrap is continuously returned to the dough feeder to be reworked. The cut shapes are continuously fed to a fryer where they are fried in vegetable oil to form thin crunchy pieces with a final moisture content of 2% by weight or less.

After frying, the product can be salted or flavoured before packing. Many different shapes and textures can be produced, using this system although control of plant efficieny is difficult.

According to Willard, a potato snack in this category is produced by mixing cooked potato solids with water and ungelatinized starch to form a dough having a moisture content of 50-60% by weight. This dough is formed into pieces that are immediately fried in vegetable oil to produce an expanded snack. The dough at the time of frying contains a mixture of ungelatinized starch and potato solids that includes a quantity of intact potato cells, and a quantity of free gelatinized starch solids. The amount of free gelatinized starch in the dough is controlled in the formulation so that on frying, the dough pieces expand to at least 1.6 times their original dimension, but not more than 3.0 times.

A product in a ring form made by this technique has been on sale since 1972. This snack, consisting of ring shaped pieces, is shaped by extrusion from direct or positive displacement equipment. A hydraulically operated ram forces dough at low pressure through dies situated at the end of a smooth bore barrel. This type of equipment is necessary for products of the type contemplated by Willard because virtually no shear occurs and the properties of the extruded dough after shaping are essentially unchanged from those of the original dough feed. As with all other food extrusion processes, the point of incidence and intensity of shear are critical to the achievement of the desired textural effect.

The extruded dough in tubular form is cut to the desired length at the die face to give ring shaped pieces which fall directly into a bath of hot frying oil where, expansion, flavour development and dehydration occur, forming a product with a cellular internal structure encased ina dense exterior of substantially reduced porosity.

The efficiency with which individual formulations can be machined into sheet form or extruded into shapes on the production plant prior to expansion and dehydration by frying or other heating means often determines the success of otherwise of the snack. Production problems not only affect output rates and therefore profits they also most importantly establish how effectively quality standards can be maintained.

In blending together mixtures of ingredients of arrive at the desired texture, mouthfeel and flavour in the finished product, it must be remembered that the physical nature of the dough produced will be affected by.

Component functionality
Interactive functionality between components
The order in which ocmponents are added
Mixing conditions time, temperature, physical shear

In carrying out this work experimentally it is often difficult ot describe cause and effect to colleagues say at another site. The simplest way to achieve understanding is to establish a basic numbering system which can then be used with reference to agreed benchmarks. For example

1. Dry, friable, powdery, can be squeezed by hand into a ball only with difficulty
2. Dry, friable, but can be squeezed into a ball
3. Easily squeezed into a ball that breaks when dropped
4. Some small agglomerates or balls obvious after mixing
5. Many aglomerates apparent after mixing. Hand formed ball does not break when dropped
6. Feels wet, easily molded, difficult to discharge from mixing vessel
7. All large agglomerates, sticks to mixer blades
8. Completely uniform cohesive dough. Discharges easily as a single loaf of nonadhesive dough. Can easily be molded by hand
9. Uniform adhesive dough like bread dough cannot; easily be discharged from mixer, sticks to the fingers

A simple uncomplicated system such as this can overcome much misunderstanding when problems arise.

Using the wet dough forming method a wide range of interestingly shaped potato nibble type snacks can be made using standard cracker making equipment with modified dough mixers. Onion, chives, parsley, etc can be included in the dough mix to add visual interest and flavor. A typical formulation for a baked product is potato granules 40 parts, potato flour 30 parts, potato starch 24.0 parts, vegetable fat 4.0 parts, salt 1.5 parts, monosodium glutamate (MSG) 0.5 parts.

In manufacture, the granules and flour are blended with the salt and MSG in a ribbon blender for 4 minutes. twenty parts of water is added and mixed for 1 minute. After resting for 1 minute the potato starch is added together with a further 25 parts of water and mixing continues for 3 minutes to form a cohesive dough.

The dough is sheeted to form a cohesive sheet about 1/2 inch (12 mm) thick followed by gentle reduction through three set of gauging rollers to produce a final sheet thickness of about 1/16 inch (1.5 mm). After cutting to the desired shape by means of a rotary cutter, the cut pieces are continuously fed to a baking oven where top & bottom heat is applied. A typical baking time is 15-20 minutes at 300°F (150°C).

The use of vegetable shortening is necessary to give the products an acceptable mouthfeel & to control toughness. Quantities can be varied to achieve the best balance between texture and mouthfeel.

The degree fo lift during baking can be inceased if a more puffed product is required by the addition of 1 or 2 parts of vegetable gum such as carrageenan. the incorporation of up to 10 parts of waxy maize starch is also an effective way to improve lift.

High shear Dry Extrusion

Fabricated snacks have been produced by this technique for more than 40 years and a great number of these are on sale throughout the world. Originally based entirely on degermed corn meal or grits, in recent years numerous and interestingly different textures have resulted from the use of potato dehydrates in admixture with both corn and rice.

The process consists of continuously feeding the selected raw materials to a single screw isothermal extruder. Various design of estruders have been developed to provide different product characteristics but the basic process requires high temperature, short time cooking at the correct moisture level for the optimum ultimate puffing effect. Extruders for these products generate heat rapidly in the extrudate by the high shearing action products between the grooved barrel and screw, combined with a relatively high screw speed (usually 300-400 rpm). They are usually a run in a "starved" condition to ensure low residence time. Typical internal temperatures of operation would be 285°F (140°C). The hot plasticized mass passes from the screw section into a pre expansion intermediate die and immediately through the final shaping die where the high temperature of the mass causes violent flashing of the moisture resulting in a puffed product having approximately 8% moisture content immediately the extruded mass reaches atmospheric pressure. The expanded extrudete is cut to the required piece thickness at the die face and is subsequently dried to a final moisture content of about 2% before surface flavoring and packing.

Potato flakes (coarse ground) and/or potato granules can be dry blended with the usual corn grit feed stock at levels up to 25% by weight to produce shaped products by this process. It is important to select materials that are sufficiently granular to ensure a consistent feed rate and residunce time in the extruder. Fine particles usually cause burn on to the screw and eventually seizure of the machine. Although the potato dehydrates may contain within them levels of emulsifier, additions of up to 0.2% of mono or diglycerides cna help with this problem. Compared with snacks extruded entirely from corn grits products containing potato solids usually have a more compact structure with less large randomly dispersed air voids.

Flavor is usually improved, mouthfeel is less sticky and shape reproduction from the extruder is more consistent.

Cross sectional photographs of the same product with and without added potato solids magnified 100 times

Low shear Pellet Extrusion

In this method a partially dehydrated, shaped piece of a starch based gel, commonly termed in the industry a pellet or collet, is puffed by exposure to rapid heating at temperatures of about 375°F (190°C), commonly by a short immersion in hot frying oil or by rapid application of dry heat. In this process typically, potato solids, either raw or dehydrated are mixed with various starches (for example tapioca or potato srarch) and water to form a dough of 28-30% moisture content. The dough is cooked or gelatinized, then held or cooled in order to reduce the stickiness of the gel before shaping into the required form by extrusion or sheeting, cut to the desired piece thickness and dried to produce a pellet with a final moisture content of between 8 and 10%. In this form the product can be stored virtually indefinitely. In the final stage the dehydrated pellets are rapidly heated to convert them to expanded structures that vary between 4 and 10 times their original dimensions depending upon the ingredients used the shape of the piece the moisture content the temperature at which puffing occurs, and the type of heating process. The presence of evenly distributed moisture in the pellet produces steam bubbles in the heated starch gel, thus creating a uniformly porous structure.

The well known tapioca starch plus dry potato solids products have, for many years, been popular in the Orient where ground shrimp is often added as a flavoring agent.

A similar product is made continuously in which fresh portatoes are blanched and added to a gel that is shaped and cut before drying.

A little nearer home the Nibbit process of Spieser and Gerkins achieves similar results. In this case, dehydrated potatoes and starch at about 65% solids are gelatinized during extrusion, cut and dried to form shelf stable collets. In this process dehydrated diced potatoes are ground to form the basic potato ingredient, whereas in most other processes based upon potato, either potato flour or dehydrated mashed potato in flake or granule form is used.

Two methods of manufacture for pellets are commonly in use, depending upon the condition of the starting materials. The first method utilizes paste making equipment and involves single screw extrusion. Single screw extruders were first applied to food processing in about 1935 for the continuous extrusion of paste products. As we know, food extruders can be broadly classified in two ways either thermodynamically or by the manner in which pressure is applied.

Using the thermodynamic approach we have:

- Autogenous extruders which generate their own heat

by conversion of machanical energy in the process itself. No attempt is made to introduce heat or cooling throgh the jacket.

- Isothermal extruders, where constant temperature is maintained throughout the extruder by cooling to remove heat generated by the conversion of mechanical energy.

- Polytropic extruders, which operate between the autogenous and isothermal extreme conditions. All food extruders are polytropic, but some tend more towards being autogenous and some more towards being isothermal.

Considering the other criterion the way in which pressure is applied, we can classify extruder types as.

- Direct or positive displacement, represented by hydraulic or pneumatic and intermeshing twin screw types both of which produce low shear.

- Nonintermeshing twin screw, which are continuous and produce high shear.

- Indirect. This type of extruder develops viscous drag and modifies the characteristics of the extruded product. There are several types of indirect extruders of which two are common.

(a) The roller extruder, which is usually used for very sticky products that do not require high pressure shaping and is of the continuous low shear type.

(b) Single screw. Of the single screw extruders commonly in use those used for forming macaroni products from a dough are the closest to the ideal in that they have a smooth or fluted barrel no solids conveying section, and usually a constant screw geometry. They are the closet to an isothermal extruder since they effect the lowest temperature rise.

In production, solids and water are metered to a continuous mixer where a dough is produced. This dough is continuously fed via the screw to the forming head and then through a die body containing up to several hundred dies of the shape required. After shaping, the product is cut to length at the die face and conveyed into a drying system. Ventilation is provided at the die face to facilitate cutting. Process conditions vary according to machine design, moisture content of dough and nature of solids used, but for comparison with dry extrusion the average conditions would be screw speed 30 rpm and product temperature 130-158°F (55-70°C).

For the manufacture of expandable potato snack pellets dehydrated ingredients that have been precooked to gelatinize the strach, such as potato granules or ground flakes are blended into a dough of moisture content 28-30%. A small quantity or uncooked potato starch is often added to facilitate extrusion and cutting. This dough is then extruded, shaped, and dried using standard pasta making equipment that has been modified to handle these more sticky natured products. By this means a large variety of shapes and textures can be produced depending upon selection of ingredient blend and die design. The cost of precooked ingredients, however, is relatively high and therefore many such products are made by the alternative cooker extrusion process.

Cooking a dough gelatinizes the starch hydrates the proteins, and changes its structure and viscosity. The condition of a cooked dough is temperature and shear rate dependent. As we know, food ingredients do not melt when they are humidified and processed under conditions of elevated temperatures and pressures as do plastics. Irreversible time dependent changes such as occur during the gelatinization of starches complicate the rheology of foods during extrusion. For these reasons we connot point to an ideal extruder capable of treating all possible types of substrates of interest of the snack manufacturer. The phsical, chemical and biochemical status of the raw materials used, the pretreatment they receive, and the treatment after cooking (That is shaping & drying) all after the process end result. Many different cooking extruders have been developed both single screw and twin screw high pressure and low pressure each of which can be used to produce certain textural effects. Considerable design work has been carried out by machinery manufacturers covering many different configurations of feeding systems mixers extrusion heads steam control mechanisms shaping dies and screws and including dryers and coolers to treat the extruded products.

To produce a desired effect the number and type of extrusion apertures as well as screw configuration, barrel design, and heating/cooling zones have to be determined experimentally.

To achieve desirable textural features with some products (for example, recipes containing high levels of potato starch), intensive shear is needed during the cooking and sometimes even the forming stages of pellet making. Without altering the screw geometry, which is usually fixed say for another product, shear can be increased by reducing moisture levels in the infeed dough. Obviously there is a minimum moisture level below which high extrusion pressure becomes unacceptable from a product shape or plant safety standpoint. This is usually at about 28.0%. Inclusion of salt in the dry dough solids is a commonly used means of increasing shear and indeed many typical potato pellet snack recipes contain up to 3.0% by weight of sodium chloride.

As mentioned, the wide range of process variable and formulation possibilities makes the pellet forming route a particularly important one for the snack maker. Continuous cooking and forming offers the best possibility for utilizing the widest range of potato and vegetable dehydrates. Adjustments to processing can be made to accommodate wide variations in raw material consistency and quality.

Textures ranging from the highly expanded light type associated with high shear systems through the range to the more dense flinty texture of natural potato chips can be achieved by raw material selection & post extrusion forming & secondary processing.

Because of the wide range of possible variables typical formulations are difficult to quote. However a reasonable starting point for a potatobased snack made by the dry pellet process is potato starch 50 parts fine ground potato flake 30 parts potato granules 10 parts monosodium glutamate 1.5 parts, salt 3.0 parts, and vegetable powder 5.5 parts (onion garlic or spinach). After premixing the dry ingredients a dough is continuously formed with a moisture content of 33.0-34.0%. This dough is then continuously cooked, shaped, cut and dried to produce pellets with a final moisture content of 8.0-10.0%.

Cross sections of these snacks magnified 100 times illustrate the difference in texture achieved by changing shape and process conditions. These pelleted products have been expanded by frying in vegetable oil typically for 20-25 seconds at 355°F (180°C).

Alternative textures with different nutritional characteristics can be achieved by continuously expanding the pellet using a solid heat transfer system. Salt preheated to about 570°F (300°C) can typically be used for this. A rotating heated drum as used for peanut roasting can be modified to suit this process. Separation of the product from the heated salt occurs by differential density after expansion which should only take 10-12 seconds.

Alternatively expansion can be carried out by hot air oven. Remember that to achieve good expansion the heat transfer to the pellet must be rapid so as to provide sufficient heat shock. A fluidized system with rapid air velocity is necessary to achieve this.

POTATO CHIP MANUFACTURE

The manufacture of potato chips (crips) may now be outlined though it is well documented in the literature.

Particular varieties of potato are chosen that have a sufficiently high (about 21%) solids content, are of regular shape and size have been carefully harvested and are subtantially undamaged. They are stored under high humidity conditions at a temperature around 46°F (8°C) at which moisture loss is minimized and the production of sugar from the potato starch is also maintained at as low a level as possible. If sugar content is too high chips are produced with too much color and so long stored potatoes may have excessive sugar removed from them before use by the expedient of increasing storage temperature to about 60°F (15-16°C) for a week or two whereupon the metabolic rate of the potatoes is increased and the excess sugar is burned off.

Following washing and destoning the potatoes are peeled (stem or lye peeling plus gentle abrasion is usual) and are then hand trimmed and inspected. Peeling is sometimes omitted in a recent manufacturing development that is claimed to result in better flavored chip.

Then the potatoes are thinly sliced, the slices are washed free of adherent starch granules and are then blanched and dried before passing on a conveyor to and into the very hot bath of vegetable oil (at about 255 F 124 C) in which they are rapidly dehyrated and cooked. Excess oil is drained off sometimes centrifuged off and the chips are cooled. They may then be salted and flavored in various ways (usually by powder adhesion to residual fat on the chips, but a spray is also possible) before packaging in moisture proof containers. These products are almost always used in the savory snack context.

SIMILAR PRODUCTS USING A BASIS OTHER THAN POTATOES

While this chapter rightly, from its title, concentrates on potato several similar products derived from cereals particularly flacked and expanded (not extrusion expanded) cereals are mentioned only briefly en passant in the cereal related and expansion extrusion chapters in this book. This appears to be an appropriate place therefore, to outline the methods used to produce flaked and "puffed" cereals.

Flaked cereals Corn flakes wheat flakes rice flakes etc. can be made from intact whole grains from part grains or from individual or from individual or mixtures of ground cereals. In the last case additives for flavoring or other purposes may be used e.g. bran powder malt sugar salt. The cereals are cooked before use whether they are to be used in whole or particulate form in the case of pelleted mixtures a dough containing all the additives is made.

The whole grains parts of grains or pelleted material are then passed between heavy steel rollers the flakes are scraped off with a doctor knife are dried on a traveling wire mesh belt and are usually toasted or browned by some form of radiant heat before packing in water and watervapor proof material.

This relatively simple and cheap technology with many variants has now been used for well over 50 years to provide a ready to eat snacks in many parts of the world.

Puffed Cereals the original means of puffing cereals was the time honored way of making popcorn. The very hot plates on to which the grains of corn were placed caused the moisture within suddenly to expand into steam and so to cause the grain to be puffed and simultaneously be cooked. This method was refined some 30 or 40 years ago by having the grain (frequently rice in this case) heated up in a quick release but hermetically sealed cylinder. After an appropriate "cooking" period, the quick release action was used suddenly to release the pressure in the cylinder whereupon the moisture in the grain caused it to puff or expand.

During the past 7 years, a new puffing method has been developed for whole cereal grains in Holland (the Presco system) and it is now possible to purchase many cereals blown up to 4 to 8 times their original size either as expanded individual grains or milled to any desired size. This provides a precooked very lightweight expanded "original texture" grain for use in many snack products.

Relatively recent advances have been made in popcorn production headed by the widespread possession of microwave ovens in the home, and there are now more then 80 U. S. manufacturers of popcorn operating and a wide range of flavors are offered in this seminal item in the history of snack foods. This expansion of popcorn consumption has yet to reach the United Kingdom and Europe.

In conclusion, it should be noted that recent innovations in the area of potato chips and similar items fabricated from mashed potato powder are now being joined by ready to eat poppadum "chips" made from the traditional urd flour plus rice flour plus savory spices and other ingredients. The introduction raises a whole host of potential products of this kind where the basis may or may not be potato but the final product simulates standard potato products in various ways.

3

HEALTH FOOD SNACKS

Within the problems of defining a snack that were discussed in the Introduction, a further difficulty of definition arises when it comes to health food snacks.

The concept of "health snacks" carries with it the inevitable question "healthier than what" All of the items included in this chapter are there because there is something comparable that is "less healthy". Exactly why and to whom the snack is healthier will vary. If you suffer from an allergy to wheat you would not consider a cornish pasty with its wheat based pastry to be healthy. On the other hand, if you suffered from heart disease and had been advised to reduce animal fat intake, you also would not consider a cornish pasty to be healthy although you would be happy to eat a low fat vegetable pasty, as would a vegetarian. If you suffered from constipation neither the cornish pasty nor the vegetable pasty would be considered, healthy if they were made from white flour, where as if the pastry were made of whole wheat flour, then your attitude would be different. Thus, what is healthy from one point of view may not be healthy from a different viewpoint. Put another way, one man's meat is another's poison.

In spite of these difficulties, the concept of the health snack is well established, even if agreement as to what constitutes a healthy snack is not. For the purposes of this chapter a health snack is one that is either sold on the basis that it is healthier than some conventional counterpart (e.g., the low fat chips), or if it is usually bought by consumers who perceive it to be healthier (e.g., carob based confectionery). This latter aspect is sometimes difficult to discern since it is not always easy to know what is in a person's mind at any given time but as a working definition such products are often sold in health food or wholefood shops, and that will help in forming the definition.

SHELF-LIFE

Like all snacks, whether healthy or otherwise, the question of storage life forms a natural division of all the various types. For the purposes of this discussion, 7 days is chosen as the arbitrary dividing line, and the snacks to be considered below will be looked at in these two categorise.

Following shelf life, the remaining divisions represent the major subcategories to be used: fruit bars granola bars nut and seed based snacks, carob based snacks, low calorie snacks, gluten free snacks, diabetic snacks, low fat snacks high fiber snacks and a miscellaneous category. Many of these categories will overlap with others and there is no way to avoid this. Where a conflict arises allocation to one category or another is based mainly on the ingredients declaration. Information on particular ingredients will be limited to those ingredients that are used primarily ingredients will be limited to those ingredients that are used primarily in the manufacture of health snacks since other ingredients will be covered in other chapters.

This chapter will end with a brief consideration of likely developments in this area.

SHORT SHELF LIFE SNACKS

Savory Snacks

The list of possible savory short shelf life health snacks is very large, and there seems little virtue in exploring them all. The main types are those encased in pastry, those encased in bread (sandwiches), and those based on rice.

The first group consists of pasties and pies and their claim to be healthy depends on either the nature of the flour used for the crusts or the nature of the filling. The pastry used can be of various healthier types such as whole wheat (which may also be organic that is produced by a long term sustainable system of agriculture that does not use man made chemicals) it may be unbleached or made from other grains such as barley or oats. The pastry may be made using polyunsaturated vegetable oils rather than the more usual hard fats or may have no added salt.

The fillings can be even more varied but usually include cheese and onion (vegetarian) lentil/vegetables (vegetarian and low fat/high fiber) as well as the more traditional meat or meat and vegetable fillings. Tofu is featured more and more in these products.

Tofu is a curd somewhat similar in texture to cottage cheese but without any significant flavour, it is produced by soaking washed soya beans in water (10:1 ratio) overnight. The beans and the water are then blended until a milklike liquid is obtained (see Fig 14.1). This liquid is then boiled prior to filtering to remove large particles, and is then mixed with 0.03-0.04 N calcium sulfate, which causes the curd to precipitate. The curds are pressed to remove much of the whey, before the tofu is sold as it is, in a fresh state or vacuum packed, in which form it can be kept under refrigeration for 3-4 weeks. The end result is a high protein curd that has some of the mouthfeel characteristics of soft cheese and is a good source of calcium as well as protein.

Tofu has a moisture content of about 80% a protein content of 11.5% and a fat content (most of it being the highly desirable polyunsaturated kind) of 4.5%. The protein is of high biologic quality similar in valuet to chicken meat. the calcium content is approximately 200-220 mg per 100 g., which compares with 60 mg per 100 g for cottage cheese, and 120 mg per 100 g for fresh milk.

Tempeh is another soya product that is useful in health

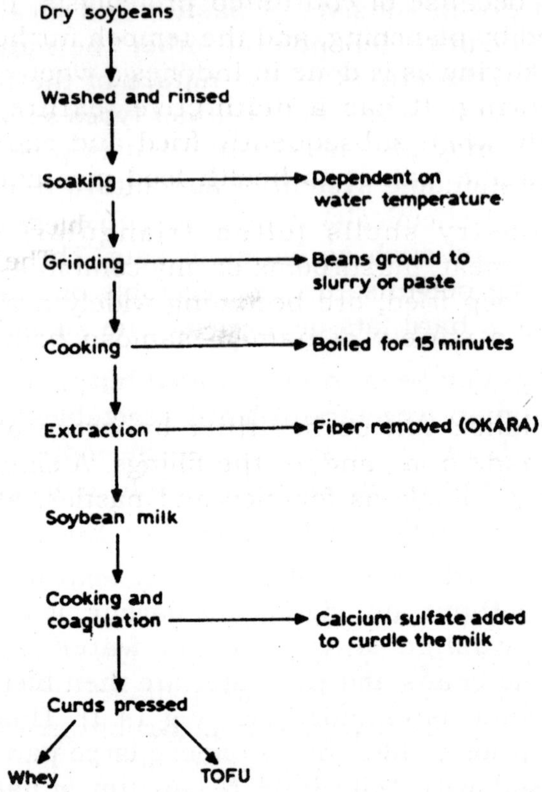

Figure 14-1 Stages in the process of converting soya beans to tofu.

food pies and pasties. To made tempeh, soyabeans (preferably organically grown soyabeans) are fist processed to remove the fibrous hull, or outer coat. During this process the bean is split into 6 or 8 pieces, or grits. The cleaned grits are cooked for 30-60 minutes. The drained and cooled grits are inoculated with a suspension of spores of the organism Rhizopus oligosporus. The grits are next packed tightly into molds, packages, or bags that allow restricted access to air, since air tends to encourage the Rhizopus organism produces spores rather than to grow. During incubation for the next 20-24 hours at 86-88°F (30-31°C) the grouth of the organism produces a proteolytic enzyme that helps to fuse the individual grits together to form a coherent mass. The wet tempeh itself is fairly unsrable, because of continued proteolysis, but this can be arrested by blanching, and the tempeh further preserved by partial drying as is done in Indonesia where it originates or by freezing. It has a distinctive texture and flavor particularly when subsequently fried and can be used to give a meatlike texture to health food pies and pastries.

Thin pastry shells (often triangular) filled with vegetables, meat, mushrooms or any combination of these, and then deep fried, are becoming widely available. They sell under a variety of names, samosa being the most common.

Sandwiches can be healthier by virtue of the bread they are made from, and/or the fillings. A similar range of choices is available as for pies and pasties, although the choice of fillings is much wider, but the shelf life is of course reduced to 1 or 2 days.

Rice based snacks are also becoming more widely available, although because of their limited shelf life and as yet limited appeal, they are usually only available in specialized outlets in major populartion centers. As with the samosa, there is a wide variety of potential ingredients but the one thing they have in common is that they are bulked out and held together by cold, precooked rice (usually brown). The mixtures may include vegetables tofu tahini (ground sesame seeds); soya sauce bulgur (precooked and dried pieces of wheat grain); cereals such as oats, wheat flour or wheat germ; seaweed' nuts, herbs; seeds' meat; or fish. They are shaped in a variety of ways, ranging from spheres to patties and even conical shapes. They are usually shallow fried after mixing and shaping, before being packed for sale. Shelf life is rarely more than 1 week, and these items should be refrigerated for optimal shelf life.

A variety of names are used, depending on the area of the world in which the manufacturer lived or obtained his recipe from: rice ball tofu patty, and vegetable kofta are some examples.

This section coul not be brought to a close without reference to a miscellaneous category, to cover those healthier savory snacks not included above. One of the more popular and widely available would be the bhajis. These are of Indian origin, and consist of wheat flour based batter mixed with different fillings, onion being the most common but also including mushrooms and other vegetables. The mix is usually seasoned, often with curry, and formed into a ball before being deepfried.

Traditional Japanese cuisine also includes a range of deep fried snacks consisting of a carbohydrate based glutinous batter enclosing vegetable pieces, prawns, mushrooms, etc.

Sweet Snacks

Healthier sweet snacks of short shelf life are also available in a wide variety of types. Depending on your definition of healthier, most housewives will have several examples in their repertoire. Most commonly oats are used to make confections of this type, the most usual being the flapjack, a mix of oats, margarine, and a sweetener that may be brown sugar, honey, or malt extract. Dried fruit may be added to the mix, or layered between it. Traditional fruit cakes can be made following the principles of healthy eating by the use of wholewheat flour, polyunsaturated margarine, and with a low sugar content, or even with no added sugar.

Fruits or fruit juices are often used in such snacks to replace the more traditional refined white sugar. The rationale for this is that sugar in fruits is better on two counts than the refined sugar it replaces. The first is that the sugar in fruit is contained within cells and is only released when the cell structure is broken down by digestion. This usually takes some time to occur after the consumption of the item which means that ingestion of the fruit does not lead to the rapid release of sugar into the bloodstream that would occur if ordinary sugar were to be used instead. Rapid absorption of sugar is not good because it tends to stimulate an overreaction of the pancreas, encouraging overproduction of insulin. Insulin is a hormone that is needed to allow the body to utilize glucose. Too much insulin too quickly tends to rapidly clear the bloodstream of glucose sometimes leading to that shaky weak feeling we have all experienced at times. This is due to the abnormally low level of glucose in the blood that can follow such circumstances. In extreme cases this is known medically as hypoglycemia. If sugar is released from digestion slowly as is the case from fruit, the likelihood of such an overreaction by the pancreas is much reduced. Long term abuse of the pancreas in this way may also be one of the contributing factors in the development of diabetes in later life.

A further benefit of fruit as a source of sweetening is that the commonly eaten fruits, such as apples and pears have much of their sugar in the form of fructose. This is one of the components of sucrose, yet it does not depend on insulin for metabolism. For this reason it is acceptable for use in diabetic foods and its use does not carry with it the risk of rapid rises in insulin level, as would be the case with sucrose itself, or with glucose. Fruit juices are therefore a valuable means of sweetening healthier snacks, although fructose itself can also be used as well, normally in snacks with longer shelf life see later.

Honey is also used as a sweetener in this type of snack. The rationale for its use in thie context is that it is considered to be healthier than refined white sugar by virtue of its method of production (i.e. its perceived "naturalness") and of its composition. Honey is a mixture of sucrose glucose and fructose (i.e., it is partially inverted) and the overall sweetening power is slightly greater than that of sucrose alone. It also contains small amounts of vitamins and minerals, though it is difficult to make much of an argument for its healthy image on the basis of this. The presence of small amounts of pollen plus traces of propolis, the waxy material used by the bee to seal the honey cell is also sometimes referred to by proponents as reasons for considering it a healthier alternative to refined white sugar.

Extract of malt and molasses are also sometimes used as alternative sweeteners on the basis of their real or perceived superior health virtues. Stronger flavour can be a problem (or an advantage depending on the circumstances) particularly with molasses.

Molasses does contain significant amounts of certain trace elements such as manganese and chromium and malt extract does contain some of the B vitamins so perhaps there is a better case for considering these as healthier sweeteners than is the case for honey. The presence of small amounts of molasses (with the accompanying trace minerals) is also used to claim a healthier image for the various incompletely refined sugars, such as muscovado or Barbados sugar, or raw cane demerara (not to be confused with London demerara, which is white sugar crystals dressed with a coating of molasses) but also because they have not been subjected to the bleaching processes used for white sugar, which may leave residues in the final product. While these traces may not be significant to most people, allergies can develop in susceptible persons.

LONG SHELF-LIFE SNACKS

As with the short shelf life types the range is infinite, although they tend to fall into more clearly defined categories, probably because the longer shelf life permits marketing activities, and this encourages manufacturers to identify specific markets, and target their products accordingly. For reasons that are not at all clear the majority of products in this category are of the sweet confectionery type, rather than the savory type that form the bulk of the short shelf life products. The preservative power of sugar at concentrations that are palateble is perhaps one of the main resons, since salt at preservative concentrations would be less palatable. This type of product therefore presents the greatest challenge to food technologists working in this area. Some of the products available fall into more than one of the following subcategories, and a certain amount of duplication is therefore unavoidable although hopefully too much repetition has been avoided. The major subcategories identified are granola bars carob products furit bars gluten free snacks low fat/low calories products diabetic snacks and a catchall miscellaneous category.

Granola Bars

This is probably the best known category of healthier snack the one most familiar to just about everyone and undeniably the major product in sales value terms. The basic product has a number of variatiosn though the underlying product remains a bar based largely on flaked cereals such as oatflakes, super markets & drug stores but also in health food stores, which have had only minimal processing. The major types of cereal bars currently on the market are the original crunchy (dry) type and the never chewy (moist) type. Within that basic division can be found variations based on the use of carob as a coating or an ingredient and the use of dried fruit and/or nuts as ingredients.

Crunchy Bars The basic formulation for a crunchy type cereal or muesli bar (as they are sometimes called) would be oatflakes, a source of edible fat or oil such as vegetable oil and a sweetener. The relative proportions will very depending on the eating characteristics required. Other cereals such as wheatflakes, rye flakes, puffed rice, or puffed other cereals may be used to vary the texture and flavor. Small amounts of dried fruit (apple flakes, apricots raisins) nuts (almonds, peanuts, coconut, hazelnut), seeds (sesame sunflower pumpkin) or carob chips (see next section) may also be added to produce variations in flavor and texture. Recent developments in ingredient technology mean are becoming available to "stick" muesli bars together without as much sugar or fat which will increase their health appeal. One combination of sorbitol fructose and hydrolyzed gelatine is claimed to allow a calorie reduction of up to 40%. The use of fructose and sorbitol as sweeteners also means that products of this kind may be also suitable for diabetics, provided glucose, sucrose, or maltose are not also used.

Chewy Bars Inceasing the total amount of sugar relative to the other ingredients perhaps adding some invert sugar to reduce the risk of crystallization and adding some sweetened condensed skimmed milk produces a softer moister chewy bar that is more pleasant to eat. The superior attractiveness of this type of product can be seen from the fact that from its inception about five years ago it has grown to dominate the granola bar sector mainly in where it is sold on the perhaps mistaken belief that it has the virtues of the original cereal bar with a pleasanter taste. The main health, criticism leveled at this type of product is that it contains much too much freely available sugar to be considered healthy yet it is widely percived as such. The sugar content of the original crunchy granola bars would have been about 15-20% total sugar content, mainly in the form of sucrose but sometimes with some added honey as well. The chewy bars on the other hand, may well have significant amounts of glucose sucrose and fructose from several ingredients (e.g., corn syrup glucose syrup, sweetened condensed skimmed milk, raw cane sugar, dextrose, invert sugar syrup) and the total amount present will be nearer 25-30%. Novel ingredients aimed at giving the chewy texture but without the large amounts of readily assimilable sugar are being developed and some have reached the launch stage, although as far as is known, none is yet incorporated into the products that are currently being marketed.

The fat content of the chewy bars can be a little lower (12-15% as against 18%) but the use of hydrogenated vegetable oil to replace polyunsaturated vegetable oil tends to negate this from the health viewpoint. Some chewy cereal bars contain more fats (up to 22-24%), than the crunchy types, so this difference is variable.

Chewy bars make use of carob chips, chocolate chips,

fruit, nuts, and seeds to provide flavor and texture just as the crunchy types do.

Carob based Snacks

Carob is a naturally sweet flour obtained from the pods of the carob tree (Ceratonia siliqua L). It has been used as a food since biblical times when John the Baptist is said to have survived on it when in the wilderness. For this reason it is sometimes known s St. John's bread. It is an evergreen tree, and is unusual for being a member of the legume family. It grows in the Middle East and also in countries such as Spain Portugal, and Italy, and produces pods about 4-8 inches (10-20 cm) long similar to broad bean pods. The mature pods are harvested in the late summer, when they are dark brown and dry. The pods are first dry cleaned to eliminate stones and foreign matter. The cleaned pods are then washed to remove adhering matter then coarsely ground or kibbled. This process liberates the beans or seeds which are then separated and used for the manufacture of locust bean gum a stabilizer much used in foods such as icecream and saled dressings. The kibbled pod material is next sieved to eliminate fines, then roasted to bring the moisture content down below 5% & to develop the desired colour & flavour. Just as with coffee & cocoa the roasting process is critical in the development of the appropriate flavor. The roasted pod material is then ground down to a flour (less than 200 mesh) before being sieved and packed for use.

Carob is noteworthy for its high content of sugar (45-50% of which glucose and fructose form roughly a third each) its low fat content (less than 1%, compared to cocoa at 24%) and its relatively high calcium content (200-250 mg/100 g). It is also a useful source of iron, containing 50 mg per 100 g. Its principal characteristic of use from the healthy snack point of view is that it has a chocolate/cocoa type flavor and appearance yet does not contain any caffeine theobromine, or other as yet unidentified constituent (s) that can trigger migraines and/or allergic responses in certain susceptible individuals. Cocoa contains over 160 mg of caffeine per 100 g and over 1100 mg of theobromine per 100 g.

Carob is used in two main ways in the production of healthier snacks either as a total substitute for chocolate in the manufacture of confectionery type bars consisting mainly or solely of carob/sugar fat or in the form of a couverture as helf or total coating on other bases such as granola fruit or nut bars or as an ingredient in such bars in the form of a carob chip. It may also be used as a flour as an ingredient in cereal of fruit bars to provide coloring and flavoring.

Confectionery Bars The use of carob in confectionery type bars is almost directly parallel to the use of cocoa powder to make chocolate bars. The basic formulation of such a product would be sugar usually raw cane a vegetable fat such as palm kernel oil carob flour wheat flour vanilla extract and lecithin as an emulsifier. Whey powder skimmed milk powder or condensed skimmed milk may be used to provide a milky contribution to the product. Carob can be used with a wide variety of other ingredients to provide flavor or texture. Additional health features may be incorporated by the use of sweeteners such as molasses or by omission of any added sweeteners at all since carob is naturally sweet. Such bars can be and often are formulated without large amounts of fat which gives them an added healthier appeal. Substitution of soya milk for cows milk either with or without added sugar provides a further attraction for those people who are intolerant to cows milk or choose not to eat or drink it.

Besides being presented in the form of a bar carob is increasingly being used for the manufacture of healthier novelty products such as Easter eggs (with features such as sugar free dairy free etc.) beans advent calendars Christmas tree decorations and figures such as Santa claus and the Easter Bunny. It is also now being used for the production of filled bars of individual bite size pieces with fondant or fruit filling and for composite nut/cereal combinations in which the other ingredients are dispersed in solid carob rather than being coated with couverture. Products mimicking buttons (flattened chocolate drops) are also now made from carob. This trend will continue as more and more people become aware of a preference for carob and virtually anything made from chocolate could and may ultimately be made from carob.

Carob Couverture In this application carob again parallels cocoa, in that it is usually used together with fat, sugar and perhaps skimmed milk powder in the form of a chocolate substitute for much the same reason as listed for confectionery type bars. Carob couverture tends to be used either to half coat or to totally enclose other bars such as granola bars (usually of the crunchy type), fruit bars or bars based on nuts and/or seeds. It may also be used in the form of carob chips, as an ingredient in granola or fruit/nut bars. Coating a cereal bar with carob couverture increases the overall fat and sugar content making the bar more appealing to eat but also reducing its intrinsic "healthier" nature. One of the more popular and widely available types of the carob based healthier snacks is carob coated fruits or nuts. The fruits include raisins apricots dates, and ginger, and the nuts include peanuts hazels brazils and almonds. The carob couverture used may contain added sugar or may be made without sugar, to allow a "no added" sugar claim. The same items are also available with a yogurt based coating consisting of sugar (optional) vegetable fat flour whey or skimmed milk powder, yogurt solids, and an emulsifying agent such as lecithin.

Fruit Bars

Fruit bars are potentially the most "healthy" of all the snacks discussed in this chapter. They are in general low in fat, high in fiber, and do not have any added salt nor much in the way of readily assimilable sugar. This feature makes the products also suitable for diabetics, although they are not usually sold as such. They are usually suitable for dieters but again they are rarely sold on such a basis.

There are a variety of types available, but the one thing they have in common is that dried fruit forms the largest ingredient. Almost any dried fruit can potentially be used but the more popular types are apricots, raisins, dates, pears, peaches and apples. Dried fruit on its own can be difficult to maintain in a soft, chewy state, so often some vegetable oil will be added to the pulverized or minced fruit. Sugar (raw cane) honey or other sweetener may be added though this will reduce the healthier claim and many products in this area are now featuring no added sugar claims. Such claims are sometimes made in relation to products sweetened with fruit juices or fruit juice concentrates something that is legally correct but still involves the addition of potentially large amounts of free sugar thus reducing or negating any healthier claim. Binders and fillers such as wheat flour potato flour apple fiber rice flour or oatflakes are all used in such products of one sort or another and rice paper is sometimes used to coat the slab or bar to facilitate handling at the point of manufacture and to reduce the problem of the product sticking to the packaging material.

Gluten free Snacks

Gluten is a mixture of two proteins called gliadin and glutenin. Together they confer on wheat the major cereal containing them the ability to form an elastic dough that can retain gas. This enables the baker to produce a light open textured bread that is pleasant to eat. Rye also contains some gluten but not enough to allow the production of a dough that retains its open texture during baking. Oats, barley, & buckwheat also contain small quantities of gluten for most people the presence of gluten in foods is of no great consequence but for an unfortunate minority the problem can be life threatening. The numbers involved are small according to the Coeliac Socity which represents such people something like 1 in 2000 people are affected by coeliac disease or gluten enteropathy as it is technically known. The number of people adversely affected by sensitivity to wheat or gluten is probably somewhat higher than this. The condition is caused by the presence of gliadin and in sensitive individuals it causes diarrhea cramps and a general irritation of the intestine so much so that its ability to absorb foods is reduced and the affected individual beings to suffer other ill effects from the lack of nuterients that this entails. Untreated coeliac disease can lead to death from malnutrition or from intestinal cancer.

The only possible treatment of such a condition is to follow a diet that rigidly excludes gluten and if this is done the patient can return to a life style that is close to normal. Some snacks, by their very nature, are gluten free such as the fruit bars without added wheat or oats, discussed above. There are also healthier snacks made specifically for people who must avoid gluten/wheat. Two main types are marketed at present, granola bars and crackers/crispbread.

The granola bars made to be gluten free can be based on soya flakes, rice flakes, or millet flakes. Apart from the replacement of wheat or oats by these items, the remaining ingredients and the manufacturing techniques will be essentially similar to those used for ordinary cereal bars. Crakers or crispbreads can be made from a variety of alternative cereals such as maize and rice, potato, tapioca or soya are other alternatives. Since wheat contributes "bite" to crackers and crispbreads, the healthier version made without wheat does tend to have less bite and be a little more crumbly, although a reasonable texture can be achieved without use of wheat or oats. Both cookies and savory crackers can be formulated in this way.

Crispbreads are more difficult to make without the use of wheat or rye. The closest product made to date is the ricecake, a product made by gentle compression and baking of puffed rice grains.

Low calorie Snacks

Considering the huge market that exists for diet pills

and tablets it is surprising that there are so few snack products promoted for use in conjunction with calorie controlled diets. Perhaps, it is because the usual concept of a snack is not compatible with the idea of weight reduction, in which the emphasis is on "good eating habits" which presumably can mean cutting out snacks. Granola bars are sometimes included in the meal replacement type products basically with the same formulation as the crunchy type products discussed eariler perhaps with added vitamins and minerals. Fruit bars are intrinsically low in calories and high in fiber and so are by definition low calorie snacks although rarely promoted as such. Low calorie bread can be made by omitting the shortening normally used and incorporating extra protein usually from wheat to assist with the retention of gas and to give a more acceptable mouthfeel to the product.

Cookies and crackers with reduced shortening content and with a cream type filling are marketed as meal replacement products again sometimes with added vitamins and minerals. Combination granola/fruit bars are marketed as low calorie snacks with added vitamins and minerals to act as meal replacements. These products are not calorie reduced in the accepted sense of the word but are packaged and promoted as a portin and calorie controlled substitute for normal food items as much their use entials consumption of fewer calories than the items they replace.

Diabetic Products

Diabetes is condition that affects large numbers of people, usually adult, in which the body does not produce enough of the hormone insulin. It is estimated that between 1 and 2% of the U.K. population and a similar proportion of North Americans is affected in varying degrees. Insulin is produced by the pancreas, and its role is to assist with the metabolism of glucose. If there is not enough insulin available in the bloodsteam, then the glucose cannot be removed for metabolism, and the blood glucose level rises. Eventually the level rises to such a degree that the kidneys cannot deal with it, and glucose "spills" over into the urine within which it can readily be detected. High blood glucose levels often lead to feelings, of fatigue and in the long term can predispose to formation of blood clots in the eyes (leading to blindness), kidneys (leading to kindney failure), or other organs. Heart disease is especially prevalent among diabetics. Various treatments are used cornerstone of all being dietary treatment designed to avoid the consumption of foods containing significant amounts of free glucose sucrose or maltose.

Diabetic snacks therefore are produced with this restriction in mind and usually rely on either fructose or sorbitol for sweetening power. Neither of these substances requires insulin for metabolism and so can be utilized by the diabetic (as well of course as the nondiabetic). Fructose is sweeter than sucrose or glucose and so less can be used to achieve the same sweetening power although the effect is fairly marginal. Its high cost means it is only likely to be used where other sweeteners are not acceptable and its use by diabetics is restricted to a maximum of 1 oz (25 g) per day. Sorbitol is a six carbon sugar alcohol made from glucose in which the aldehyde group has been converted to an alcohol group by hydrogenation. It also is fairly expensive compared to sucrose. It is absorbed more slowly than sucrose or fructose and is converted to fructose for further metabolism. Its slow absorption means that significant amounts can accumulate in the intestine creating osmotic disturbances that can lead to diarrhea. For this reason its use is limited. In practice products containing either fructose or sorbitol are usually labeled with the statement best eat less than 1 oz of sorbitol/fructose per day.

Substituting either or both of these sweeteners for conventional sweeteners means that a range of diabetic snacks can readily be produced and in practice this is the case. Granola bars boiled sweets chocolate bars and couverture are all produced and marketed as suitable for diabetics. Some cereal bars now marketed contain relatively new derivatives of glucose produced by polymerization. The polymerization means that much of the glucose is unavailable for digestion and hence does not yield as many calories per ounce as glucose itself (28/oz as compared to 112/oz) and it does not stimulate insulin production in the same way and nor does it cause an increase in blood glucose levels in diabetics. It is therefore, suitable for diabetics, as well as being low in calories, and noncariogenic (i.e. it does not promote tooth decay). Combinations of sorbitol, fructose, & hydrolized protein are also now becoming available for this use. The combination gives superior stickiness without the need for the same amount of carbohydrate as conventional granola bars, thus allowing a reduction in total calories. The end result is a lower calorie granola bar that is suitable for diabetics, as well as those needing a reduced calorie bar for whatever reasons.

A somewhat different approach to the formulation of snacks for diabetics follows from research that shows that the use of viscous gels can help reduce the rate of absorption of food constituents & help to reduce the peak levels of boold sugar that might other wise arise. Small amounts of highly viscous gels, such as guar gum xanthan gum, or glucomannan, help to slow down the rate of absorption of sugar molecules, probably by increasing the viscosity of intestinal and stomach contents, so as to inhibit the movement of solute molecules to the absorption surfaces. Guar gum is already marketed in this way, in the form of a snack bar containing glucose, raisins, soya flour, cocoa butter, milk powder, fructose and dried apple, as well as sorbitol, glycerol, and 2.5% guar gum. Guar gum is also used in the formulation of cookies, crackers, and crispbreads for diabetics.

Miscellaneous

Such a group of products as this defies any description save to say they do not fit into any of the foregoing categories and yet have one or more aspects which qualifies them for the description "healthier snack". Vitamin and/ or mineral fortified products such as soup, aimed at the elderly or convalescent, and fortified milk powder based drinks for the same market and calorie packed vitamin/ mineral/amino acid fortified milk based drinks intended for body builders are good examples. Other snacks for body body-builders, such as high-calorie chewy bars, or isotonic drinks, could also be considered as being healthier snacks.

Licorice, while used in traditional candy products, also has a role in healthier snacks, either in the form of a licorice juice stick (the juice extracted from the licorice root and dried into a bar shape) or as the licorice root stick itself, sold as it is a chewable "natural confection". Licorice itself is naturally sweet (indeed, one of the noncaloric sweeteners under development currently is derived from licorice) and the root when chewed releases the sweet flavor of licorice and hence makes a healthier snack. Mixing licorice extract with molasses and wheat flour leads to the production of a chewy licorice snack bar that is popular with both children and adults.

Other medicinal herbs or plants are also sometimes used in the form of confectionery, and as such can be considered "healthier". Extract of coltsfoot is used to make a coltsfoot candy traditionally used to treat cought's and still sold to day. Horehound. another herbs used for the relief of coughs, is used in the form of a candy bar, together with extracts of capsicum coltsfoot and ginger, and oil of peppermint and aniseed to produce a herbal candy sold on the basis of its (undefined) medicinal properties. Even potato chips can and do fall into this category either on the basis of the use of organically grown potatoes the use of polyunsaturated vegetable oil for frying the retention of the peel on the potato used for the chip (higher fiber claim) or on the basis of a lower fat content. This latter aspect can be quite significant with reductions of up to 30% and in a high fat product such as potato chip such a reduction can be a valuable aid to a healthier snack claim. The basis process used is to partially fry the crisp at a somewhat higher temperature than normal. The part fried crisp at a containing some residual moisture is then dried without further use of frying. Different techniques are available for this ranging from microwave cooking to hot air drying. The end result is a lighter colored lower fat crisp that still retains much of the crisp texture and flavor. Demand for these products is rising and the presence of such snacks seems to be attracting new purchasers into the market place rather than just being used in place of the existing high fat crisps.

The list of healthier snacks can go on almost indefinitely depending largely on definition and the way a product is marketed. The types listed above represent the major indentifiable categories availanle at present, but the picture is evolving repidly, as the health aspects of snack foods (and indeed all other foods) gain more recognition. Observation of the market place is probably the only way to maintain a current perspective.

4

SNACK FOOD PRESERVATION AND PACKAGING

The definition of snack food adopted in the Introduction to this book prechudes the consderation here of every single food used as a snack but includes consideration of the majority of those that depend for safety, longevity, and maintenance of characteristic organoleptic qualities upon the kind quality, and methodology of their packaging. Twenty years ago there was no difficulty defining a snack because only a few products (e.g. potato chips, nuts, cookies, etc.) were regarded as such. With the spectacular growth in this market largely due to the advent of extrusion cooking we need to further separate liquid (instant soups, pot noodles) from solid snacks that require either no or minimal heating or ot satisfy the requirement of a hot meal. Cooked foods verging on full meals are now embraced by the wider definition of snacks and it is here that much packaging development has taken place, catalyzed by the mushrooming invasion of microwave ovens into the domestic kitchen.

This is based on studies in which their "snack food" definition has one additional major constraint that is not in the definition used in this book that the snack must be an "impulse" purchase, a constraint that is somewhat irrelevant in the context here. But it is a wider definition than most and includes the following.

Conventional Snacks
Potato chips
Corn Flakes and other forms of corn

Sayory/extruded
Nuts
Salted/savory crackers

Newer Snacks
Instant hot (pot snacks and cup soups)
Cereal bars/mixes
Meat
Novel (ethnic and filled)
Countline confectionery items
Dairy beverages (milk, yogurt, fermented)
Sweet baked items including cookies

This includes quite a large proportion of the snack foods discussed in this book some notable exceptions being fish per se, cheese, fruit, and fruit based snacks, and snack adjuvents such as pickles, dips, sauces etc. However, it is a usufully broad upon which demands on packaging snack foods can be based, and incidentally happily includes packaging appropriate to the few items not explicitly included in the Frost & Sullivan definition.

PACKAGING MATERIALS FOR MAINTAINING PRODUCT INTEGRITY

All products should satisfy the requirements of protection from handling, distribution, and retailing, which determine the need for primary, secondary, and tertiary packaging. The primary packaging protects the basic product and is typically a bag, carton, or tube. Secondary packaging or shipping container as it is sometimes referred to is designed to contain a group of primary packages and is commonly a corrugated box. The third level of packaging rears its head when a number of primary or secondary packages are assembled on a pallet for handling as a unit load for storage in a warehouse for eventual distribution. An overall packaging specification may further include the need to apply strapping either over or without shrinkwrapping or some other plastic overwrap. A unit in manufacturing terms generally refers to the secondary pack, which is to be distinguished from a unit pallet load.

Because of the high costs involved in, for example, refrigerated distribution and storage, major cost savings are frequently possible by ensuring that the dimensions of the primary and secondary packs result in maximum utilization of pallet space. It is also important to make sure that the precautions taken to ensure the integrity of the product within the package are not so excessive or inconvenient as to give rise to difficulty of opening or even considerable risk of damage by the consumer in gaining access to the product. In one area of this context singly oriented plastics are more useful than bioriented ones but it is a problem that is not by any means universally surmounted. Scissors or a knife are by no means routinely available and a Fort Knox situation is more undesirable.

FACTORS RESPONSIBLE FOR LOSS OF QUALITY IN SNACK FOODS

Product quality is compromised if consumer acceptance decreases during storage. The mechanisms of deteriorative changes that can be arrested by packaging may be summerized as.

Moisture gain or loss

Oxidation due to residual oxygen in the sealed pack

Photolytically induced oxidation and other reactions from the ultraviolet (UV) light component of natural sunlight or/and from artificial lighting used in retail cabinets

Microbial action mainly enzymic

To some extent there is an interaction among the different mechanisms in the sense that or example moisture gain in cookies and crackers not only results in rejection for its obvious effect on texture but can also result in microbial activity. Many microbiologic organisms cannot sustain growth if the moisture level (or more basically the water activity equal to the equilibrium relative humidity (ERH) expressed as a percentage) is below certain values. Bacteria cannot generally propagate at water activity of less than 0.95 (95% ERH) yeasts require a water activity of <0.85, and molds <0.70. To play safe, the lower the water activity, the less likely is it that microbial activity will limit the shelf life of the product. Clearly, water vapor permeation characteristics of the primary packaging are an important controlling element in packaging design.

Oxidation generally relates to the interaction between the product and oxygen within the pack and may manifest itself as a development of rancidity of fatty constituents. Oxygen from air trapped within the pack is thus capable of leading to product rejection. Another type of oxidation is due to the generation of free radicals from the effects of UV light. Excluding the use of antioxidants, which would tend to fall under the emotive headling of "additives" both effects can be eliminated by judicious selection of packaging materials and exploitation of controlled atmosphere packaging (CAP) or vacuum packs.

The injurious effects of UV light on microorganisms may be exploited with advantage where surface sterilization is possible by exposing a product in a transparent package to intense UV irradiation produced by mercury discharge lamps. Because of the harmful effects of strong UV light on skin surfaces and especially eyes the face needs to be protected when working close to the source of the light even from rays reflected by the ceiling unless the discharge tubes are enclosed in an opaque tunnel. Glass (but not quartz), or close-fitting goggles or plastic face visors need to be worn if working close to UV light that is not covered. UV irradiation is an elegant form of in line surface sterilization (provided the UV light has direct access to all parts of the product and the packaging film is substantially transparent to UV light at the germicidal wavelength of 2537 A) which is well suited to snack foods requiring a high water activity to maintain organoleptic and textural properties. In line surface sterilization of primary packaging that will come into contact with the food product is also practiced for cartons formed continuously from reeled film.

Bacteria are most sensitive to destruction by UV (2537

A) and some spores, algae, and protozoa are most resistant. Table 17.3 indicates doseges for inactivation of a wide range of microorganisms. Surface sterilization may be applied to products that are thermally processed, where the surfaces become recontaminated between emergence from an oven or extruder and eventual packaging. Various highly reflecting materials used in the construction of a UV sterilizing tunnel (or batch sterilizer) will enhance access by the UV to all parts of the surface, and thereby improve the level of sterility of the packaged product this is particularly important where the product surface to be sterilized has a high roughness factor. There is no value in applying surface sterilization with UV light if the interior of the edible product lacks sterility at the stage of packaging.

BARRIER PROPERTIES OF PLASTIC FILMS

Films can be divided into two categories those based on cellulose and those based on thermoplastics. The regenerated cellulose based materials may be uncoated (PT) or coated with a layer of nitrocellose (MST) or polyvinylidene chloride (MXXT). Even uncoated dry cellulose films are excellent barriers to gases, but not to moisture. When they are coated, moisture pick up can still occur via the raw trimmed edges. Sealing is achieved by a variety of energy, intensive steps to create fusion by flaming use of heaters, hot wires, ultrasonic, impulse, rediofrequency or high frequency energy. Heat sealable coatings may be exploited that also serve to increase the barrier properties of a laminate.

The four most important gas permeabilities are those for water vapor, carbon dioxide, nitrogen, and oxygen. The relative permeability values do not follow the simplistic relationship suggestive of Grahams Law of Diffusion. Density, tensile strees, elongation and softening points are additional parameters that characterize the suitability of a plastic for a particular duty. The review of plastics in packaging is recommended for detailed data on relevant properties. Table 17.4 contains permeability data of plastics

TABLE 17-3. APPROXIMATE MINIMUM DOSE IN J/M^2 OF ULTRAVIOLET RADIATION AT 2537Å REQUIRED FOR THE 90% DESTRUCTION OF VARIOUS MICROORGANISMS

Bacteria		**Yeasts**	
Bacillus anthracis	45	Common yeast cake	60
B. megatherium (veg.)	11	***Saccharomyces ellipsoideus***	
B. megatherium (spores)	27	(bakers yeast)	60
B. parathyphosus	32	***Saccharomyces cerevisiae***	
B. subtilis	70	(bakers yeast)	60
Spores	120	***Torula sphaerica*** (as found	
		in milk and icecream)	23
Clostridium tetani	130		
Corynebact diphtheriae	34	**Various algae**	
Eberthella typhosa	21	Diatoms	
Escherichia coli	30	Green algae	3600–6000
Leptospira spp.-Infectious		Blue algae	
jaundice	32		
Micrococcus candidus	61		
Micrococcus piltonencis	81	**Protozoa**	
Micrococcus sphaeroides	100	*Paramecium*	640–1000
Mycobacterium tuberculosis	62		
Neisseria catarrphalis	44	**Worms**	
Phytomonas tumefaciens	44	Nematode eggs	400
Proteus vulgaris	26		
Pseudomonas aeruginosa	55		
Pseudomonas fluorescens	35	**Mold spores**	
Salmonella enteriditis	40	***Aspergillus amstelodami***	
S. typhosa (typhoid fever)	22	(meat)	667
S. paratyphi (enteric fever)	32	***Aspergillus flavus***	600
S. typhimurium	80	***Aspergillus glaucus***	440
Sarcina lutea	197	***Aspergillus niger*** (bakeries)	1320
Serratia marcescens	24	***Cladosporium herbarum***	
Shigella dysenteriae		(cold stores)	600
(dysentery form)	22	***Mucor mucedo*** (meat, fat,	
Shigella flexneri (dysentery		bread, cheese)	650
form)	17	***Mucor racemosus***	170
Shigella paradysenteriae	17	***Oospora lactis***	50
Spirillum rubrum	44	***Penicillium digitatum***	440
Staphylococcus albus	18	***Penicillium expansum***	130
Staphylococcus aureus	26	***Penicillium chrysogenum***	
Streptococcus hemolyticus	22	(fruit)	500
Streptococcus lactis	62	***Penicillium roqueforti***	130
Streptococcus viridans	20	***Rhizopus nigricans***	1110
Mycobacterium tuberculi	100	***Scopulriopsis brevicaulis***	
Vibrio comma (cholera)	34	(cheese, etc.)	800

for nitrogen, oxygen, carbon dioxide, and water vapor.

In seeking to protect a snack food with gases to provide a controlled atmosphere it is necessary to distinguish between an inerting effect designed to exclude oxygen (and thereby prevent oxidation reactions) and a positive antimicrobial effect due to the gas itself. For example, unlike the single inerting effect of nitrogen, carbon dioxide exerts three effects.

1. It may act as a displacer of oxygen.
2. It may inhibit microbial growth by exerting a toxic effect on the microorganisms. The gas is particularly effective against Gramnegative aerobic spoilage bacteria such as Pseudomonas spp. which, cause off flavors.
3. If moisture is present it will react with water to produce hydrogenions which in turn inhibit microbial growth. Bacteria generally do not propagate at pH values below 4.5 whereas yeasts and molds grow quite happily at pH values as low as 1.

The fact that carbon dioxide is readily soluble in both water and any lipid component within the pack must be recognized in setting the initial gas composition. If carbon dioxide on its own is used in a pack then, with a moist or/ and fatty snack, a partial vacuum eventually forms and due allowance must be made to prevent collapse of the primary pack. Mixing carbon dioxide with introgen reduces the effects of dissolution into the food components. Conversely, if it is known that packs are to be delivered to

TABLE 17-4. PERMEABILITY OF FILMS TO GASES

	Permeability (ml/m²/MPa/day)[a]				Ratios (to N_2 permeability		
Material	N_2 at 30°C	O_2 at 30°C	CO_2 at 30°C	H_2O at 25°C 90% RH	O_2/N_2	CO_2/N_2	H_2O/N_2
PVdC (Saran)	0.07	0.35	1.9	94	5.0	27	1,400
PCTFE[b]	0.20	0.66	4.8	19	3.4	24	95
Polyester (Mylar A)	0.33	1.47	10	8700	4.5	31	27,000
Polyamide (Nylon 6)	0.67	2.5	10	47,000	3.7	15	70,000
PVC unplasticized	2.7	8.0	6.7	10,000	3.0	25	3,800
Cellulose Acetate (P912)	19	52	450	500,000	2.8	24	2,700
Polythene							
(d=0.954–0.960)	18	71	230	860	3.9	13	47
(d=0.922)	120	360	2,300	5,300	2.9	19	44
Polystyrene	19	73	590	80,000	3.8	32	4,200
Polypropylene (d=0.910)	—	150	610	4,500	—	—	

From Paine and Paine

[a]All permeabilities calculated for 25-μm thick film. Units are millilitres per square meter per megapascal per day.

[b]Polychlorotrifluoroethylene.

TABLE 17-5. RATE OF MOLD GROWTH IN CRUSTY ROLLS PACKAGED UNDER VARIOUS GASES INCLUDING THE PRESENCE OF OXYGEN ABSORBERS

Headspace atmosphere	Delays to mold growth
Air	5–6
CO_2/N_2 (60 : 40)	16–18
N_2	9–11
Air + oxygen absorber	>60
CO_2/N_2 + oxygen absorber	>60
N_2 + oxygen absorber	>60

a geographic region several thousand feet above sea level, then carbon dioxide partially dissolved in the food components prevents pack failure caused by the lower external pressure on the pack.

CAP is to be distinguished from "modified atmosphere" packaging (MAP) in that the former is a controlled atmosphere throughout storage, whereas the latter (generally not applicable to snacks and applying to living food cells that releavse carbon dioxide during storage) is adjusted at the onset of storage. For snack food packaging the objective is to select the most impermeable film (s) consistent with satisfying obvious cost considerations. The effects of gases on controlling mold growth in crusty bread rolls stored at 77°F (25°C) is clearly demonstrated in Table 17.5.

The absorber or "getter" in this instance was iron oxide. Its efficacy demonstrates spectacularly the effect of creating an essentially anaerobic environment (<0.05% oxygen) in order to suppress the growth of common bakery organisms. Without doubt the use of getters for creating the ideal gas environment for processed snacks, coupled to the use of highly impermeable single or laminated film, will invade much of the more sophisticated technology in CAP in the next few years.

Many developments in gas packaging have been prompted by advances in lamination technology that enable downgauging of thermoformable films by as much as 30%. Five layer lamination is not unusual. One commercial converter supplies film having a five layer construction composed of polymide-polyolefin-polyamide-polyolefin-polyolefin produced in line. This combination allows the polyamide supporting layer to exhibit pliability and impact penetration resistance combined with flexibility and to be downgauged without loss of properties of the polyolefins. Polyolefin layers provide sealing character and water vapor impermeability and are selected from polyethylene (PE) ethylene vinyl acetate copolymers (EVA) or ionomer, while ethylene vinyl alcohol copolymer (EVAL) is incorporated to provide a low oxygen transmission rate. It is the co-extrusion process of lamination tailored to the barrier quality required that determines the level of downgauging of the overall film thickness. The theory of downgauging is twofold it exploits the barrier properties of the adhesives (generally polyolefins with grafted on polar groups such as OH or OOOH to give adhesion to the polar barrier polymers) between the laminae as well as reducing the effects of parmeable patches by avoiding overlap. Films sensitive to moisture uptake in turn receive protection thus maintaining their sought after properties by being sandwiched between moisture resistant polymers. Thermoplastics possess measurable oxygen transmission rates so that the incorporation of polyvinylidene chloride (PVDC) or EVAL in the laminates increases the barrier properties sufficiently to give shelf lives of at least a year to most pasteurized or sterilized products.

Product protection from the effects of oxidation is also practiced by resorting to vacuum packaging and relying on high barrier films to preserve the vacuum during storage. This method of preservation is tending to give way to CAP partly for aesthetic reasons. Other disadvantages of vacuum packaging include.

- Lack of resistance to mechanical damage to product
- Allowing anaerobic spoilage to take place
- Total dependence on perfect sealing

While vacuum packing will continue to be exploited with certain nonsnack foods such as raw meat its application to snack foods is severely limited.

At the less sophisticated end of the packaging spectrum there are several materials that may be more cost effective in their application. Experts have assembled a working table (Table 17.6) that provides a ready method of reckoning the type of packaging to use for different types of snacks. Products having a high fat level are more likely to raise the question of chemical transfer between packaging and the product. This subject has become so sensitive in recent years that the criteria of acceptable materials based on processing/product need to be constantly updated. Recent evidence of the formation of dioxin albeit at the parts per billion level during the age old process of bleaching fibers during the paper making process has raised difficult

TABLE 17-6. A COMPARISON OF SOME PROPERTIES OF THE COMMON FLEXIBLE PACKAGING MATERIALS (QUALITIES GRADED FROM 0 TO 10 WHERE 10 IS THE HIGHEST GRADING AND 0 SIGNIFIES THAT THE QUALITY IS NONEXISTENT)

	Resistance to:					
	Water vapor	Gas transmission	Odor	Water	Oil or grease	Chemicals
Polythene (PE)	7	3	3	10	5	10
PVC	2	5	5	9	8	6
PVdC copolymer	9	8	8	10	8	8
Polyester	4	6	8	10	8	10
PT cellulose	0	6	6	5	10	3
MSAT cellulose	5	6	6	6	10	2
MXXT cellulose	6	9	9	6	10	3
PE/MSAT cellulose	8	8	8	6	8	8
Cellulose acetate	1	2	2	6	6	3
Kraft paper	0	0	0	2	0	0
Sulfite paper	0	0	0	2	0	0
Glassine	0	3	3	3	4	2
Waxed glassine	4	5	4	5	6	4
PE coated paper	7	3	3	6	5	7
PVdC coated paper	8	8	8	6	8	7
0.009 mm Al foil	10	10	10	10	10	5

questions about its continued practice where food comes into contact with board products particularly where there may be a concentration effect in chemical transfer to a fatty component of a snack food.

METALLIZED FILMS

The packaging system selected for a specific product must take into consideration not only the product (composition, mechanical strength, sensitivity to oxygen and moisture uptake/loss, etc.) but also marketing and distribution factors. Marketing embraces the image, which may be affected by the condition of the product at the point of sale and any subsequent storage within the home. Visual impact and printability of the packaging materials also affect the image. In recent years there has been a move towards the use of metallized films both for functional (blocking of light & high gas barrier) properties and sometimes purely for aesthetic reasons.

Metallization of a film consists of evaporating a suitable metal by means of heat and condensing on to the surface to be coated under high vacuum. The film (or paper) is unwound over a large chilled drum below which is a series of "boats" or crucibles in which the metal usually aluminum or zinc is evaporated. To produce stripe metallization a mask is placed in front of the metal source typical thickness level of the deposited film are of the order of 0.05 m. The reasons for using metallized film fall into three categories.

Cosmetic improvements. The highlyb refletive finish of metallized materials, particularly films offers unique marketing advantages. Foil laminates are yesterdays technology, while metallic inks come a poor second on grounds of appearance.

Cost savings. Because of the low metal requirements in any metallizing treatment a given material has a lower cost than laminating it with aluminum foil. In many cases the use of metallized film leads to faster wrapping speeds than when using foil laminate.

Improvements in performance specification. With certain plastics and cellophane films metallization enhances barrier properties and retains them unlike foil laminates when the packaging is crumpled and flexed. However foil laminate does retain an advantage in its dead fold characteristics where such is required e.g. where double end fold wrapping individual items is a requirement. Because of the low thickness of application typically 0.1 g/m^2 as opposed to 22 g/m^2 for aluminum foil laminate metallized film and paper can be used as a direct substitute for the umetallized material as the mechanical handling properties will be virtually identical.

Both gas transfer through films and UV light transmission are generally the limiting factors controlling the shelf life of packaged product. In instances where transparency in the primary packaging is a requirement improved impermeability and UV reflection may be achieved by processes known as ion plating and magnetron sputtering. Superficially the effect is similar to metallization in that metal atoms end up as a thin coating on the substrate (plastic film or bottle) so thin that it may not even be visually evident. Nevertheless the coating improves impermeability to gases and is substantially opaque to UV radiation whilst transmitting visible light. The method of application of the coating may be extended to include metal oxides.

BAGS

There are essentially four types of paper bags used in packaging flat, gusseted, self opening satchel, and rose bottom. Sulfite papers are for general purpose and kraft bags are used where strength is a particular requirement. Resistance to flavor loss and to greases is achieved using vegetable parchment or glassine, and wet strength is achieved by waxing. The use of films (plastics) has increased the applications of begging quite considerably, particularly when used in combination with paper. Indeed greaseproof waxed and vegetable parchments are now largely supplanted by film materials in bagging applications.

Low and high density polythene, cellulose, polypropylene, polyester, vinyl, and Saran coated films are more generally used where moisture barrier and grease resistance are required.

MACHINERY

The type of machinery of relevance to the packaging of snacks includes form fill seal (FFS) gas inerting, bagging, and cartoning.

Form-Fill-Seal (FFS) Machines

FFS machines use a reel of flexible material that can be paper film or laminates and form it into a tube and then seal fill and seal off the contents. Alternatively the machine may fold the material lengthwise and seal it at right angles to the fold of from a series of pockets that are filled and then selaled. The first type of machine produces pouches with a seal at each end and down the center of one face while the latte type forms sachets with three or all four edges sealed. FFS machines are of three types.

- *Vertical* machines in which the material is formed into a circular section over a forming collar.
- *Horizontal* machines where the material is formed into a rectangular section through a forming box.
- *Sachet-forming* machines that either use a single web folded in half and then cross sealed or use two webs that are brought together and initally sealed on three sides.

Containers are frequently produced from reels of material by thermoforminga series of trays in a web filling then feeding another web over the open tray that is then heat sealed to the base. The sealed pack is then punched out to provide discrete units or cut at intervals to provide multipack units.

This latter facility is capable of reducing unit costs and is popular with the consumer, it makes FFS machines an essential requirement in modern market oriented packs.

The step of drawing into the mold may be with vacuum or compressed air and with or without plug assistance. When using compressed air, forming pressures of 6-8 atmospheres are common. Compressed air generally gives a more uniform wall thickness than resorting to vacuum forming. For complicated shapes, mechanical prestratching may be required as part of the forming sequence.

FFS machines are generally used in gas packaging. The required mixture of gases can be produced and stored in a conventional gas cylinder or produced on demend by a mixter installed on the packaging machine. If exclusion of oxygen is the objective and that applies to the vast majority of packaged snack foods then it is ocnsiderably more economical to link to packaging machine to a supply of bulk gas rather than suffer the high cost of cylinder rentals. Many food processing operations may already be using bulk gas for freezing of chilling foods. In the case of liquid nitrogen (LN) the gas that is continually evaporating from the storage vessel may be used for inerting. Enhanced vaporization facilities on the storage tank enable the demand to be matched with the supply of the inerting gas. Where precise mixtures are required equipment is available based on dialing a preset mixtures. Mixers for three or more gases have separate dials for each gas. Gas packaging machines are basically FFSs with lances projecting inot the partially formed packs, attached to the gas metering units. Major suppliers of the integrated machines include Multivac, APV Baker, Tiromat, Lark Valley, Fuji, Ilapak, Aucouturier and Dynapack all supplying microprocessor controlled machines capable of handling a variety of films and laminates. The more advanced machines provide a continuous readout of the oxygen content of the package.

Bagging and Cartoning Machinery

The unit steps involved in bagging include feeding the flat bag to the loading point, opening the bag and preparing it for acceptance of product and finally effecting the closure. Initial opening is generally achieved with the aid of mechanical fingers assisted by compressed air. Either the product is then moved into the bag or the bag is manipulated over the product the latter being preferred to minimize mechanical damage to the product. Closures may be effected by use of ties clips staples tapes or heat sealing of laminated bags.

A cartoning system generally linked with a specific manufacturers machinery/board supplier constructs from a flat blank the erected carton for filling and sealing. Commercial systems are sophisticated and totally automated with many aiming to produce long life packs lasting several months. Systems may be supplied that will erect fill and close either a prelined or a laminated carton or that make their own liners on the machine. Before committing an operation to a particular system consideration should be given to multisourcing of the packaging as a barrier against price rises flecxibility of machine to cope with different pack sizes with minimal downtime space requirements and expansion capabilities.

COMPUTER APPLICATIONS IN SNACK PACKAGING

Exploitation of the benefits of computer analysis and control in packaging has only really progressed in the last seven or eight years. The computer has yet to make its full impact on production and distribution. In a recent appreciation of the subject on which this section is largely based Nyman lists several areas that have started to exploit the cost benefits of both on line and off line computer techniques in packaging. These include.

- Prediction of shelf life based on moisture gain or loss
- Cost of plastic packaging based on material permeability and product requirements
- Structural designs of cartons or cases
- Optimization of paperboard sheet layout
- Optimization of pallet patterns or truck or rail car loading
- Specification writing
- Prediction of compressive resistance of primary or

secondary packaging or both together
- Graphic design and layout
- Color enhancement in graphics
- Typography selection
- Visual reqresentation of graphic design in real life situations
- Packaging line layout

In effect the desktop computer has enabled accurate answers to be obtained to the myriad what if situations. Spectacular cost savings have been achieved by a number of companies simply in recognizing applying and exploiting three dimensional geometry in the stacking of regular shaped secondary packs of product on to a pallet. The high costs of transport and distribution make a 1-5% overall saving possible simply from computerized selection of scondary pack dimensions leading to improvement of the utilization of pallet space. Commercial computer programs exist for effecting such cost savings which may be of the order of $30,000 per unit percent increase in pallet loading per product line. Such savings have greatest impact where the cost of distribution becomes enhanced by refrigerated storage. The predominant benefits of programmable controllers and microcomputers over previous monitoring and control methods and improved speed accuracy and reliability. According to Nyman these are achieved through.

- Display screens with instruction prompts to guide operators during startup changeover and operation.
- Memory capabilities that can retain the variable operations and settings required for running different products.
- On line calculations that can monitor machine and production performance and provide instant status reports.
- The ability of microprocessors to communicate with each other or directly through a host computer.

Self diagnostic tests that can identify failure areas and recommend corrective action in both the control system and the machinery
- Use of plug in circuit boards and modules to provide

fast and easy expansion or repair.

Changing packaging machine operations through software rather than hardware changes.

The phenomenal speed of data retrieval from commercial databases coupled with the integration of several production lines via a supervisory computer enables rapid changes to be implemented whenever dictated by technical market and legislative forces. Planning product launch involves product and package development in conjunction with packaging machinery suppliers factory space allocation, promotion advertising & soon integration of these concurrent activities into a structured form is possible on a desktop computer with one of the commercial programs that allow the effects of perturbations on the overall operation to be quantitatively assessed and used in conjunction with just in time (JIT) production criteria whose principal spin off results in minimizing capital tied up on raw material stocks.

Perhaps the most exciting development resulting from exploiting the computer in packaging is simulation of the deteriorative changes accompanying distribution and ageing of the packaged snack. The physical laws governing the properties (e.g. gas or vapor transmission) and strength of packaging materials are precisely known and therefore may be programmed into a relevant simulation from which the all important information may be displayed on the state of the packaged product under a wide range of possible and probable exposures which in turn may be used to compute the most cost effective packaging. Storage and rapid retrieval of designs used in the past are one of the most attractive features of computer generated design saving in development costs all round. A three dimensional shape may be used to optimize pallet pattern layout and quantify tolerances on gauge thickness of the secondary packaging.

With the facilities of modern graphic displays it is now possible to produce format type position logotypes pictorials and color. The candidate design may be placed in a computer generated shelf display of a store to portray exactly how the packaged product will appear in real life. When a satisfactory design is eventually evolved it is possible to transform the design into camera ready art so that the whole design process is reduced to hours from the weeks or months used in the conventional development of design and artwork. Computer software is available that will design complex folding cartons in seconds as opposed to the hours taken to design such cartons manually.

The incentives for installing computer control systems include manufacturing cost reduction improved production efficiency improved product quality process control enforcement and safer process operating conditions according to Nyman. The fact that computers in the packaging industries now justify whole conferences and seminars is the indelible writing on the wall of the way the packaging industry is being forced to move otherwise known as progress.

5

DETAILS OF PLANT, MACHINERY & EQUIPMENTS FOR SNACKS FOOD

Snacks and snack foods usually share with convenience foods (with which there is an obvious overlap) the need for a wide range of processing operations to bring them to the final marketable and/or consumable state. This is particularly so in the case of snack foods where individual portions may become of individual "bite" size each of which may require all the operations carried out on it that are used on a "meal portion" convenience item. Therefore many more unit processing operations may well need to be carried out per pound of food on snack items than on regular and convenience equivalents. The potential here is for a very large cost factor to enter the equation (labor) which could price such products off the market. Consequently the food industry machinery manufacturing companies have stepped in to provide many machines that can markedly reduce the labor cost component in the manufacture of snacks and snack foods.

Machines have been introduced that can transform "scraps" (in the sense of perfectly edible and good quality material that is small in size to be used in its regular form) into a snack form where shape and size deficiencies do not preclude its use.

Others can produce and handle much smaller items than used to be able to be made others can combine various ingredients in a carefully measured shaped and sized way into most attractive "bite" sized snack units. In this context it should be remarked that colour-sorting macjines have many branches of snack food production. Here raw materials (pulses cereals etc.) may vary in color to such an extent that the absence of sorting can completely spoil the appearance of any final product in which they feature. Dark or blackened rice grains for example can be disastrous and not very long ago all polished rise had to be hand sorted for rogue grains. Nowadays it is all done electromechanically and has even gone to the extent of color analysis and sorting in terms of shades of color of fast moving ingredient streams. And there are very many more ways in which specialized food machinery can be and is being created to reduce or ameliorate the ever increasing costs of manual labor.

This machinery is slowly but surely becoming interdisciplinary a machine developed for one sector (e.g. bread or cookie production) may be found to be adaptable to and most useful in another role such as meat manufacture and this overlap in use may and sometimes does extend from food to pharmaceutical and to chemical industry machines. Furthermore this overlap is relevant not only to marginal operations such as packaging but to intrinsic ones such as the use of coating pans and specialized methods of drying.

COMMINUTION AND PARTICLE SIZE CONTROL

Because snack foods are usually eaten without implements for cutting them up it is frequently necessary especially for not so tender stranded or perhaps somewhat tough ingredients to be appropriately cut up before reaching the mouth otherwise the problem frequently encountered with the beef sandwich made from not so tender roast beef will continue to arise If this were to be translated to the beefburger it is unlikely that it would survive long. Likewise overlarge hard particles in a snack food detract from the pleasure of eating it and such particles should be reduced in size.

In both the above circumstances a choice of methods is available all with their own advantages and disadvantages.

Comminution of Raw Meat Fish and Similar Materials Starting with the same piece of raw material it is very surprising what a difference can be produced in the final judged organoleptic quality of finished cooked product by varying the way in which meat is cut into small pieces. The commercially impossible ideal is hand chopping of say beef with a very sharp knife. The second best is mechanical flaking (Comitrol(R)) again with a sharp cutting blade. The third is the use of the ubiquitous bowl chopper which usually provides rather a large variation in size of piece if medium size pieces are to be eliminated. This machine has the potential advantage however of giving a very wide range of piece sizes of being able mix as well as cut and of being able to be chilled and/or run under vacuum in appropriate versions so that for example fat pieces are cleanly cut and air is not incorporated.

The final and most usually used (because easiest and least expensive) is the miner or meat grinder which tends to use brute force rather than very sharp blades and very significantly disrupts texture. Cooking shrinkage is usually greatest in the last case as well as texture and usually previewed flavor being poorer. There are also other differences that it would take too long to go into here.

Comminution of cooked meat (or fish) is not nearly as critical from a quality viewpoint as of the raw materials and the method of chopping or milling it can best be judged on the uniformity of particle size and range of sizes produced by whatever cutting or milling machine (e.g. paste mill) is used.

These considerations of course are particularly relevant to the manufacture of burgers pates rissoles sausages of all types pastes or spreads meat pies and other meat filled snacks.

Comminution of Low-moisture Snack-Foods or Snack Food Ingredients : This is governed largely by two factors. The first is the eventual mouthful of the product and in particular the discrimination between particle sizes by the tongue (for particles above about 20 m in dimension). The second is the necessity or desirability of effecting some form of separation of the component parts of the material being size reduced. The eventual quality of many foods can be materially affected by what is done at this stage.

Machinery available for "dry" comminution consists of items that will tear, cut, crush and operate by impaction, sometimes combining two or more actions in the same machine.

The most interesting of these machines are some of the most primitive and account in part for the emphasis that has been applied to food textures throughout the ages stone milling machinery. The lower millstone of a pair remains stationary. The upper stone rotates, with a small adjustable gap between the two. The feedstock goes to the center of the pair of stones, the output proceeds centrifugally to the periphery. The feedstock is briefly retained by the roughness of the lower millstone, the upper stone both crushes and tears the feedstock, simultaneously separating any structured and nonbrittle parts of the feedstock (e.g., integument or skin) from the brittle and crushable part (frequently endosperm).

This forms the essence of flour, spice and several other commodity comminutions and while it is unchanged and essential in a variety of applications, particularly spice milling it has been largely replaced by the roller mill fluted, differential speed rotating steel rolls as the tearing and crushing medium followed by smooth steel roll crushing to produce size reduction. However, smooth stone rolls are not unknown, being used, for example, in the melangeur for crushing mixing and refining.

The original gritstone (or alternative abrasive material) mill, however, provides opportunity for the manufacture of some very superior snack foods. Pieces of dried fish or meat may be shredded in such a mill and subsequently provide a very much more satisfactory texture in a product than would pulverization. For example, fish cakes composed of shredded dried fish plus mashed potato powder plus rusk plus dried egg make a most acceptable snack that is readily produced (merely by the addition of water and frying). The use of fish powder, however acceptable it may be in fish soup formulations, is not at all appropriate here.

The steel roller mill has a great number of useful attributes relating to the final texture of many snack foods. It has a variety of variables, all very controllable, which include smooth of fluted pairs of rolls, differential or equal speed to rotation of rolls and feed rate and can effect (with subsequent screening) separations at the same time as size reduction that affect final characteristics of products very markedly. Besides size reduction, rolls can also be used for changing the shape of pieces of foodstuffs (e.g. flaking following appropriate conditioning to avoid fracturing on crushing) and there are many forms of flaked snacks for example rolled or flaked oats used as snacks by travelers, explorers, mountaineers, and suchlike as well as by the general public in muesli.

The smoothness or perceptible texture of such items as chocolate and some other forms of confectionery snacks is frequently achieved by a succession of pairs of smooth rolls.

Impact Milling or Hammer Milling: This is achieved by high speed impact of a rotor with a piece of the foodstuff frequently enhanced by a narrow clearance between a part of the rotor and the casing in which it operates. The material can only emerge from the mill by passing through a screen with appropriate apertures, so that maximum particle size is assured. This process has little relevance in general to snack foods but is widely used in the food industry.

Comminution to Produce Suspensions and Emulsions Comminution of solids suspended in liquids and of water with fats or oils to produce creamy emulsions requires special processes that are widely used in snack food production.

Production of a particulate suspension of a solid component in water or oil can be done by the commercial equivalent of the domestic liquidizer, though the commercial versions are usually more sophisticated in design. Multiple sharp blades or other form of rotor running at high speed and frequently with a baffle to intensify the action are frequently used for the purpose. In addition to reducing the size of solids within a liquid, such machines can also emulsify water in fat or fat in water, though here the emulsifier or homogenizer (very high pressure, very small aperture size) is frequently used as for example in "homogenized" milk and on icecream mixes. The particles, in this case globules, of the noncontinuous phase of the emulsion, are made very small indeed. Homogenization can also be used to enhance and control viscosity in a great variety of products.

LAMINATION

A great variety of snacks and snack foods appear as laminates multilayer items in which the layers may all be the same or may vary in a multitude of ways. Very varied machinery has been developed and is still being developed to mechanize this requirement.

In the area of a laminated form of a single constituent for example "puff" pastry "mille feuille" cakes "butter puff" crackers, the method of manufacture has changed in bulk production from hand or machine rolling of special doughs, manually folding them, and then rolling out and further folding and rolling until the desired extent of lamination has been achieved, into a machine process that does all of this automatically. In many cases of this type the layers must be prevented from fusing together again and hence an oiling of the sheets is frequently necessary between foldings and this is accomplished in dough laminating machines. Other materials (e.g., dried fruit) can be automatically sprinkled between the laminated sheets to form such traditional products as lerdy cake.

In considering other laminations where the layers differ, it is usual to attempt to meld the layers and the use of a separating ingredient (e.g., oil or fat) is frequently not required. Machines are available to extrude, simultaneously, differing layers of paste that can then be rolled to cause them to adhere and if desired, to reduce the overall thickness of the laminate before it is cut to sizes required. Many chocolate confectionery bars are formed in this way before being enrobed and within the laminations there can be enclosed items such as nuts and dried fruit to enhance the texture and flavour of the bar.

The Japanese Rheon company has been very active of late years in the field of developing laminating machinery with considerable success, and there is still wide scope for the development of new types of laminated products that are attractive by reason of color, texture, and flavour variations and combinations that may be achieved with them.

SIZING AND SHAPING

Before going into any detail here it is appropriate to mention the very big influence that the use of PTFE has had in recent years as a coating on the parts of food machinery that come into direct contact with the product. It has significantly affected what is possible and what is not in the handling of difficult (e.g., sticky or tender) mixes. Coated rollers, knives, conveyors etc. can now be used satisfactorily on items that previously needed liberal (and usually manual) dusting with a dry material such as flour or icing sugar or what have you. In many instances they allow the full mechanization of operations that previously had to be manual, and messy manual operations at that. It has incidentally been possible largely to eliminate the use of silicone and other mold release agents.

A large proportion of snacks and snack foods consist of mixtures of various kinds that are initially produced in bulk. Others are pieces of individual items (e.g., meat) that require size reduction and eventual shaping and/or sizing. According to the nature of the material it may first have to be rolled to give a standard thickness dimension and then cut with knives (plain or PTFE coated, circular rotating, knives) to arrive at the final bite piece or bar dimensions.

Alternatives to the knives are saws (e.g. in wafer production), wires, air-knives, or punches and dies (including stamping). An alternative to rolling is extrusion to a given shape (square, rectangular, circular) with some form of cut off to provide the third dimension. Thin creams can be portioned and applied through metered jets, thicker creams can be treated similarly except that the jets can be shaped. For both creams a low pressure pumping system is necessary.

In the case of solid, nonrollable, or nonextrudable material such as slabs of cooked or raw meat, knives are the usual shaping, sizing and trimming tools. This includes some of the machines previously mentioned under comminution, which is after all a sizing (small particle size) operation.

The most difficult shape to achieve in forming is the sphere, ovoid, or egg shape, but food engineers have succeeded most satisfactorily in this area, mainly by the use of PTFE-coated rolls of various kinds set at various angles and planetary motion tables and the like to achieve the desired shape from initially angular flat sized pieces or from cylinders. Systems using molds are also used.

There has been quite a lot of cross-fertilization between the food machinery engineers making equipment for the bakery and confectionery industries and for the meat patty, burger, etc. area because their problems have a great deal of similarity dough dividing and handling being very similar to the making of patties, rissoles, and burgers.

COATING

The coating of snack foods is carried out for a great variety of very good reasons and in an equally great variety of ways. It can be a single and simple coating or multiple and difficult.

Take first a simple and classic case - the Scotch egg. Here one starts with an initially "coated" raw (or rather cooked) material a hard boiled shelled egg which consists of a discrete yolk center coated with a firmly set albumen layer. This is then coated with a layer of sausage meat this is lightly coated with raw egg white, which is again coated with breadcrumbs or rusk before the whole is deep fried. The end result is a rich, brown, crispy outer shell with a cooked sausage layer next, followed by white albumen and then by orange yellow yolk. Attractive textures, colours and complementary flavours.

However, the Scotch egg has been miniaturized into a single bite and could be said to have been improved in flavour because the hard boiled egg part has been chopped and blended with mayonnaise & condiments to act as the centre of what is otherwise a normal miniature variant. The manufacture of the normal Scotch egg has until very recently been quite labour intensive; however, because of the recent development of special machinery for multicoating, the manufacture of the miniature variant is much lower in labour requirement.

The present situation is that, provided the rheology (viscosity, flow, etc.) is satisfactory or can be made satisfactory by adjusting oil and/or water content, nature of solids and their state of comminution, temperature chemical state (particularly related to combined H_2O) then automatic multicoating or multlilayers can be arranged for a very wide range of composite snacks or snack foods to emerge in piece size from small bite upwards. This can be accomplished on machines of the Rheon range and by similar machines.

Beside this style of coating there are many others to suit differing circumstances and differing needs in the manufacture of snacks.

Enrobing is the technique used for single coating with chocolate or couverture (which may be repeated to provide extra thickness) of the enormous variety of materials that serve as centers of box chocolates as well as of confectionery bars in great variety. For total enrobing tempered warm chocolate flows down over the fondant and other pieces or bar centers carried on a wire mesh belt while similar chocolate is pumped up from beneath to cover the bottoms of the pieces or bars. Excess chocolate is blown off and the pieces or bars then chilled before wrapping or packing. Alternatively, tops or bottoms of pieces may be coated alone.

Similar in many ways, *liquid spray coating* may be used on snacks, sometimes also being used to spray a coating with adhesive properties to ensure the firm adherence of a subsequent layer of coating. The spray may be generated from a pressurized nozzle or perhaps preferably from a revolving disk or dish.

Dusting or passage through a container or tunnel in which there is a suspended or agitated particulate coating material is a further method of coating snacks. Such contains are frequently a basis for flavor addition for example nuts are frequently flavoured this way the nut oil providing a basis for adhesion of the coating.

Immersion in liquid may also be a means of coating provided that the base product does not seriously absorb the liquid, whether it is only or water based.

Panning is a versatile method of coating, originally relatively small scale (used in the manufacture of sugar coated pharmaceutical tablets) but now automated so as to be applicable to large bulks of throughputs of confectionery snack items in particular. The usual basic material in panning is a sugar (sucrose) solution that can be dried off to provide a hard, dense coating that can then be polished, if desired, with beeswax or similar edible polishing material. The panning material can be colored of flavored if desired. The process, on the original small scale, is carried out in copper pans of truncated pear shape with internal baffles and an open top and capable of being swivelled in various directions. Spraying of sugar solution on the tumbling contents of the pan is followed by air drying using forced circulation and this is repeated until the necessary amount and kind of coating has been achieved.

Among the first snack food items to be offered in a sugar coated panned form were nuts particularly almonds but now such items are legion. Most of them are produced on automated panning equipment.

A varient of the above "hard" panning is "soft" panning, less used but useful when an easier eating form is required. In the same way as soft icing on an iced cake may be achieved by the addition of a little glycerol to icing mix, so the hardness of sugar coating in panning may be modified, but a final hard coat or two is desirable from many points of view.

Decorating of Snacks Decoration connot really be classified in any way. It may include an assembly of different colored shaped. and sized pieces their bonding with another ingredient the glazing of the whole and so on. The provision of machinery to do such jobs cannot be justified without large bulk or long run requirements for such items among which are found canapes in great variety.

DEWATERING AND REMOVAL OF LIQUID FAT

It is frequently required in the manufacture of snacks to remove water or fat from products either water or fat that has been in use for processing or juices that are not necessary or desirable in the particular context of the use of the food or are nutritionally undesirable. In other cases it may be that a liquid is required freed from unwanted solids.

Three basic methods may be chosen all with their own advantages and disadvantages that must be related to the materials and the job to be done. The centrifuge has the facility to separate items of differing specific gravity largely irrespective of particle or globule size. With the dewatering press, liquids of all kinds may be expressed from solids containing them. The filter, pressure or vacuum (or neither), is sensitive to particle size, clogging, etc., but may be suitable in many cases. All have their own niches in the wide variety of such operations that arise in snack food manufacture and there are of course other less used methods such as evaporation or osmosis for use in special circumstances.

HEAT TRANSFER

Heat transfer is necessary in a great variety of snack food processing. Probably the most direct method of heating is by injection of steam, largely used in pasteurization or sterilization of food and sometimes also of packaging. Immersion in a heating or cooling liquid (water, oil, brine) is also used widely, as is stirring or mixing of a product against a heated or cooled surface, including sometimes scraping the surface that is being heated or cooled on the other side-contact heating or cooling. Radiant heat and its obverse where the foods heat is radiated to cool walls is another method, as is the use of air or a gas for heating or cooling a food (e.g., nitrogen or carbon dioxide in freezing).

The speed of heat transfer is frequently very important, for example, in minimizing ice-crystal size in freezing and in rapidly passing the destruction point when disposing of enzymes (in blanching, etc). It is likewise most important in the tempering of chocolate.

MECHANICAL AND ENGINEERING FACETS OF ORGANOLEPTIC QUALITY CONTROL OF SNACKS

It is said that the proof of the pudding is in the eating. And in the eating all the factors that account for acceptability (or the lack of it) come into play-appearance, taste, smell, texture. A great variety of mechanical aids are now accepted as being essential to a consistent and reproducible assessment of perceived characteristics, but however good the trained assessors may be they can be rendered largely unreliable by inappropriate working conditions and equipment.

Ambience

The test panel room should be accurately temperature controlled, it should have no windows; it should be lit by lamps of controllable and strictly controlled intensity and spectral distribution; and it should be kept furnished with a continuous flow of air passed previously through an activated charcoal bed to remove any extraneous odors.

Colour measurement of the food in this room can be dynamic (e.g. trichromatic colour analysis of a rotating sample) or static, and can also measure reflectance and gloss, requiring quite sophisticated equipment and lighting control; all this in addition to normal visual assessments.

The test panel room is also used for individual and personal odour and taste assessments, which do not have an engineering component.

Texture assessment requires the use of such machines as tenderometers and other penetrometers viscosity meters various kinds and several other types of mechanical hydrostatic and similar machines designed for carrying out special requirement tests on specific foodstuffs.

In many instances the use of chromatographic equipment may be desirable to confirm or deny some of the test panel conclusions especially where taints or any unaccustomed trace flavors or odors may have obtruded or been suspected. Electronic engineering plays a major part in a great deal of the modern equipment needed in these areas.

In any new snack food introduction appropriate standards must be laid down for the product, with permissible deviations to allow for inevitable and continuing problems of quality characteristics maintenance in the factory, and the QC test panel is an essential part of establishing such introductions.

WEIGHT AND/OR VOLUME CONTROL OF SNACK FOODS

The manufacture and packing for sale of snack items falls between the Scylla and Charybdis of being on the right side of the law in maintaining minimum weight or volume standards, and by "giving away" the minimum of excess weight or volume possible and so maximizing profit. Therefore spending on first class weight or volume packing machinery and on the ancillary weight or volume checking machinery is sound policy.

There can be no generalization here except that liquid volume fill and check is usually relatively simple compared with weight fill and check weighing especially where fragility (as in potato chips), poor flow characteristics large unit pieces (but not so large as to constitute countlines) and other complications arise.

It should also be noted that weight may be used and frequently is as, a check on volumetric filling, occasionally the reverse may take place.

The recent trend in legislation towards the concept of a minimum net average weight or volume of a number of unit packs of a product rather than each individual pack having to be of the minimum claimed or prescribed weight or volume is a realistic and helpful factor and faces up to the fact that under factory high speed conditions the imposition of a universal "every unit" concordance with the standard is really impracticable with the best of goodwill from all quarterrs. Both consumer and manufacturer are adequately protected by an "average" system-in Europe signified by the **e** sign.

MOISTURE CONTROL

For many decades, in fact ever since adulteration of foods with chalk and other cheap bulky ingredients became illegal, it has been cynically stanted that the food manufacturer should sell in his product the maximum amount of air and water possible. In the present day legislative and competitive situation this statement has become a nonsense but there is nevertheless a narrow margin within which manipulation of water-content and water retaining ingredients can afford minor textural and financial advantages to the competent food manufacturer. The narrowness of the operative limits in any one case can depend on a great variety of ·factors including those that are or could be obvious. Principally, those of microbiologic stability and proneness to texture change on storage (e.g., crystallization, separations etc). are the controlling factors and are quite severe constraints with failure leading to unsaleability in many cases. So accurate moisture control is imperative in very many cases and it is now fortunate that (mainly) electronic engineering permits of so many alternative methods (capacitance conductivity ovening etc.) for the rapid and frequently continuous monitoring or moisture both in processing and in final products.

Many products used in manufacturing snack foods (e.g. fruit juice or fruit concentrates have a large proporation of their value assessed on their total solids content, here measure is for all practical purposes a moisture measured by brix (A specific gravity (SG) measure) however, this SG measure for the particular product concerned and so falls into the classification of a rapid and reasonably accurate moisture measure too.

Many products that depend on sugar concentration for their preservation (e.g. fruit preserves) must have a minimum of 62.5% of sugar present if they are to keep well. In this case the sugar content is measured continuously during manufacture by refractometry but as in the case of SG above it all boils down (no pun intended) to moisture content.

Consideration above has been given to total water content the relatively recent concept of water activity in a food can often be very much more important than total water content in that only unbound or active water in a food is really important in very many areas of a foods potential stability in chemical microbiologic enzymic etc. terms.

HYGIENE CONTROL

Pasteurization has become one of the principal bastions available for control of micrologic growth in foods and has spawned a variety of very sophisticated engineering processes being possible in so many forms ranging from strictly controlled (time and temperature) heating to radiation in many forms X rays electron beams radioactive isomers ultraviolet light etc. Both spoilage and pathogenic bacteria are concerned also pasteurization may be used to terminate the lives and actions of certain snack foods some cheese for example.

If a greater degree of hygiene control in a food is required by engineering means then sterilization may the employed as in canning. Obviously both pasteurization and sterilization measures require back up. Once a sterile product is exposed to the air it normally quickly becomes nonsterile and engineering comes to the rescue again providing aseptic filling and closing of presterilized packs. Thus arise many of the long shelf life high moisture products with which we are all familiar.

Hygiene is not nearly so difficult with overall low moisture or alternatively low water activity products so long as moisture levels are not exceeded then the product is usually safe.

The fact of having several efficient ways of dealing with microbiologic dangers in food does not excuse the necessity for ensuring (by engineering including civil engineering again) that the factory areas used for processing and production can be and are maintained in a suitably hygienic state.

The maintenance of hygienic control, on raw materials processing and final product has been completely transfermed during the last few decades. Mechanical and electronic engineering, have permitted the ever more rapid measurement of the microbiologic status of all the above mentioned areas with ever lessening manpower requirements and ever increasing rates of throughput of more and more samples. Capital expenditure has increased in this area but many laboratory technicians have frequently been replaced by one electronic engineer with overall major savings in the laboratory.

COMPOSITION CONTROL

At the present time with ever increasing requirements for product labels to contain compositional data calorific values etc. It is necessary to have such continuing data available in order to ensure legal conformity. As so often happens in this overall area the development of rapid and accurate (and cheap) analytical methods usually by mechanization of one sort or another is father to the establishment of legal requirements (cf. lead and cadmium.).

The pattern of development of analytical methods has closely paralleled that of microbiologic methods mechanical and electronic engineering with the necessary chemical and physical science background and it must be said also that quite a large part of this development stemmed from the enormous demand placed on hospital laboratories where multiple detailed analyses of body fluids are so very important in diagnosis. There is a large common area between food analysis and the hospital analyses.

As in the case of moisture control compositional control is necessary for incoming raw materials as well as for finished product and in many cases for intermediate process control and is an essential and frequently legally necessary back up microbiologic checks.

CONTAMINANT AND FOREIGN BODY CONTROL

In addition to visual control many engineering based methods are available for removal of foreign bodies that may have accidentally made their way either into raw materials or finished snack food products. Basically there are four types of method available.

Size. A screening or sieving operation may be used to remove foreign bodies of untypical size and shape and for that matter unwanted extra large or extra small individual components. This method is widely used in ports and factory reception areas and on items such as cereals and pulses and is also used in grading of fruits and vegetables as well as removal of foreign matter from them.

Specific Gravity. A typical example of this technique can be observed in the separation of stones from potatoes or other root vegetables in a stream of flowing water. The potatoes are carried over a weir, the stones are retained.

There are many variants on this theme, particularly those concerned with air lift separation. The low SG materials are carried over in the air stream, the higher SG items are not. Air lift separation may also be refined to carry over the smaller particles of a powder and to retain the larger particles. A liquid variant is the use of brine or other salt solutions of varying SG in "float or sink" separations.

Magnels. A very widespread source of foreign materials found in food products arises from ferrous metals used in ships holds conveying machinery processing plant and the like. These can be usually are removed by magnets placed on conveyors, the material removed ranges from small particles of iron and steel to nuts and bolts and even larger items. For nonferrous metallic objects the electronic "treasure hunter" type of device may be and is frequently used as well as magnets.

X-Ray Examination. This is a somewhat expensive but nevertheless most valuable engineering means of finding and removing atypical materials from a flour or meal a typicallity being defined in terms of a material that obstructs or permits the passage of X rays more than the normal material being checked.

6

INSTANT NOODLES

Noodles having been originated in China more than 5,000 years back are being recognised as global food item. It is also gaining popularity in Indian population too. Basically it has been defined as a product made from flour, water and salt and formed into thin, string like spices. Various types of noodles can be seen on the shelf of a super market in big cities like Chinese Noodles, Wanton Noodles, Hokkiens Noodles, Dried Noodles, Instant Noodles etc. Noodles can be divided into three categories.

* Dough stretching Type. (Hand made type)
* Douth sheeted and Cut Type
* Dough Extrusion Type (Like Pasta, Spaghetti, Macaroni)

The instant fried noodles have become extremely popular in the recent years with many MNCs being the major players in the market.

Ingredients : The basic ingredients in the instant noodles making are : Flour, water, salt, alkali, phosphates, stabilizers and anti-oxidants.

Flour : The wheat flour used for noodle making should be of good quality because flour constitutes 95% of the total solids in the noodles. Flour is a mixture of various components such as starch, protein, minerals, lipids, fiber, pigments, enzymes and other minor constituents. The wheat protein is known as gluten and is responsible for elasticity and extensibility in the finished product. The gluten quality and quantity both are important. The gluten content should be 10-14% starch forms 67% of the wheat flour, it helps to form a matrix in noodle making. The other constituents also affect the noodle quality.

Water : Water hydrates and softens gluten and forms a viscons liquid phase in dough. Too little water will result a noodle structure which is porous and too high water will give dough sheets which are sticky.

Salt : Salt strengths the gluten, thus gives strength to the noodles. It controls dough consistency and retards the microbial growth in the finished product and it also adds taste to noodles.

Alkali : It is a mixture of sodium and potassium carbonate. It is called Kansui. It gives more elastic dough with less extensible characteristics.

Phosphates : It gives good water holding properties and reduces oil pick up during frying.

Mixing : The ingredients other than flour are predissolved in water and stored in storage tank. The pH of water is 7.2 to 7.5 and temp. is 20 to 35^{0}C. The wheat flour is weighed and mixing water is added into batch mixer. The mixing water is added into batch mixer. The mixing time is 5 to 7 mins. in high speed and 18 to 20 mins. in low speed mixers.

Rolling and Noodle Formation : After mixing crumbly dough pieces are compressed into continuous sheet by passing through pairs of rolls and sheets are reduced to desired thickness and cut into noodles. The reduction process develops the gluten. The width and shape of noodles strands are determined by dimensions of cutting rolls.

Steaming : The cut and wavy noodle strands are conveyed to a stem chamber to cook the noodles.

Molding : Cooked noodles are cooled with a cooling fan, cut into one serving size (based on weight). The cut noodles are placed to a molder before being fed to tunnel fryer.

Frying : The molded noodles are dehydrated in a fryer. The usual frying conditions are 60 to 70 sects, at 145 to 150°C. frying removes excess water in noodles, incorporates oil in the noodles and gelatinizes the starch.

Packing : As the temperature of fried noodles is very high, so it requires immediate cooling to avoid rapid oil oxidation. At the some time excess oil is drained away. Then these cooled noodles are packed into normally polypropylene, polyethylene film into cups with cup filling machines and sealed with shrink film.

Keeping Quality : Instant noodles have low moisture content and high fat content. This limits shelf life of packed noodles in generally five to six months due to oxidative rancidity of lipids. Polyunsaturated acids are involved in auto-oxidation reactions. The lipids in wheat flour have around 65% polyunsaturated fatty acids, so even if noodles are fried in fully saturated fat, oxidative rancidity will still limit shelf life of noodles. The oxidative rancidity of instant noodles is evaluated by sensory tests or by hexanal conent determinations which is produced in auto-oxidation reactions. The rancidity in instant noodles can be retarded by use of anti-oxidants like BHA or TBHQ, which inhibits the lipid oxidation process.

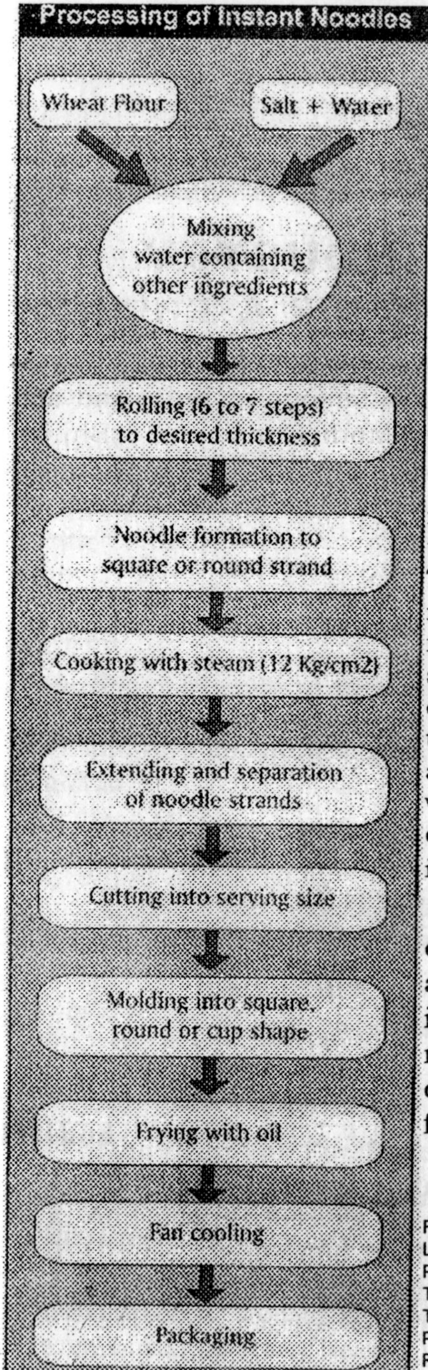

Future Prospects : In this article we have just tried to give the basic knowledge about the instant noodle technology but lot of work still remains to be done on:

* Selection of wheat flour on producing good quality noodles.
* Effect of gluten content on final product.
* Effects of processing parameters on quality of end product.

Oil pick up during frying, reduces breakage, gives shine in the surface and soft inside core. The running of dough on the machines like rollers and noodle former is improved. Specially stabilisers have now been developed and are available in the market for Instant Noodles and allied products like pasta, vermicelli, macaroni, sphagetti etc. to be used as noodle improvers.

Anti-Oxidants : The commonly used anti-oxidants are BHA, TBHQ. These help in increasing the shelf life of noodles by retarding the oxidative rancidity in the finished product.

Investment

Rated Plant capacity	=	1.50 Ton/Day
Land & Building	= Rs.	16,75,000.00
Plant & Machinery	= Rs.	15,25,000.00
Total Capital Investment	= Rs.	61,36,759.00
Turn Over/Annum	= Rs.	1,44,00,000.00
Profit Sale Ratio	=	15.53%
Rate of Return	=	36.45%
Break Even Point (B.E.P)	=	56.50%

7

NAMKEEN INDUSTRY
(DALMOTH, CHANACHUR & BHUJIA)

Namkeen Products are quite famous in India and are consumed in good quantity. Dal Moth, Chanachur & Bhujia are the important names enhancing the flavour & taste as processed foods. These are food products having no historical background & becomes in market and in social & cultural synonym as the society became more advanced.

Initially in long-long ago, people did not heard the name of Dal moth, chana-chur or Bhujia like food products. But now a days it is well known not in India but world wide. These are mainly consumed during breakfast period & are very much during social & cultural periods. These are used as tasty & flavored food as well as in medicinal way, however, a little it may be, according to ayurveda) because of their carminative stimulative digestive properties. India produces almost all these types of salty processed food products of grains all these types of salty processed food products of grains like Grams, Pulses etc.

The main raw materials for these products are Gram, pluses & spices. The various food additives & colours may be used to provide sophistications in the products. The raw material are frequency available in India.

MANUFACTURING PROCESS

The manufacturing process of these food products are nearly same with a little difference. The various food products is i.e Dal Moth, Chanachur & Bhujia, manufacturing processes are given below individually :-

Dalmoth:

The process comprises soaking of pulses (Arhar, Moong, or whatever it may be) in water and washing in a washing tanks. It is adaptable or batch or continuous processing or a combination of these processes. The outer skin is then peeling off in a skin peeling barrel drum. The peeling may also be done by sharp bamboo stick. The skin peeling is necessary to facilitate removal of moisture.

The pulses are then dried. The drying may be done in sun but sundry takes a long time for which an electrically drier is best suited. The drier may also be corn grined with steam heating arrangement. Generally, the pulses are loaded in a trolley fitted with suitable trays & fed to the drier. The drying temperature is around 50-60°C.

After drying, whole of the pulses are fried in deep edible hydrogenated oil at 100-180°C for about 60-90 seconds. Excess oil is drained from the pulses. These are mixed with common salt, powder and spices mix. These are them packed in polythene bags. Storage can be prolonged by preventing rancidity, adding antioxidant and a synergost to the frying oil.

Chanachur:

The processing's of chanachur differ from Dalmoth upto frying & mixing with spices.

Initially, the required amount of chana is soaked in water in washing tanks and then it is beaten by light hammer it can be done manually but manual beating will take more time and will not be economical. Machine hammering is to be preferred for this purpose. When all came in flattered round shape then it is send to frying section where these are fired with in edible hydrogenated oil. Then these are mixed with common slat powder & other spices mix. These are then sent to packing section where these are packed in polythene bags, Before packing addition of antioxidant and synergies can be done.

Bhujia :

Both yellow and white varieties of maize can be used for preparation of Bhujia, but the bhujia made from yellow maize will yield dense colour. Wheat & Gram can also be used to prepare bhujia. The gram or maize seeds are cleared and sintered and then these are polished, so that any foreign material deposited on its upper surface are removed. Then seeds are sent to pulverizer. The ground flours coming from pulverizer, which pass through sieve of mesh no. 1, are good for the purpose.

Then, dough is made frcm flour and other spices ingredients etc. i.e. floured spices and ingredients are mixed with water herewith in this stage. When a thin dough has been formed then it is fried on a deep edible oil contained in a pan heated with a local furnace or electrically or automatic furnace. The thin dough is passed through a siever having dient aperture. The aperture should be selected as per requirement. The frying is done around temp. 100 - 180°C. Then the fried material (bhujia) is placed into a shape & size maker where required size can be get through it. Ultimately it should be sent to packing section where these all have been packed in polythene bags.

Dal Moth

Roasted or fried pulse	-	50 Parts
Black pepper	-	2 ,,
Fenugreek	-	1 ,,
Cumin powder, white	-	1 ,,
Cumin powder, black	-	1 ,,
Turmeric	-	1 ,,
Salt	-	3 ,,
Vinegar of mustard oil	-	2 ,,
Chilli	-	1 ,,

Chanachur

Chana (gram)	-	20 Parts
Salt	-	2 ,,
Black pepper	-	1 ,,
Mustard rye	-	1 ,,
Cumin black	-	1 ,,
Lemon Oil (Terpeneless)	-	1 ,,
Chilli	-	1 ,,

Bhujia

Flour	-	50 Parts
Salt	-	4 ,,
Lemon Oil (Terpeneless)	-	2 ,,
Black pepper	-	2 ,,
Cumin	-	1 ,,
Chilli	-	1 ,,

FLAVOUR & ESSENCES

The following flavour & essences may be used to provide flavour and aroma to the final product:-

Lemon Flavour Essence

Lemon oil	-	28 Oz.
Orange oil	-	8 Oz.
Amyl acetate	-	6 Oz.
Amyl butyrate	-	16 Oz.
Ethyl acetate	-	40 Oz.
Alcohol	-	16 Oz.

Orange Flavour Oil

Lemon oil	-	4 Oz.
Amyl acetate	-	4 Oz.
Ethyl acetate	-	2 Oz.
Sweet orange oil	-	12 Oz.
Amyl butyrate	-	12 Oz.
Alcohol	-	16 Oz.

Universal Flavour Essence

Amyl butyrate	-	4 Oz.
Ethyl formate	-	12 Oz.
Amyl acetate	-	12 Oz.
Ethyl acetate	-	20 Oz.

Wheat Flour Grades

There are four grades of flours available in the market.

1.) Straight Flour

These are flour of flour containing all the four streams of the milled product is 100% of the extraction is called straight flour.

2.) Patent Flour

A better grade of flour having lower ash content and lighter in colour than straight flour is called patent flour. Short patent represent about 70-80% of the total extraction while fancy patent is only about 40-60%.

3.) Cut Straight Flour

A flour from which only a part of the middlings have been removed is called cut straight flour.

4.) Clear Flour

The portion of the straight flour left after the removal of patent is called clear flour. It is darker and stronger than patent flour from the same wheat.

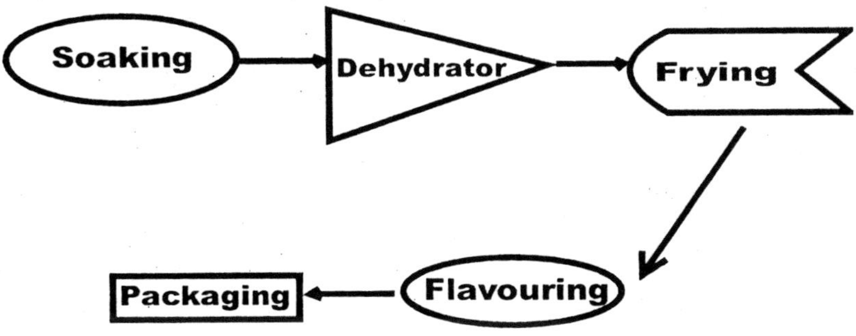

PROCESS FLOW CHART FOR NAMKEEN-DAL

PLANT ECONOMICS

Rated Plant Capacity = 100.00 Kgs/Day

LAND & BUILDING

Land Area 200 sq.mt. = Rs. 2,00,000.00

PLANT & MACHINERY

1. Pulveriser
2. Disintegrator
3. Drying oven
4. Sieving machine
5. Skin peeling barrel drum
6. Filling and sealing machine
7. Weighing machine

FIXED CAPITAL

1. Land & Building	Rs.	2,00,000.00
2. Plant & Machinery	Rs.	87,000.00
3. Other Fixed Assets	Rs.	60,000.00
TOTAL	Rs.	3,47,000.00

RAW MATERIALS

1. Grains
2. Other ingredients
   (Like spices, chemicals etc.)
3. Oil (Edible oil as groundnut oil, sunflower oil)

TOTAL WORKING CAPITAL/MONTH

1. Raw Material	Rs.	30,400.00
2. Salary & Wages	Rs.	11,160.00
3. Utilities & Overheads	Rs.	12,000.00
TOTAL	Rs.	53,560.00

TOTAL CAPITAL INVESTMENT

Total Fixed Capital	Rs.	3,47,000.00
Total Working Capital for 3 Months	Rs.	1,60,680.00
TOTAL	Rs.	5,07,680.00

TURN OVER/ANNUM

Receipt by sale of 1/2 kg. Packs (30000 kgs.x 2 = 60,000 Packs)	Rs.	10,20,000.00

PROFIT SALES RATIO = Profit/Sales x 100 = 22.49%

RATE OF RETURN = Operating Profit/T.C.I x 100 = 45.19%

BREAK EVEN POINT (B.E.P) = 53.03%

8

NAMKEEN AND SWEETS

Namkeens as well as sweets are gaining eminence in modern times and their demand is also increasing considerably to cater to the taste of people. Among the namkeens, the prominent items are dal moth, bhujia, moong dal, navratna mixture etc. These are becoming most versatile as for their relish and palatability is concerned. Now a days these items are well known not in India, but world wide. These are used as tasty & flavored food. India produces almost all these types of salty processed food products of grains like Grams, Pulses etc. Namkeen aid in digestion and adsorption of food possesses anthelmintic and properties.

The main raw materials for these products are Gram, pulses & spices. The various food additives & colours may be used to provide sophistications in the products. The raw material are frequently available in India.

Namkeen which are salty food products get abroad market in foreign countries. These products are very much popular not only in India but also in overseas countries. Hence, there are a lot of scope and market of these products & there fore, it will provide a very much profitable business.

Regarding sweets, there are various varieties and Laddu is one of the traditional Indian Sweets prepared in every home, sweet stalls and consumed by every Indian in every special occassion like Diwali, Holi, Dussera, Pongal, Janmashtami, Ram Navmi, Siv Ratri, Teej and other various festivals.

Laddu serves the purpose of sweets lovers. All ages people men, women, young, old , children boys, every body like it due to sweet taste.

Laddu is prepared by different ways, different types as Besan Laddu, Khoya Laddu, Suji Laddu, Khoya mix Suji Laddu, Atta Laddu, etc. There are other variety of sweets Peda, Burfi, Rasgolla, Chamcham, Gulab Jamun, Gazzak, Jalebi, Paneer Ki Jalebi, Malai Chap etc.

There are several processed food that are exported to foreign countries to satisfy there needs. India is exporting so many types of processed food with longer shelf life i.e. Jam, Jelly, Biscuits, Processed and Canned fruits & vegetables, Cheese, Butter, other milk products, several variety of sweets.

MANUFACTURING PROCESS OF NAMKEEN

Dalmoth:

For the manufacture of dalmoth, pulses (Arhar, Moong, or whatever it may be) are soaked in water and washing in a washing tanks. It is adaptable or batch or continuous processing or a combination of these processes. The outer skin is then peeling off in a skin peeling barrel drum. The peeling may also be done by sharp bamboo stick. The skin peeling is necessary to facilitate removal of moisture.

The pulses are then dried. The drying may be done in sun but sundry takes a long time for which an electrically drier is best suited. The drier may also be corn grind with steam heating arrangement. Generally, the pulses are loaded in a trolley fitted with suitable trays & fed to the drier. The drying temperature is around 50-60°C.

After drying, whole of the pulses are fried in deep edible hydrogenated oil at 100-180°C for about 60-90 seconds. Excess oil is drained from the pulses. These are mixed with common salt, powder and spices mix. These are then packed in polythene bags. Storage can be prolonged by preventing rancidity, adding antioxidant and a synergost to the frying oil.

Chanachur:

For the manufacture of chanachur the processing's of chanachur differ from Dalmoth upto frying & mixing with spices. Requisite quantity of chana is soaked in water in washing tanks and then it is beaten by light hammer it can be done manually but manual beating will take more time and will not be economical. Machine hammering is to be preferred for this purpose. When all came in flattered round shape then it is send to frying section where these are fired with in edible hydrogenated oil. Then these are mixed with common salt powder & other spices mix. These are then sent to packing section where these are packed in polythene bags, Before packing, addition of antioxidant and synergies can be done.

Bhujia:

Both yellow and white varieties of maize can be used for preparation of bhujia, but the bhujia made from yellow maize will yield dense colour. Wheat & Gram can also be used to prepare bhujia. The gram or maize seeds are cleared and sintered and then these are polished, so that any foreign material deposited on its upper surface are removed. Then seeds are sent to pulverizer. The ground flours coming from pulverizer, which pass through sieve of mesh no. 1, are good for the purpose.

Then, dough is made from flour and other spices ingredients etc. i.e. floured spices and ingredients are mixed with water herewith in this stage. When a thin dough has been formed then it is fried on a deep edible oil contained in a pan heated with a local furnace or electrically or automatic furnace. The thin dough is passed through a siever having dient aperture. The aperture should be selected as per requirement. The frying is done around temp. 100-180°C. Then, the fried material (bhujia) is placed into a shape & size maker where required size can be get through it. Ultimately it should be sent to packing section where these all have been packed in polythene bags.

Dal Moth

Roasted or fried Pulse	-	50 Parts
Black Pepper	-	2 ,,
Fenugreek	-	1 ,,
Cumin powder white	-	1 ,,
Cumin powder, black	-	1 ,,
Turmeric	-	1 ,,
Salt	-	3 ,,
Vinegar of mustard oil	-	2 ,,
Chilli	-	1 ,,

Chanachur

Chana (Gram)	-	20 Parts
Salt	-	2 ,,
Black Pepper	-	1 ,,
Mustard Rye	-	1 ,,
Cumin black	-	1 ,,
Lemon Oil (Terpeneless)	-	1 ,,
Chilli	-	1 ,,

Bhujia

Flour	-	50 Parts
Salt	-	4 ,,
Lemon Oil (Terpeneless)	-	2 ,,
Black Pepper	-	2 ,,
Cumin	-	1 ,,
Chilli	-	1 ,,

FLAVOUR & ESSENCES

The following flavour & essences may be used to provide flavour and aroma to the final product:-

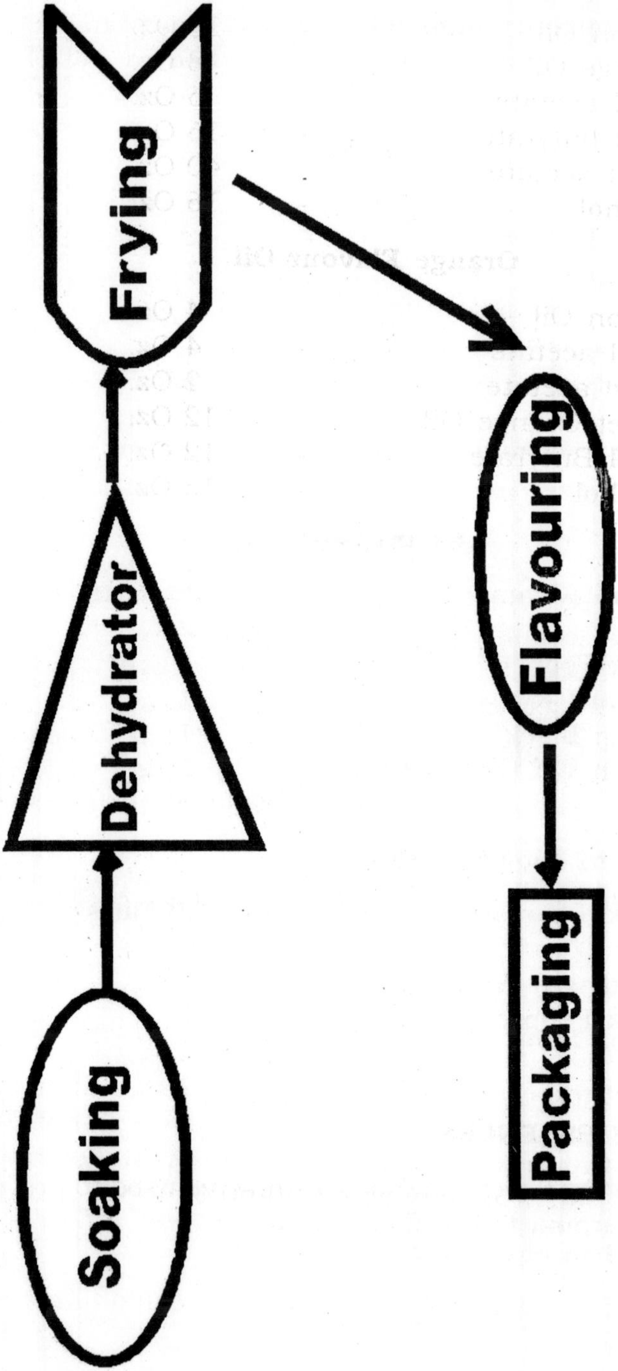

PROCESS FLOW CHART FOR NAMKEEN-DAL

Lemon Flavour Essence

Lemon Oil	-	28 Oz.
Orange Oil	-	8 Oz.
Amyl acetate	-	6 Oz.
Amyl butyrate	-	16 Oz.
Ethyl acetate	-	40 Oz.
Alcohol	-	16 Oz.

Orange Flavour Oil

Lemon Oil	-	4 Oz.
Amyl acetate	-	4 Oz.
Ethyl acetate	-	2 Oz.
Sweet Orange Oil	-	12 Oz.
Amyl Butyrate	-	12 Oz.
Alcohol	-	16 Oz.

Universal Flavour Essence

Amyl butyrate	-	4 Oz.
Ethyl formate	-	12 Oz.
Amyl acetate	-	12 Oz.
Ethyl acetate	-	20 Oz.

Wheat Flour Grades

There are four grades of flours available in the market.

1) Straight Flour

Three are flour of flour containing all the four streams of the milled product is 100% of the extraction is called straight flour.

2) Patent Flour

A better grade of flour having lower ash content and lighter in colour than straight flour is called patent flour. Short patent represent about 70-80% of the total extraction while fancy patent is only about 40-60%.

3) Cut Straight Flour

A flour from which only a part of the middlings have

been removed is called cut straight flour.

4) Clear Flour

The portion of the straight flour left after the removal of patent is called clear flour. It is darker and stronger than patent flour from the same wheat.

PREPARATIONS OF SWEETS

Moong Dal Ladoos

Formulation	Quantity (gms)
Moong Dal	600 gm
Ghee	500 gm
Sugar	600 gm
Cardamom	5 gm
Crushed Dry Fruit & Saffron	q.s

Process

Soak dal overnight and grind it coarsed, Heat the Ghee and brown the dal till golden in colour, keep stirring. Add the ground sugar to the dal. Add crushed cardamoms saffron dissolved in little milk and finally crushed dry fruit wait till Cool. Add the remaining ghee in the dal and form the ladoos.

Besan Ladoos

Formulation	Quantity (gms)
Gram flour (very fine)	600 gms
Sugar (Ground finally)	400 gm
Cardamom	5 gm
Pure Ghee	50 gm
Chopped nut	100 gm

Process

Fry the besan in ghee on a very low fire till lightly browned. Remove from fire and add the ground sugar immediately mix well. Add little quantity of ghee to bind it so that it forms ladoos after the besan has cooled. Do not add too much ghee. Crush nuts and cardamoms finely and mix in the besan before forming the ladoos.

Mysore Pak

Formulation	Quantity (gms)
Besan (gram flour)	200 gm
Sugar	500 gm
Ghee	250 gm
Cardamom powder	15 gm

Process

Roast the gram flour on a very low fire. Melt the ghee and mix the roasted flour with 200 gm ghee. In a Separate vessel make a sugar syrup with one thread consistency and slowly add the ghee, flour mixture and stir constantly. When add the mixture is poured keep stirring adding the 50 gm of ghee slowly without the mixture burning or sticking to the entire ingredient is poured on a greased thali and cool. It is later cut into diamond shape as per customer's appeal.

MOONG DAL HALWA

Formulation	Quantity (gm.)
Moong dal	500
Mava or Khoya	400
Milk	400
Sugar	600
Ghee	400
Saffron, Rose water, Kewra	q.s.

Process

Either soak dal over night and grind it in the morning or ground the dal to a very fine after soaking for a few hours. The paste should be absolutely fine. Heat ghee and fry dal till it become brown exactly. Add the milk and fat, it cook till the milk evaporates. Add crushed khoya in the dal and stir on a low fire till well blended. The sugar dissolve the sugar in 1. cup water, add saffron and boil it to one thread consistency. Put in the dal and stir briskly.

Rash Bara

(Badar Dipped in Jaggery syrup)

Formulation	Quantity (gm.)
Urad Dal	200
Jaggery	200
Aniseed (Powdered)	5
Ghee	q.s

Process

Soak Dal in cold water for 7-8 hours. Grind it finally. Stir until it become sticky and add ground aniseed. Make bara and fry one by one in Ghee. Now dip them in syrup mate by boiling the Jaggery in 1[illegible] cup of water till well blended and syrupy.

Boondi Ladoo

	Quantity (gm.)
Gram flour (Very fine)	600
Sugar	400
Large Cardamom Dana	50
Melon seeds (Kharbuja Giri)	50
Ghee (for frying)	q.s.

Process

Mix the gram flour with water and make a thick batter. In a separate vessel make a sugar syrup of one thread consistency and now sieve the batter through a boondi Jhari and fry the boondis. Add them to the syrup as you fry. Then pour the fried boodies in the sugar syrup along with large cardamom Dana and Melon seeds and make Ladoo hands.

Manufacture of Petha.

For manufacture of petha, raw green petha is taken. Then peel and slice the same. Then soak it into milk of lime solution for 3-4 hours and cook it to semi cooked conditions. It is then withdrawn from the cooking vessel and washed with clean water 2-3 times. Then it is soaked in sugar syrup for 0.5-1 hours. Then it is placed on the sieve to remove excess sugar syrup. Then it is packed in polyethene pouches.

Similarly for manufacture of Angoori and kesar petha, raw petha is peeled and sliced in cylindrical shape of equal size. It is then soaked in milk of lime for 2-3 hours, and cooked like plain petha. It is then with drawn from the vessel and dipped in the flavoured sugar syrup. It is then placed on the sieves to remove excess sugar syrup from it. Then it is packed in the polyethene pouches.

Sone Papadi

Sone Papadi is prepared from either maida or Besan as per customers requirements.

		(Kgs.)
Maida/Besan	=	70
Sugar	=	30
Refined Vegetable oil	=	15
Flavour	=	q.s.
Ilaichi	=	0.02
Dry fruits (Kaju, Badam, Pista)	=	2

Process of Manufacturing

1. Procure all the raw materials from market by checking good quality.

2. Prepare maida or besan paste by mixing maida/besan, sugar, (Powdered) with water.

3. Warm the refined vegetable oil in a Stainless Steel Pan.

4. Then mildly cook the maida/besan paste in the oil by pulling or extruding the pastes into thin fine hair like shapes.

5. Then remove from the oil, cool and Strain to remove excess oil.

6. Then to it add the ilaichi roasted dry fruits, flavour etc.

7. Then cut this into small pieces and pack in the polyethene pouches or plastic or cardboard packs in sizes 250 gms, 500 gms, 1 kg size.

RAW MATERIALS

Sugar, flour, besan, colour, milk, khoya, dry fruits, ilaichi, flavour, ghee, butter, drinking chocolate etc. Polyethene films, Aluminium foil, wax paper, cardboard boxes, cartons, labels, wooden booden boxes.

MANUFACTURING PROCESS

1 - For 1 Kg. Laddu

Flour	-	0.25 kgs.
Milk	-	2 lits
Desi Ghee	-	100 gms.
Coconut Crushed	-	100 gms.
Flavour	-	3 gms.
Dry Fruits	-	50 gms.
Sugar	-	250 gms.

Preservative mix - (0.032 Butylated itydroxy Anisol+2gm. pot. sorbate+8.1 gm NISIN)

First of all milk is boiled and evaporated to concentrate form.

In the second step Flour is fried in the desi ghee till it obtains a slight brown colour. Then water is added, sugar is added and stirred it. Then crushed coconut is added and also concentrated milk. It is homogenized. At this stage, Dry Fruits (Raisin, Cahewnut, Almond, Pistachio etc.) are added as per the taste. This is again mixed. The mixing pan is cooled gradually. Here preservative mix is added. The product is moulded into spherical Laddu form by semi automatic moulding machine. This product laddu is now ready for packing. The laddu is weighed of quantity 1 kg , 2 kg, 5 kgs and packed into wax paper envelope. The envelope made of wax paper is previously impregnated with 0.25% scorbic acid. The Laddu packed in wax paper is kept in HDPE bags/pouch of capacity 1 kg, 2 kgs, 5 kgs as per requirement and sealed by semi automatic vacuum packaging machine. This packet is now kept in cardboard box and packed in cartons or wooden boxes for export purpose.

Preservative mix for 1 kg Laddu is = 0.032 gms Butylated Hydroxy Anisole + 2 gm potassium sorbate + 0.1 gm NISIN.

Formulation II for 1 kg Elaichi Laddu

Milk (Fullfat)	-	5 litrs.
Sugar	-	200 gms.
Coconut Crushed	-	100 gms.
Flavour	-	3 gms.
Ilaichi	-	5 gms.

Preservative mix - (0.04 gm Butylated Hydroxy anisol+2 gm. Potassium sorbat+0.1 gm NISIN.

Formulation - III For 1 kg Cashewnut Laddu

Milk (Full fat)	-	5 litrs
Sugar	-	200 gms
Coconut Crushed	-	50 gms
Cashewnut	-	50 gms
Flavour	-	3 gms.
Ilaichi	-	2 gms.

Preservative mix. The quantity as in formulation (II).

Formulation IV - Pistachio Laddu

Full fat Milk	-	5 litrs
Sugar	-	200 kgs.
Suji	-	100 gms.
Ghee	-	50 gms.
Pistachio	-	50 gms.
Ilaichi	-	3 gms

Preservative	-	Quantities as in formulation

Formulation - V (Raisin Laddu 1 kg)

Milk	-	5 lits
Sugar	-	200 gms.
Raisin	-	50 gms.
Ilaichi	-	3 gms.
Flavour	-	2 gms.
Preservative	-	As in Formulation (II)

Coconut Laddu of different flavour, Rose flavour, orange flavour, kewda flavour.

Formulation - VI

Milk	-	5 lits
Sugar	-	200 lits
Ghee	-	50 gms.
Coconut Crushed	-	120 gms.
Flavours (Rose, Kewda, orange, pine apple)	-	10 gms.

Preservative - As in Formulation (I).

In the formulations from II to VI processing is as follow.

The milk is first evaporated into concentrate form. Then sugar is added also crushed coconut is added and properly. The ghee as mentioned in which formulation is added and mixed till homogenized. Then ilaichi, dryfruits etc. are added and homogenized. The product is gradually cooled and the desired flavour is added to it. After mixing it properly, the product is moulded into spherical Laddu form. The Laddu is now first packed in wax paper impregnated with 0.25% potassium sorbate or scorbic acid. This pack is kept in HDPE bags or pouches and vacuum packed with semi automatic vacuum packaging machine. Its self is checked and the product packets are kept in card board box and again packed in wooden boxes or cartons for export purpose.

Pulveriser

Disintegrator

PLANT ECONOMICS

Rated Plant Capacity = 3.00 Ton/Day

LAND & BUILDING

Land Area 250 sq.mts = Rs. 22,21,500.00

PLANT & MACHINERY

1. Pulveriser
2. Disintegrator
3. Drying oven
4. Sieving Machine
5. Skin Peeling barrel drum
6. Manual Filling & Sealing Machine
7. Otis lift
8. Bhatti
9. Fryer
10. Ink Jet Printer
11. Pouch Packing Machine
12. Mixer
13. Effluent Treatment Plant
14. Chimney
15. Weighing Machine
16. Exhaust Fan
17. Computer

FIXED CAPITAL

1. Land & Building	Rs.	22,21,500.00
2. Plant & Machinery	Rs.	38,30,750.00
3. Other Fixed Assets	Rs.	6,15,000.00
TOTAL	Rs.	66,67,250.00

RAW MATERIALS

1. **For Namkeens:-** Grains & pulses & gram, peas
3. Oil (edible oil as ground nut oil, sunflower oil etc.)
4. **For Sweets :-** Gram Flour, pulse
5. Sugar
6. Dry fruit, saffron, food colours, khoya etc.

7. Edible oil/pure ghee, raw petha, milk
8. Misc. Consumables
9. Packing materials

TOTAL WORKING CAPITAL/MONTH

1. Raw Material	Rs.	22,50,500.00
2. Salary & Wages	Rs.	1,62,925.00
3. Utilities & Overheads	Rs.	95,000.00
TOTAL	Rs.	25,08,425.00

TOTAL CAPITAL INVESTMENT

Total Fixed Capital	Rs.	66,67,250.00
Total Working Capital for 3 Months	Rs.	75,25,275.00
TOTAL	Rs.	1,41,92,525.00

TURN OVER/ANNUM

Sale of Namkeens of various types
600 Tons and Sweets 300 tons Rs.6,60,00,000.00

PROFIT SALES RATIO = Profit/Sales x 100 = 49.26%

RATE OF RETURN = Operating profit/T.C.I x 100 = 229.09%

BREAK EVEN POINT (B.E.P) = 12.45%

9

PROCESSED PRODUCTS FROM POTATO

Most of the potato processing is presently confined to the developed countries and it is only in the initial stage in India. However, fast growth in potato processing is expected to occur in India due to increased urbanization, preference of new generation for easy-to-prepare and fast foods, rising per capita income, increase in number of working women and expanding tourist trade. Among the processed potato products, chips and French fries are the most popular forms in different countries. In Indian, chips are very popular in the urban areas, while French fries are not commercially available in the market. They are served in the restaurants or at fast food outlets and are sometimes prepared fresh at home.

In India many processing plants with an annual capacity of 25000 tons have been installed and now it may have increased to about 50000 tons/annum. The installed capacity of potato of potato chips in organized sector was 6,000 tons in last decade and several brands of chips (vies. Haldiram, Aggrawal's, Bikaner, Rameshwar's, Frit-Lays, Unclechips etc.) are available in the market. In India, processing of potatoes construction. But, there is a considerable scope for expansion of processing in India.

Processing of potatoes is an imperative necessity in India to avoid gluts and the consequent different of storing large quantities of potatoes during period of extremely high temperature. Moreover, the abundant solar energy available in the plains of India can be used in the development of dehydrated products at no extra cost and can work as a cottage industry in rural areas.

The change from fresh to processed potatoes in developed countries is partly due to enhanced efficiency in processing, which reduced the relatively high cost of canned, dried and frozen forms and partly due to factors such as increased demand for convenience foods, fast foods and picnic snacks. However, the situation is quite different in India. Potatoes as a raw material are not cheap except for a few weeks just after harvest. The costs of frying medium, processing, packaging and transportation add further to the cost of the finished product and it is beyond the reach of a common man. To make processed products available to the common man, it would be desirable to develop appropriate technology for the production of dehydrated products such as dehydrate chips, dices, granules and flour. Dehydrated dices can be cooked along wit other vegetable in households. Potato granules and flour can be used for preparing tikkis in the fast food outlets and extruded products like papads as a cottage industry. Potato flour can also be used in the preparation of idli and alu bhujia etc.

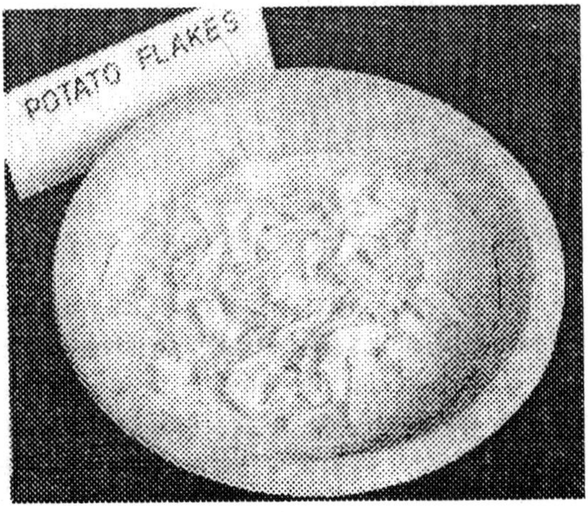

CLASSIFICATION OF PROCESSED PRODUCTS

Processed potato products can be classified as follows:-

1. Fried products, which include potato chips, frozen French fries and other frozen products.

2. Dehydrated products, such as dehydrated chips, dices, waris, flakes, granules, flour, starch, potato custard powder, soup or gravy thickener and potato biscuits.

3. Canned potatoes: The quality of processed products is mainly influenced by the morphological characters, dry-matter and reducing sugar content of potatoes. There are different tuber quality requirements for various types of processed products. Large size potatoes having high dry-matter and low reducing sugars are suitable for the preparation of chips and French fries, while small potatoes with low dry-matter are preferred for canning.

FRIED PRODUCTS

Potato Chips

Potato chips, a fried snack food is most popular in the urban class. Potatoes are washed, peeled and sliced to about 1-1.5 mm thickness and then fried in the cooking oil at about 180-200°C for about 2-3 min until 2% moisture is achieved. The product should have a light yellow colour and possess pleasing and desirable flavour with a crispy texture. To get a finished product of good quality, it is necessary that potatoes destined for chipping should be fully matured, healthy, without any mechanical injury, uniform size (40-60 mm), round to oval, firm with shallow eyes and free from any internal or external defects.

French fries

French fries are potato strips of 1x1 cm in cross-section and 6-7 cm in length. They are fried in the cooking oil at about 180-120 C for about 4 min. Frying is considered complete when a sample breaks cleanly to show fully cooked tissue, the water content usually being 60%.

Nine potato varieties grown at Jalandhar in Punjab plains were evaluated for French fries immediately after harvest. Peeling losses varied between 10.4 and 16.5 % and the total losses including nubinns and slivers ranged from 12.6 to 21.2%. The yield of French fries ranged from 44.8% (Kufri Sindhuri) to 50.7% (Kufri Lauvkar) (Table 2). Two recently released varieties Kufri Chipsona 1 and Kufri Chipsona 2 gave a recovery of 59.3% and 58.3% French fries, respectively. Based on colour, texture and yield of French fries, Kufri Lauvkar, Kufri Chpsona 1 and Kufri Chipsona 2 among Indian varieties and Atlantic, FL 1533 and FL 1625 among exotic cultivars were considered most suitable for processing into French fries.

DEHYDRATED PRODUCTS

Dehydration is one of the major means of preserving potatoes and, giving products like dehydrated chips, dices, potato starch, potato flour, granules, flakes.

Dehydrated potato chips, dices and waris

Solar energy can be utilized by the housewives to dehydrate potato slices, dices, waris and papads etc. Dehydrated potato dice is an ingredient in processed foods such as canned meats, meat stews, frozen meat pies and potato salad. The procedure for the preparation of dehydrated chips consists of cutting 2-3 mm thick raw slices with a hand slicer in cold water, followed by blanching in hot water for 1-5 min, and then spreading in the sun to dry at the end of the day. The dried product can be stored in air-tight containers or sealed in polythene bags for 6 months. Likewise, dices and waris of different size and shape can also be prepared from potatoes. A cabinet for solar drying of 20 kg of blanched potato slices was developed at the Central Potato Research Station, Jalandhar which was found to be quite efficient and produced better quality solar-dried products than made in the open sun. Later on large solar concentrator and home solar dehydrator were also developed by the Central Potato Research Institute, Shimla. Solar dehydrated is also used in some parts of the country to dry cook potato slices. The procedure is similar to the one used for drying raw potato slices, except that potato tubers are cooked in boiling water for about 8 min, before peeling and slicing. During dehydration as such slices take longer time but they take up much less cooking medium during frying than raw slices. Studies conducted at the Central Potato Research Station, Jalandhar showed that the dehydrated chips made from 7 Indian varieties and 5 exotic cultivars after 4 months of storage in the evaporatively cooled potato store, when fried, produced acceptable colour with crispy texture and good taste as against unacceptable dark colour and bitter taste chips made from cold stored potatoes. The recovery of dehydrated chips from exotic cultivars ranged between 15 and 17% as against 11.2-15.7% in Indian varieties.

Potato flakes and granules

Potato flakes and granules are convenient foods both for domestic and large scale use. The processes for flakes and granules preparation can use rejected potatoes, as they have less stringent raw material requirements. Flakes of good quality were prepared from 4 varieties namely, Kufri Jawahar, Kufri Lauvkar, Kufri Pukhraj and Kufri Sutlej. These were prepared at the Central Potato Research Station, Jalandhar and the recovery was 17.3, 11.5, 12.8, and 16.2%, respectively.

Potato starch

Potato starch is used by paper manufacturers for beater sizing, tub sizing, calendar sizing and surface coating. It is also used in the textile industry in the sizing of cotton, worsted and spun rayon warps. Much of the potato starch in developed countries is utilized in the food industry in bakeries, specially in Swedish and German style breads, crackers and matozoth. It is also used as a thickener in soups and gravies. Potato starch has been successfully used to make puddings. Pregelatinized potato starch is used in considerable quantities in instant puddings, in which its properties are preferable to those of cereal starches. Starch is used in confectionery industry as a medium for molding cast candies such as jelly beans and gum drops, as a thickening agent in synthetic jellies and as a dusting agent mixed with powdered sugar, for candy gums, chewing gums etc. It is also used in producing adhesives and dextrins, as a fermentation raw material, binder for tablets and binder and extender for sausages. The highest annual potato starch production is in the Netherlands, while French, Germany, Poland and Russia are important producers of starch.

Sub-standard potatoes like too small, too large, misshapen, damaged, cull and surplus potatoes not fed to livestock can be used in starch manufacture. For the extraction of starch, potatoes were peeled, washed, cut into small pieces and macerated in a domestic electrical mixer at low speed for 4 min. or in a locally made motorized grinder. The recovery of starch in the motorized grinder was less but the extraction rate was fast. The slurry taken in container and the starch was allowed to settle. The residual starch was dried, ground into fine powder and then sealed in the plastic containers.

Work on utilization of potato starch for the development of different products was initiated at the Central Potato Research Station, Jalandhar long back in 1966. Three products like custard powder, soup thickener and biscuits based on combinations of potato starch with flour were developed which were found to be highly acceptable. The main ingredients in all the 3 products are potato starch and flour.

Potato flour

Potato flour is used by the baking industry, especially in the baking of bread to retain its freshness. It also imparts a distinctive, pleasing flavour and improves toasting qualities.

The generally accepted level of potato flour in the bread is 6%. It is also used as a combination thickener-flavouring agent in products such as dehydrated soups, gravies, sauces and baby foods.

Potato flour was prepared from 10 Indian varieties by 2 methods at the Central Potato Research Station, Jalandhar. In the first method, fresh potatoes were peeled, washed, cut in 2 large pieces, dipped in water containing 0.25% sodium metabisulphite and pressure cooked for 10 min. The cooked pieces were mashed thoroughly and dried in the oven at 60°C. The dried product was ground into fine flour by using a grinding mill. The second method consisted of blanching the raw cut slices in water containing 0.25% sodium metabisulphite, followed by drying and grinding. The mean recovery of flour by the first method was higher by 2.3%. Among the varieties, maximum recovery was obtained from Kufri Sherpa (16.6% on fresh weight basis). However, for large- scale production of flour, a faster way of drying the slices by using a kiln or a flow drier has to be adopted.

Table 1. Important processing qualities of some freshly harvested Indian potato varieties

Variety	Dry-matter (%)	Chip colour	Reducing sugar (mg/100 g fresh wt.)
Kufri Badshah	16.9	7	298
Kufri Bahar	16.7	6	240
Kufri Chandramukhi	20.7	6	208
Kufri Dewa	19.8	6	228
Kufri Jawahar	19.3	6	246
Kufri Jyoti	17.8	6	264
Kufri Lalima	20.6	8	332
Kufri Lauvkar	19.2	3	128
Kufri Sindhuri	18.8	7	278

*On a 1-10 scale of increasing dark colour. Chip colour score up to 5 was acceptable

Potato custard powder

Custard powder was prepared from several combinations of potato starch and potato flour in 2 colours and flavours.

Custard pudding prepared from pure potato starch and potato flour-starch combination (1:9 and 1:4) tasted equally goods as corn custard powder mix, the custard pudding gave a typical potato taste which was not pleasant. In appearance, the light yellow custard powder with vanilla flavour were well comparable to the commercially available corn custard powder. Addition of 10% potato flour in the custard powder mix, apart from economizing the cost of production, also improved the taste and texture of the custard pudding.

Preparation (ingredients): Potato starch, 90%; potato flour, 10%; edible salts, 0.3%; permitted colour and flavour as per requirement.

Potato flour was mixed with starch thoroughly and homogenized after addition of edible salt, permitted colours and flavours. Custard powder was prepared in 2 colours-light yellow and light pink and in 2 flavours-vanilla and strawberry.

Soup or gravy thickener

Various combinations of starch and flour prepared from potato were tried to develop soup or gravy thickener. Addition of 2% potato starch or 2% potato flour-starch combination (1:1) proved to be good thickening agents and were effective in bringing the desired consistency in the tomato and chicken soups when compared with commercially available corn flour.

Based on taste, colour and homogeneity of tomato soup, the panelists rated tomato soup prepared from 2% potato starch as the best, followed by corn flour and potato flour-starch combination. Therefore, potato starch can be a good substitute to the corn flour or corn starch in the soups.

Preparation (ingredients): Potato starch, 50%; potato flour, 50%; edible salts, 0.03%.

Potato biscuits

Biscuits of improved taste and texture were made when half of the wheat flour (maida) was replaced either by potato starch or potato flour. However, biscuits prepared from pure potato starch were very soft and left a residue in the mouth after eating which was not very pleasant. Like-wise, biscuits prepared from pure potato flour gave a typical taste and flavour and were not acceptable.

Preparation (ingredients, for approx. 1.4 kg of biscuits): Potato starch/flour, 300 g; wheat fine powder (maida), 300g; sugar, 180 g; hydrogenated vegetable oil, 330 g; milk powder, 100 g.

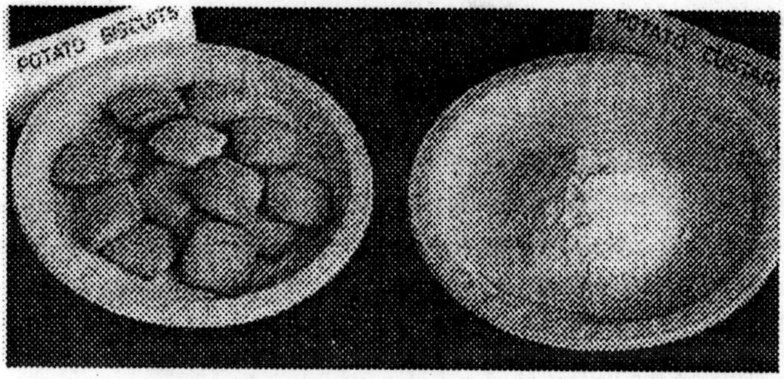

CANNED POTATOES

Canning of potatoes on commercial scale is not carried out in this country mainly because of the high cost of can. However, some quantities of potatoes are canned to meet the requirements of the armed forces. It is reported that potatoes with a specific gravity of less than 1.075 or < 20% dry-matter are preferred for canning and can be canned without disintegration or sloughing during processing even without the use of calcium salts.

Inspite of the vast scope for processed products, India lags behind in indigenously developed infrastructures for modern industries, suitable varieties for different processing and storage technology, proper packaging and transportation facilities and awareness need to be improved to enhance the efficiency of processing and to reduce the cost of processed products. Development of appropriate technology for dehydrated products for the rural sector will not only ensure remunerative returns of their produce to the small farmers, but would also boost the processing industry.

Table 2. Losses during French fries preparation, processing quality and yield of fries prepared from some Indian varieties

Variety	Peeling loss (%)	Trimming and cutting loss (%)	Total lossess during processing (%)	Quality of fries		Yield of French fries (%)
				Colour	Texture	
Kufri Badshah	10.8	1.8	12.6	MB	Soggy	49.5
Kufri Bahar	13.4	2.6	16.0	LB	Soggy	46.6
Kufri Chandramukhi	12.2	2.3	14.4	LB	Mealy	46.6
Kufri Dewa	14.7	4.2	18.9	L	Mealy	47.6
Kufri Jawahar	13.0	3.8	16.8	GY	Pasty	47.8
Kufri Joyti	10.4	3.4	13.8	L	Mealy	47.5
Kufri Lalima	14.4	2.9	17.3	MB	Mealy	48.3
Kufri Lauvkar	12.6	2.3	14.9	L	Mealy	50.7
Kufri Sindhuri	16.5	4.7	21.2	L	Mealy	44.8

L, Light, LB, light brown; MB, medium brown; GY, golden yellow. Peeling loss is the weight of skin removed during peeling

Trimming loss includes the weight of residual skin, eyes and discoloured area removed from peeled potatoes

Cutting loss includes the weight of slivers (thin slices) and nubbins (short or broken pieces) separated from the product after cutting of French fry strips

10

PAPPAD AND BARIYAN PLANT

The Word "PAPPAD" is quite familiar with Indians. Pappad is a common Indian food normally taken with meals. Some time before, pappads were made at home by the ladies and most of them know the process of making them. At present also some of the housewives are making these, but their number has decreased considerably.

Pappad's are of different types i.e. made from urad dal, potatoes, rice etc. However, process of making all of them is very simple and absolutely identifical except the formulations which may change according to one's taste. Pappad's may be made by using red or black pappers and their quantities may also be altered to make the product strong or light in chilly.

Base for all types of pappad in is Urad's pulse. Good quality pappads are made by urad only whereas in cheap quality pappads beson is also mixed.

Bariyan are traditional have name made item. It is generally consumed by either making Lussy or by adding in curry as per required charge of taste. The bariyan are manufactured from different cecal variety edible product. The bariyan are generally prepared in all Indian houses from Urad dal, Moong dal, Soyabean and others. These are tasty things and add taste to the lunch and dinners.

PROCESS OF MANUFACTURE OF PAPPAD

Pappad may be manufactured by a single type of pulse flour or combination of various pulse flour. The rice flour is also added to reduce the cost of the pappad. However, following formulation is suggested for the pappad making.

Urad Pulse Flour	1000 Parts
Black Pepper	25 Parts
Sodium Bi Carbonaye	10 Parts
Zeera	15 Parts
Hing Water	10 Parts
Salt	25 Parts

All the ingredients are first taken according to their weighted quantities and then pre mixed. Now, the premixed mass is taken into a dough kneading machine. Required quantity of water is added and the whole content is kneaded at minimum speed to get homogenous lump of the dough. After 30 minutes resting it is divided into balls of about 6-8 kg mass. Now, this ball is placed on the conveyor belt of the automatic dough sheeting machine. The belt is moved to and thickness is gradually decreased using the lever handle till the final thickness of about 2.5 to 2 mm sheet is obtained. The conveyor belt takes the sheet to the sheet cutting machine.

The sheet is now cut into round shaped and tailing materials are then again mixed fed to the sheeting machine. After round cut of the pappad, the pappad is sent for sun drying or a drying chamber in which hot air at 27-30°% of moisture content.

The pappad are then packed into the printed plastic packs. This plastic back may contain about 100 pappads or as per market requirements.

MANUFACTURING PROCESS OF BARIYAN

Urad Dal/Moong Dal	-	100 kgs.
Red chillies powder	-	1/2 kgs.
Salt	-	2 kgs.
Hing	-	100 gms.
Other spices	-	100 gms.

First of all soak the Urad dal or Moong dal for a night in a vessel with 1.5 times the clear water. The dals are first thoroughly washed and left off all the night for soaking. In the morning stain out the dals from that vessel and pass through grinding machine. Then add the previously mixed ground spices and salts and again homogeneously mix it. The pasty mass is now ready for extension. As the quantity of mass is extruded from the machine, it is placed on PP or PE flim to dry either in sun or using special drying chamber. The dryed bariyan are now ready for packing in polyethylene. Packets with suitable brand name. Then sold in the market.

PACKAGING OF PAPPAD

Papad should be packed either by count (25, 50 or 100 to a pack) or by weight (250 g 500 g 1kg) or in any other suitable manner. The material used for packaging of Papad should be moisture-proof and non-toxic, such as, pouches made from PET/LDPE and BOPP/LDPE.

AUTOMATIC PAPPAD PLANT & MACHINERY

Complete new line of Pappad Plant of 250 kgs./8 hour Shift complete with Dryer.

Dough Mixing Machine Stainless Steel SS 304 Lined capacity 20 kg. with 2 HP Electric Motor & Gear Box.

Dough Sheet Extruder Unit : With independent 1 HP Drive and Reduction Gearing.

Inter Table : SS 18 Swg Line for Sheet transport between Extruder and Gauge Rollers.

3 Pairs of Gauge Rollers : Three pairs of precision gauge rollers heavy duty duly hard chromed with independent adjustment of sheet thickness between gauge rollers.

Two sets of Dough sheet transport rollers with Drives.

Two sets of Stainless Steel Knives to Gauge rollers.

One set rotary cutting rollers.

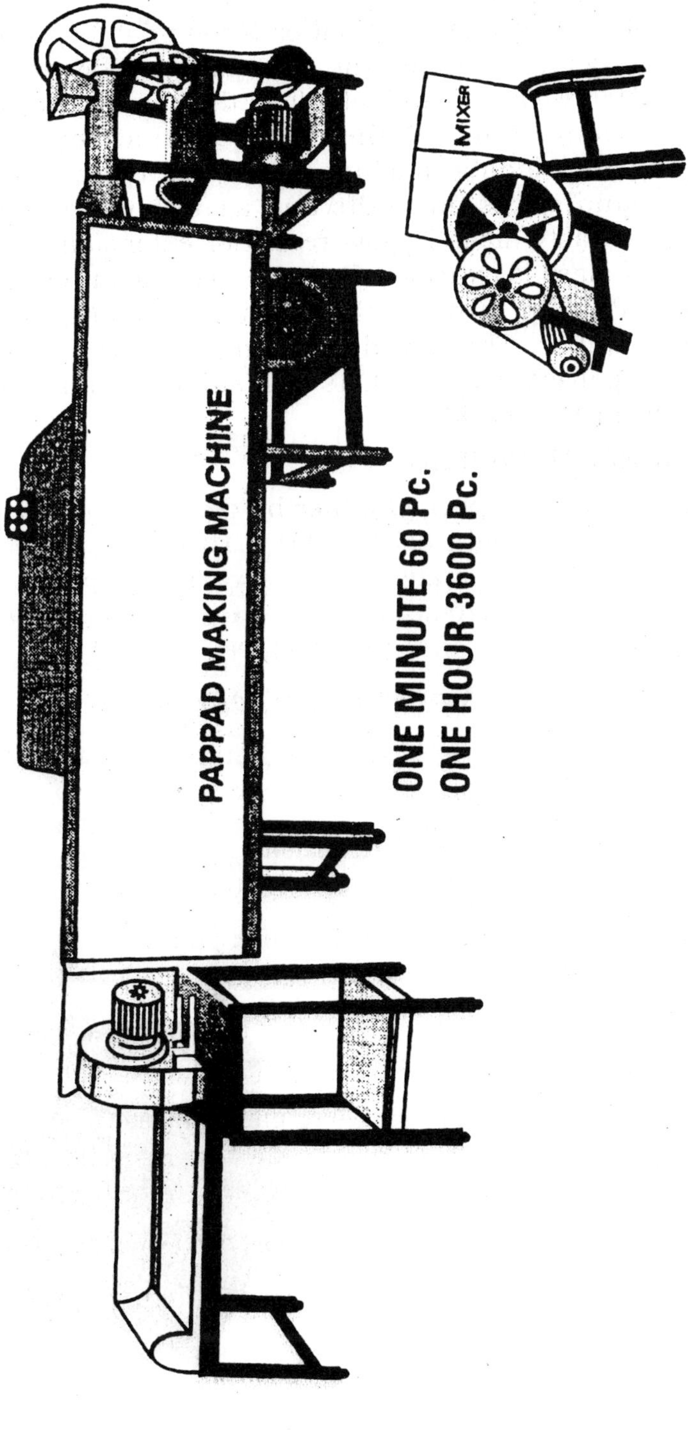
PAPPAD MAKING MACHINE
MIXER
ONE MINUTE 60 Pc.
ONE HOUR 3600 Pc.

One set rubber rollers to cutting rollers.

One food grade conveyor system for conveying Pappads to Dryer.

One combined Pappad & Wadi Dryer.

Size 6' x 4' x 6.5' High capacity 150 Kg. Wt. 1200 Kg. gross including 4" insulation.

Oil consumption 17 ltr. in 12 Hrs. *(Summer)* 24 ltr. in 15 Hrs. *(Winter)*

Insulation Mineral Wool

Electric Motor 1 HP 3 Phase 1400 RMP

Tray Size 1 Meter x 1 Meter

Side Sheeting Covering : 18 Gauge Galvanised or S.S as per order (Optional)

The dryer can be heated Electrically or with LPG. The electrical heating load is 6 kw. The electrical load of Drive Motors is 6.5 HP i.e. Mixer 2 HP, Extruder 1 HP, Sheeter 2 HP, Air Blower .5 HP. Oven Drive 1 HP. Total 6.5 HP.

Note : Above stated dryer is suitable for drying of Pappads as well as for drying of Wadi's

The estimated price of above complete automatic pappad making plant complete with dryer for an output of 250 kg. Pappads of Lizzat (5.5) size per 8 hours shift would be approx. Rs. 5 Lacs. Automatic Pappad Packing Machine Pouch Type would be around 3 lacs.

Wet Grinder

PLANT ECONOMICS

Rated Plant Capacity = 1.10 Mt./Day

LAND & BUILDING

Land Area 1000 Sq. = Rs. 9,50,000.00

PLANT & MACHINERY

1. Sifter
2. Dough mixer
3. Automatic dough sheeting machine
4. Automatic sheet cutting machine
5. Air drying chamber
6. Pack sealing machine
7. Weighing balance/machine
8. Wet grinding machine
9. Automatic extruder for making bariyan
10. Miscellaneous Equipments

FIXED CAPITAL

1. Land & Building	Rs.	9,50,000.00
2. Plant & Machinery	Rs.	13,60,000.00
3. Other Fixed Assets	Rs.	2,10,000.00
TOTAL	Rs.	25,20,000.00

RAW MATERIALS

1. Black urad, dal, flour
2. Black pepper
3. Sodium bicarbonate
4. Zeera
5. Hing water
6. Salts
7. Urad dal
8. Moong dal
9. Red chillies power
10. Other spices
11. Hing
12. Packing materials

TOTAL WORKING CAPITAL/MONTH

1. Raw Material	Rs.	3,16,138.00
2. Salary & Wages	Rs.	35,624.00
3. Utilities & Overheads	Rs.	39,000.00
TOTAL	Rs.	3,90,762.00

TOTAL CAPITAL INVESTMENT

Total Fixed Capital	Rs.	25,20,000.00
Total Working Capital for 3 Months	Rs.	11,72,286.00
TOTAL	Rs.	36,92,286.00

TURN OVER/ANNUM

Sale of 180 ton of Pappad & 150 ton Bariyan	Rs.	81,60,000.00

PROFIT SALES RATIO = Profit/Sales x 100 = 28.66%

RATE OF RETURN = Operating profit / T.C.I x 100 = 63.35%

BREAK EVEN POINT (B.E.P) = 38.92%

11

POTATO CHIPS/WAFFERS

Potato chip is a snack-food item very popular for picnics, cinema halls, journeys, evening tea and may be served at any time. These are much consumed by all age group children. This profile provides a small scale plant which requires few capital investment. The whole plant and machinery are fluently available in India and almost in every state of India. Few addresses have also been added in this book to enable the entrepreneur for buying these machines.

Snack food like potato chips in recent years have made impressive trends in food industry. The approximate composition of chips is as follows:-

Moisture	-	2%
Protein	-	6.7%
Fat	-	37.1%
Carbohydrate	-	51.1%
Minerals	-	3.00%

For chips manufacture sugar contents of potatoes should be over S.G (Specific Gravity) 1.080 i.e (minimum 20% solids content).

STEPS IN THE PROCESS OF MANUFACTURE EMPLOYED AS FOLLOWS:

1.Inspection of feed stocks and manual removal of obviously trash on a conveyor belt.

2.Mechanical washing and stoning of potatoes using

brushes with gravity separation of stones in a vertical fume.

3. Steam or water peeling of potatoes usually by steam jet surface loosing of the skin followed by a dry abrasive skin removal treatment and then the use of brushes and water sprays thus minimize water usage and concentrating the skin residues.

4. Inspection and triming by hand in a conveyor belt.

5. To maintain continuity of production a buffer tank is usually provided at this point containing a weak solution of SO_2 or sodium meta bisulfate to avoid enzymic blackening during the holding period.

6. Slicing of potatoes to the desired thickness using multiple knives.

7. Washing slices free of starch and use chemical separation of slivers and nubbins concominatantly with dewating the slices.

8. Blanching of the slices in steam or hot water (160°-200°F) (71-93°C) which amounts to a partial pre cooking. blanching times will depend on slice thickness and the blanch temperature and can be from 3 or 4 times upwards.

9. Drying the slices by shaking and by air blast to avoid a water carry over and to start the dehydration continued in the next stage.

10. Frying or cooking on a conveyor in a thermostaticaly controlled bath of oil, the oil subjected to continuous re-circulation and filtration and indirectly heated by a mineral oil caloriefier with strictly controlled cooking time to ensure consistent product quality and colour.

11. Defaulting of crisp by shaker and by hot air blast.

12. Flavouring and salting of chips by dusting on the seasoning whilst the defaulted chips are being timber conveyed.

13. Cooling of the finished chips.

14. Packing of the chips as soon as possible in small sophisticated laminate package designed to prevent. The ingress of both oxygen and moisture.

During the processing of the potatoes to chips; the moisture contents of the potato has been reduced from 79% (Approx.)to 5% (Approx.) and of the 95% of dry malts in the chips 35-40% will be fat.

Taking into account peeling trimming and other small losses in the plant and the up take of fat the conversion ratio of potatoes the chips is around 4:1.

PROCESS OF MANUFACTURE

Potatoes received from fields are first checked for quality on conveyor belt. The spoiled ones are removed from the lot. The good potatoes are then washed well and with jet of water to remove mud and other materials. Then the clean potatoes are moved into the peeling section.

The peeled potatoes are sliced in a conscious slicing machine. The peeled potatoes are feed to the hopper of the slicing machine and are discharged out to dual potato slicing machine. The dual slicer are used to handle more potatoes continuously. Each slicer are separately powered by a variable speed gear head motor. The feed to the dual slicer are arranged in such a way that slice cutting rotor in either slice may be changed during operation. Rotary type slicer are used in most chips plants. Slice thickness varies from (1/15 to 1/30mm). Potato slices are washed in rotating reels in the additional jet of water under high pressure to remove starch from the potato slices.

The washed potato slices are dried in a dryer to remove moisture content.

The dried potato slices are treated chemically with sodium bisulfate alone or with phosphoric acid, sodium citrate or citric acid to prevent the formation of dark chips during trying. In this chemical treatment water or solution is heated up to 200°F and after rinsing slices are placed in the above hot solution for one or two minute and then sent into frying kettles.

For frying two types of process are in general use.

1. Batch frying
2. Continuous frying.

The simplest method for frying in batch frying provides for a slicer to be mounted on a batch directly above the frying vessel. This vessel may be either rectangular or flat bottom. Flat bottom tank with burner beneath or the tank may be of the immersion tube type.

After frying the chips are hand salted and packed. A uniform application 1.5 to 2 lbs of salt is applied to 100 lbs of chips. Mono sodium glutonate is used for flavour. One part of mono sodium glutonate to 10 parts of salt provides a good mixture.

Then the chips are packed to protect the content against development of rancidily.

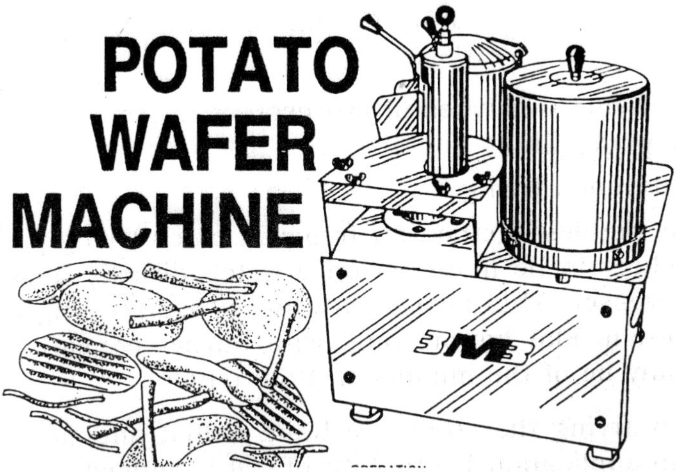

Details of Machinery

This comprehensive machine (Picture is given) has been specially designed and constructed, keeping in mind the small tiny wafer manufacturing unit. Since it is low cost, individuals with limited funds can also invest in it and make a decent margin from the proceeds.

This machine combines three operation viz. peeling, Slicing and dehydration on a common base and drive, thus effecting a considerable saving in space and energy requirements.

The machine is sturdy and very easy to operate thus no extra skill or efforts are required.

Operation

Potatoes are fed into the peeling drum which has a special internal lining that peels off the potato skin which ratation. After this process is over, the peeled potatoes are fed from the hopper into the slicing section where the potatoes are sliced even by and quickly. These are then thoroughly washed and fed into the dehydrating stainless steel drum. On rotation the moisture from the potatoes is practically removed and they are ready for frying.

Technical Specifications : Single Phase
Motor : 1/2 HP
Capacity : 200 Kgs. of Potato per 8 Hours
Dimension : 23" x 23" Height 36"
Sali Blade Chips : Medium & Thick

PLANT ECONOMICS

Rated Plant Capacity = 0.50 MT/Day

LAND & BUILDING

Land Area 500 sq.mt = Rs. 6,75,000.00

PLANT & MACHINERY

1. Potato peeler
2. Power operated slicing machine
3. Blancher
4. Electrical Heater
5. Weighing machines
6. Hydro extractor
7. Deep Fat Fryer
8. Automatic packing cum sealing machine

FIXED CAPITAL

1. Land & Building	Rs.	6,75,000.00
2. Plant & Machinery	Rs.	1,50,000.00
3. Other Fixed Assets	Rs.	1,10,000.00
TOTAL	Rs.	9,35,000.00

RAW MATERIALS

1. Good potatoes
2. Edible oil
3. Other chemicals
4. Packing materials

TOTAL WORKING CAPITAL/MONTH

1. Raw Material	Rs.	1,90,000.00
2. Salary & Wages	Rs.	54,000.00
3. Utilities & Overheads	Rs.	18,000.00
TOTAL	Rs.	2,62,000.00

TOTAL CAPITAL INVESTMENT

Total Fixed Capital	Rs.	9,35,000.00
Total Working Capital for 3 Months	Rs.	7,86,000.00
TOTAL	Rs.	17,21,000.00

TURN OVER/ANNUM

Sale of 150 MT of 30 per kg.	Rs.	45,00,000.00

PROFIT SALES RATIO = Profit/Sales x 100 = 20.86%

RATE OF RETURN = Operating profit/T.C.I x 100 = 54.03%

BREAK EVEN POINT (B.E.P) = 45.39%

12

POTATO CHIPS (AUTOMATIC PLANT) WITH IMPORTED MACHINERY

Potato chips are basically used for snacks purposes. They are produced by rapid dehydration of potato slices by direct contact with hot fact. Its crispness and special palatability make it the favorite of people of all age group.

Different varieties of potatoes are usually used for chips. In India, almost all part of the country produces it but the main share of the total production comes from Uttar Pradesh, Bihar, West Bengal & Orissa.

Packaging Requirements for Fried Potato Chips

Snack foods like chips, in recent years, have made impressive trends in food industry. Potato chips, which form one of the popular items in snack foods, are prepared by frying thinly sliced potatoes for 3.5 minutes in oil at 95-110°C. After frying, the chips are thoroughly drained off the oil, salted and cooled before packaging to prevent it from sweating and sogging. The approximate composition of potato chips is 2 percent moisture, 6.7 percent protein 37.1 percent fat, 51.1 percent carbohydrates and 3.0 percent minerals. Generally flexible pouches based on regenerated cellulose or paper or plastics are used for packaging.

A functional package for chips has to protect the contents against development of rancidity, ingress of moisture, loss of odour, pick-up of foreign flavour and should offer physical protection from breaking, crushing, etc. Besides, it has to perform the job of "customer's eye catching" by its attractive design and printing, should be free from oil staining, provide easy opening and reclosing facilities, etc. The product is generally offered in consumer packs weighing from 25 to 250 g.

Physico-chemical Changes during storage

Rancidity : High fat content and large surface area of the product present a serious problem of rancidity. Use of BHA and BHT upto 0.02 percent by weight on the residual oil basis to retard oxidation has been allowed. Light and oxygen enhance the rate of deterioration [1,2,3] and this is further accelerated by temperature, presence of metals like copper and radiation by UV rays. Hence, the packaging materials, preferably having an oxygen barrier less than 16 cc/sq.m/day/atmosphere at 75°F4, is considered suitable.

Moisture: Potato chips containing moisture above 3.5 percent are found to be organoleptically unacceptable and further increase poses greater problem than rancidity. Packaging materials with water-vapour transmission rate of less than 6.2g/sq.m/day at 90 percent RH and 38°C may be expected to offer a reasonable shelf-life to the product.

Transparent and Opaque Package

It is reported that chips exposed to light becomes unsaleable in shorter period compared to one that is shielded from light.

Since on rancidification is a major source of development of off flavour in potato chips, the UV light barrier offered by opaque packaging materials provides superior flavour protection. However, in advanced countries, the total sales are evenly divided between opaque and transparent ones. Transparent packages are 'sparkly' for 'glossy', offer product visibility and thus enhance sales appeal. In view of longer shelf life to the product, there is growing trend to prefer and favour opaque materials.

Packaging Materials

Some of the functional flexible packaging materials, which come to forefront for consideration for packaging of potato chips, are waxed glassine, polymer coated cellophane, cast and oriented polypropylene (OPP), high and low density polyethylene and their laminates including aluminium Foil.

Pouches of waxed glassine are opaque, grease resistant and particularly suitable for oily chips. Though wax coating reduces oxygen permeability, its poor transparency and other inadequate physical strength properties of paper are undesirable features. But it is economical and has rigidity for good machinability. Glassine with OPP combination offers improved performance on automatic packaging machines and its high strength enables the structure to withstand breakage. Newer developments include PVDC coated glassine, PVDC coated glassine laminated to OPP and sulphite paper laminated to OPP.

Similarly, opaque packaging materials like aluminium foil laminates of the type cello/PE/foil, foil/PE, glassine/ wax/ foil/glassine, foil/PE/PVDC coated glassine have been used because of their good barrier properties for water vapour and other gases.

Transparent packaging materials such as duplex cellophane combination, window type cartons and PVDC coated cellophane offer desired protection but suffer from low flex endurance and become brittle under low temperature conditions. In recent years, there is growing trend to use cellophane laminate as this offer advantages like increased stiffness, reverse printing and flexural resistance. Some of the typical laminates are cello/ coating/cello, cello/poly/cello, cello/adhesive/cello, etc.

Other transparent materials of importance are cast and oriented polypropylene (OPP) which offer advantages such as clarity, good barrier properties to oxygen, water vapour, grease resistance, machinability, resistance to low temperatures. Balanced OPP has increased stiffness, low coefficient of friction, offers better slip and machinability. Gloss and clarity of the film are equal to that of cellophane.

High density polyethylene and its laminates are relatively new comers to the field of potato chips packaging and are receiving widespread attention. Some of the laminates used are HDPE/adhesive/coated cello, HDPE/adhesive/coated glassine, HDPE/adhesive/OPP, coloured HDPE, etc.

Packaging and Storage studies

At present, in the country, pre-made grease-proof paper pouches are extensively used for packaging of freshly prepared potato chips. There is a growing trend in trade to offer the product for sale in sealed pouches in 25, 50 and 100g units, specially in restaurants, theatres, recreation centres etc., in different packaging materials. Hence, it was felt desirable to undertake an investigation on the keeping quality of chips in different flexible packaging materials. The data on the sorption behaviour of the product and storage life in consumer packs are presented in this communication.

Storage Studies: It can be seen that at accelerated condition of storage of 92 percent RH and 38°C, the potato chips attained critical moisture level of 3.5 percent within three days in unit pouches in all he packaging material studied. Under normal conditions of storage, i.e. 65 percent RH and 27°C, the extrapolation of results suggests that it will take 12, 12, 15 and 17 days to attain the critical moisture level in 100 gauge HDPE cello/poly laminate, 300 MXXT and 200 gauge low density polyethylene unit pouches respectively. thus, it can be inferred that in the above packaging materials, fried potato chips will have a half-life of about 2 weeks in 50 g unit pouches of size 13 x

15 cm. It may be pointed out that the above observation is with respect to loss of crispness by moisture pick-up by potato chips, which is a major problem than oxidative rancidity in short-term storage of the product. Even here use of packaging materials having low transmission rate to oxygen is advisable, However, for long-term storage, the problem has to be viewed from both moisture pick-up and development of oxidative rancidity of the product.

Organoleptic evaluation of the stored chips at the end of 10 days at 65 percent RH and 27°C has indicated that the chips are quite acceptable with reference to both crispness and off flavour due to rancidity.

MANUFACTURING PROCESS

The common step in the manufacturing process of a typical potato chips manufacturing unit working on either indigenous or imported machinery.

(1) Sorting, Cleaning & Washing:

The potatoes received from fields are first checked for quality. The spoiled ones are removed from the lot. The good potatoes are then washed well with jet of water to remove mud and other materials. Then, the clean potatoes are fed into the peeling section.

(2) Slicing and Washing

Several slicing arrangements are employed in the industry. Peeled potatoes fed in the hopper, discharges them into a dual potato slicing unit mounted on a continuous slice washing machine. The dual slicers are used to handle more adequately the large volume of potatoes that are sliced. Each slicer is separately operated by a variable sped gear fitted motor. The feed to the dual slicers is so arranged that slicer cutting motor on either slicer may be changed during operation. Rotary type slicers are used in most chip plants. The most widely used types have three blades mounted on a circular plate.

Slices are washed with additional jets of water under

high pressure to remove starch from the cut surface and to separate slicers from each other. Slice washing equipment consists of a rectangular S.S. Tank with S.S. wire mesh cylinder and drum. The drums is rotated within the washing machine tank and is positioned. So that potato slices from the slicer assembly discharge in to the receiving and of the washing machine tank.

(3) Drying of Slices:

In the frying process water is removed to the extent that finished chips contain 1.5 to 2% moisture. Its surface moisture is removed from the slices before frying. It helps to shorten the frying time and hence to increase the capacity of the kettle and also to save fuel. A number of water removal methods are employed. The most common ones are perforated revolving drums sponge rubber covered squeeze roller, heated air etc.

Treating with chemicals:

Some chemicals treatments are done on potato slices for preventing the formation of dark chips during frying. Water and solution of the following chemicals are used. Sodium bisulphite alone or with phosphoric acid, sodium citrate or citric acid etc. In all the treatments the water or solutions to be heated to the temperature of 200°F. After this slices are placed in the above hot solution for one minute and then dropped into the frying kettle.

Chip Frying:

Method of chip processing may be divided in two categories, (1) the etch method (2) the continuous method.

Batch Frying method

The simplest method of batch frying provides for as slicer to be mounted on a frack directly above the frying vessel. This vessel may be either rectangular, flat bottom tank with burner beneath or may be tank of the immersion tube type.

Method of Batch processing:

Raw peeled potatoes are sliced into a tub of cold water and allowed to soap. The slices are removed from the water and placed in a centrifuge to remove excess surface water before frying. They are then discharged from baskets into the fryer. Finished chips are removed from the fryer and placed in a centrifuge to remove excess surface oil. The chips are salted and packed. A uniform application 1.5 to 2 lb. of salt is applied to 100 lb. of chips. Monosodium glutamate intensities the flavour of potato chips. One part of monosodium gultamato 10 parts of salt provides a good mixture.

Packaging:

A functional package for chips has to protect the contents against development of rancidity, increase of moisture, loss of odour, pick up of foreign flavour and should offer physical protection from breaking crushing etc. Besides it has to perform the job of customers eye catching by its attractive design and printing. It should be free from oil staining, provide easy opening and reclosing facilities etc. The product is generally offered in consumer packs weighing from 50 to 250 gram.

Working of Imported continuous Potato Producing Unit

Wright machinery company of U.K produces a number of potato making machineries with varying capacities. Machinery are arranged in series.

Potatoes come to the drum peeler from crate dumper through distribution hopper, washer destoner and vertical lift. Peeled potatoes move to inclined feeder through an inspection conveyor where spoiled potatoes are separated out. Inclined feeder transfers the potatoes to the rotomation potato slicer. Fines from the slices are removed and the rest passes to cold water washing drum. Then chemical treatment to avoid decolourisation during frying is done. Dewatering process is carried out by the use of dewatering conveyor. The dewatered slices are then fed

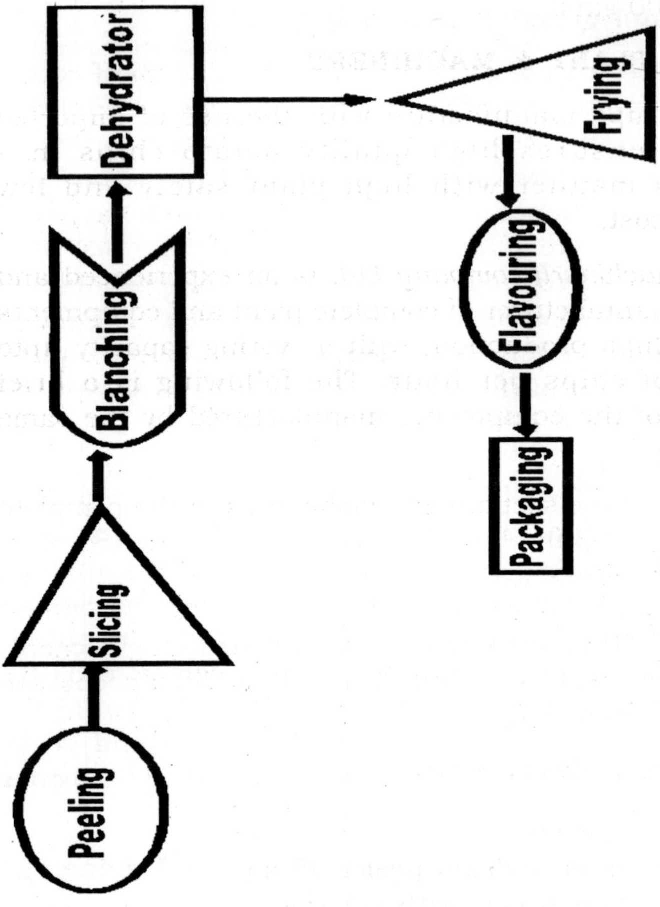

PROCESS FLOW CHART FOR POTATO CHIP LINE

to the fryer.

The thickness of the slices before frying will be in the range of 0.85 to 1.7 mm thickness. Hydrogenated vegetable oil is used for the frying purposes. The fryer has an external high efficiency heat exchanges which may be gas or oil fired. This ensures an efficient heat transfer, with considerable economics in fuel costs, whilst accurately maintaining the temperature of the cooking oil in the fryer. Properly fried potato chips are then transferred to flavour tumbler for flavouring the chips. Then using the packing equipments, the properly salted and flavoured chips are packed in proper bags of 50 gm,

100 gm & 200 gms.

IMPORTED PLANT & MACHINERY

Potato Chips manufacture with the use of imported machinery ensures high quality potato chips in a continuous manner with high plant safety and low production cost.

Wright machinery company Ltd. is an experienced and expertised manufacturer of complete plant and equipments for potato chips production, with a varing capacity upto 2270 Kgs of chips per hour. The following is a brief description of the equipments manufactured by the same company.

There are three sections of machineries in the complete plant (1) Potato chips line. In this section, raw, unpeeled, uncleaned potatoes are fed in one side and fried salted potato chips are taken from the other end. (2)Optional equipments. This section include flavouring equipment. (3) Packaging section. Salted and flavoured chips are packed in air tight bags.

Description Machineries

I. Potato Chip Line

1.	Hand fed abrasive drum peeler 25 kg. Capacity drum peeler with variable retention time	1 No
2.	Potato Inspection conveyor stainless Steel frame, food quality PVC conveyor, Fixed feed drive	1No
3.	Belt slicer feed elevator. All stainless steel reserve hopper and inclined PVC belt elevator with level control probes.	1 No
4.	Rotormotion potato slices, Three cutting head Flat plate type potato slicer complete with spare head	1 No
5.	Slice wash Tank. Cold water wash tank to remove surface starch and potato cut offs.	

POTATO CHIP LINE

Full self-clean — 1 No

6. Blancher Designed to operate at 87°C to dilute concentration of reducing sugars in potato slices. Full self clean and extended drain sections
7. Potato Chip Fryer.
   Including paddles and product hold-down belts each with own variable speed

drives. Full fines removal, clean-in-place system and salt applicator

8. Heat Exchanger. Remote direct heating unit with fully moduting burner suitable for firing with gas or light fuel oil, including main pump group
9. Control console push button control unit with temperature chart records
10. Oil Reserve Tank. Mild steel tank and stainless steel filter basket with sufficient, capacity to hold cooking oil from entire system
11. Chip Inspection conveyor. Mild steel frame, food quality PVC belt and fixed speed drive
12. Flow master Hopper with inclined conveyor 0.15^3 stainless steel hopper with vibrating tray feeding flighted incline belt conveyor. fixed speed drives inclined conveyor operating on demand from bag maker complete with dual discharge chute and three position pneumatically controlled gate
13. Bag makers High speed twin tube bag maker with conventional mechanical weighing scales. Each side independently driven 1 No

Optional Equipment Available

Processing Section

1. Wet End control Panel Push button control console for equipment preceding slicer feed elevator
2. Electronic remote control facility For paddles and hold-down belt
3. Flavour tumbler stainless steel flighted tumble drum 1.8 m x 0.3 m
4. Dry ingredient Distributor. Powder metering system mounted inside tumble drum. Provides even wall of flavour falling onto tumbling chips

5. Tumble Washer Perforated 8.5 drum with internal helix to control flow of product. Unit complete with full self-clean and drain extensions. Free starch and potato cut-off removed system for use where blanching is not required
6. Electrical pre-wiring. All starters, isolators and cable supplies fitted and cut to size

Packaging Section

1. External stroke Adjustment. Remote bag length adjustment.
2. Additional Tube formers, Required for each different bag with to be produced.
3. Bag Takemay conveyor
4. Rotary each off Table
5. Codemaster Overprinters suitable for printing date or batch code.
6. Gas Flushing

INVESTMENT

The project cost depends on the size of the plant, few managerial decisions, Govt. fiscal policies etc. However, with certain assumptions with regard to automisation & to the size of the plant to produce 100 Kgs./Hrs. of Chips, the total cost of the project is estimated at about Rs. 2.25 Crores, in which Rs. 1.25 Crores worth of plant & machineries included. The balance Rs. 1 Crore is attributed to buildings, preoperative expenses & margin money for the working capital.

However, we are also providing another project cost of different capacity.

POTATO CHIPS (IMPORTED PLANT)

Rated Plant Capacity	=	1200 Ton/Annum
Plant & Machinery	=	Rs. 1,62,00,000.00
Total Capital Investment	=	Rs. 2,75,00,000.00
Rate of Return =		60%

13

READY TO EAT PROCESSED COOKED FOOD

Ready to eat food viz; Instant curried Dal mix, Ready Suji Halwa mix, Ready vegetable pulav mix etc. are gaining enormous eminence in modern era.

It is consumed by the defence forces in an appreciable quantity. Apart from being consumed in bulk quantities by defence personnels. These "ready to eat" foods also serve the ease of their availability to people during outing, in picnics etc, where they relish these ready to eat food. The future scope of these ready to eat food is very bright.

Ready Suji Halwa Mix

The ready Suji-Halwa mix shall be of light amber-brown colour, free from any charred or burnt particles. It shall have a light roasted aroma and shall be free from any gritty taste. It shall be free from any unpleasant rancid, musty, tallowy or any other stored odour or flavour and any insects or fungus infestation or microbial deterioration. It shall also be free from any added colours and artificial sweeteners. Permitted flavours may however, be added.

When the ready Halwa mix is boiled with water for 5 minutes, it shall attain the characteristic gel structure of freshly prepared Halwa free from cooked lumps or any other textural defects.

Ready Vegetable Pulav Mix

The ready vegetable Pulav mix shall have a uniform

distribution of various ingredients. It shall be free flowing, devoid of any lumps, dirt or any other foreign matter and excessively broken rice grains. The mix shall have a pleasant aroma and shall be free from musty, rancid or any other stored odour. The fried onions, if added, shall have a light brown colour and shall be free from burnt and scorched pieces. The fried peas and potatoes shall have a characteristic pleasant taste and aroma and shall not be excessively fragmented. The material shall be free from any signs of insect or fungus infestation or microbial deterioration. The mix shall be free from any synthetic colours and added flavours.

When the ready vegetable pulav mix is boiled with water, it shall be reconstituted after 15 minutes into freshly prepared Pulav, free from textural and flavour defects.

The ready vegetable pulav mix shall contain not less the 17.5% of total vegetables and the salt content shall not exceed 4% when dried fruits have been added to the ready, vegetable pulav mix, these shall not be less than 4% by mass on dry basis

Ready Khichdi Mix

The ready khichdi mix shall have a uniform distribution of various ingredients. It shall be free-flowing, devoid of any lumps, dirt or any other foreign matter. The mix shall have visible grains of rice and dals and shall not be an excessively fragmented powderous material. The mix shall bave a pleasant aroma and shall be free from musty, rancid or any other undesirable or stored odour. The fried onions, if added, shall have a light brown colour and shall be free from burnt and scorched pieces. The material shall be free from any signs of insect or fungus infestation or microbial deterioration. The mix shall be free from any synthetic colours and added flavours.

When the ready khichdi mix is recooked with water it shall reconstitute into a preparation having a characteristic flavour, texture and consistency of freshly made khichdi. It shall reconstitute within 12 minutes and the reconstituted product shall be free from uncooked particles.

Salt content shall not exceed 4 percent when tested.

When dried fruits have been added to the ready Khichdi mix, these shall not be less than 4 percent by mass on dry basis when tested.

Ready Upma Mix

The ready upma mix shall have a uniform distribution of various ingredients. It shall be a slightly brownish-white or amber colour. It should have a characteristic flavour of roasted Semolina and added spices and shall be free from burnt or charred particles. The product shall be free from any unpleasant rancid or any other undesirable stored odour. The dry vegetables shall have a characteristic colour, taste and flavour of fresh vegetables and shall not have undergone browning and dis-colouration or excessive shrinkage. The material shall be free from any signs of insects or fungus infestation or microbial deterioration. The mix shall be free from synthetic colouring matter.

When the ready upma mix is boiled with water for 6 minutes, it shall be reconstituted into freshly prepared Upma, free from textural and flavour defects.

Salt content shall not be less than 3.5 percent and shall not exceed 4 percent when tested.

When dried fruits have been added to the ready upma mix these shall not be less than 4 percent by mass on dry basis.

Instant Curried Dal Mix:-

The instant curried dal mix shall have a pleasant aroma, free from musty, rancid, tallowy or any other unpleasant stored odour. The appearance of dal shall be characteristic of the dal from which it has been prepared and shall not be excessively powdered. The fried onions, if added, shall have a characteristic light brown colour and shall be free from burnt and scorched pieces. The dal shall be free from any signs of infestation and microbiological or any other spoilage. The product shall also be free from artificial colours and added flavours.

Salt content shall not be more than 4.0 percent by mass when tested.

When the instant curried dal mix is boiled with water, it shall be reconstituted into a slurry within 15 minutes and shall not have any uncooked hard dal particles.

REQUIREMENTS FOR READY TO EAT FOOD

Requirements for Ready Suji Halwa Mix:- Table

Sl. No.	Characteristic	Requirement	Method of Test, Ref to
(1)	(2)	(3)	(4)
1.	Moisture, percent by mass, max	4	Annex B of IS 12569: 1989
2.	Total ash (on dry basis), percent by mass, Max	0.4	Appendix D of IS 4684: 1975
3.	Acid insoluble ash on dry basis, percent by mass, Max	0.1	Annex C of IS 12569: 1989
4.	Fat (on dry basis), percent by mass, Min	28	Annex D of IS 12569: 1989
5.	Sugar (on dry basis), percent by mass, Min	35	Clause 8 of IS 6287: 1986
6.	Acid value of extracted fat, Max	1.2	Clause 7 of IS 548 (Part 1): 1964
7.	Protein (N x 6.25) on dry basis), percent by mass, Min	4.0	IS 7219 : 1973
8.	Uric acid, mg/100 g, Max	10	IS 4333 (Part 5): 1970

Requirement For Ready Vegetable Pulav Mix:- Table

Sl. No.	Characteristic	Requirement	Method of Test, Ref to
(1)	(2)	(3)	(4)
1.	Moisture, percent by mass, max	8	Annex B of IS 12569: 1989
2.	Total ash (on dry basis), percent by mass, Max	6	Appendix D of IS 4684:1975
3.	Acid insoluble ash (on dry basis), percent by mass, Max	0.25	Annex C of IS 12569: 1989
4.	Fat (on dry basis), percent by mass, Min	18	Annex D of IS 12569: 1989

5.	Protein (N x 6.25) on dry basis), percent by mass, Min	4.5	IS 7219 : 1973
6.	Uric acid, mg/100 g, Max	10	IS 4333 (Part 5): 1970

Requirements For Ready Upma Mix

Table

Sl. No.	Characteristic	Requirement	Method of Test, Ref to
(1)	(2)	(3)	(4)
1.	Moisture, percent by mass, max	5	Annex B of IS 12569: 1989
2.	Total ash (on dry basis), percent by mass, Max	2.5	Appendix D of IS 4684: 1975
3.	Acid insoluble ash (on dry basis), percent by mass, Max	0.25	Annex C of IS 12569: 1989
4.	Fat (on dry basis), percent by mass, Min	10	Annex B
5.	Acid value of extracted fat, Max	2.0	IS 548 (Part 1): 1964
6.	Dehydrated vegetables including green chillies coriander or curry leaves and other vegetables, percent by mass, Min	7.5	Annex D of IS 13264:1991
7.	Uric acid, mg/100 g, Max	10	IS 4333 (Part 5): 1970
8.	B-N-oxalyl-amino-L-alanine	Absent	Appendix A of IS 2400:1976

Requirement For Ready Khichdi Mix

Table

Sl. No.	Characteristic	Requirement	Method of Test, Ref to
(1)	(2)	(3)	(4)
1.	Moisture, percent by mass, max	8	Annex B of IS 12569: 1989
2.	Total ash (on dry basis), percent by mass, Max	6.5	Appendix D of IS 4684:1975
3.	Acid insoluble ash (on dry basis), percent by mass, Max	0.25	Annex C of IS 12569: 1989
4.	Fat (on dry basis), percent by mass, Min	6	Annex D of IS 12569: 1989
5.	Protein (N x 6.25) on dry basis), percent by mass, Min	10	IS 7219 : 1973
6.	Uric acid, mg/100 g, Max	10	IS 4333 (Part 5): 1970
7.	B-N-oxaly-amino L-alanine	Negative	Appendix A of is 2400:1976

Requirements For Instant Curried Dal Mix:-

Table

Sl. No.	Characteristic	Requirement	Method of Test, Ref to
(1)	(2)	(3)	(4)
1.	Moisture, percent by mass, max	8	Annex B of IS 12569: 1989
2.	Total ash (on dry basis), percent by mass, Max	6.5	Appendix D of IS 4684:1975
3.	Acid insoluble ash (on dry basis), percent by mass, Max	0.25	Annex C of IS 12569: 1989
4.	Fat (on dry basis), percent by mass, Min	10	Annex D of IS 12569: 1989
5.	Uric acid, mg/100 g, Max	10	IS 4333 (Part 5): 1970
6.	B-N-oxaly-amino L-alanine	Absent	Appendix A of is 2400:1976

PROCESS OF MANUFACTURE OF READY SUJI-HALWA MIX

The process of making halwa from the ready mix, involves adding appropriate quantity of water to the mix and mild heating. Due to ease in cooking and the convenience it provides the ready mix is gradually gaining popularity.

Ready Suji-Halwa mix is prepared by roasting the wheat semolina cooking and drying various ingredients and subsequently dry mixing various ingredients so as to provide a homogenized mixture having a characteristic flavour of roasted semolina and light amber brown colour. Roasted dry fruits like Cashewnuts, almonds, raisins and permitted flavour may also be used as optional ingredients. The product is then packed.

The essential ingredient of ready suji - halwa mix are wheat semoliva edible fat or oil, sugar and the optional ingredients are dry fruits and nuts, flavour and cardamom.

Though preservative is generally not required as packaging condition is sterilized by irradiations to check the bacteria, yeast and mould growth. Still 0.05% of sodium Benzoate is added to the ready to each suji - Halwa mix to increase the shelf life without quality deterioration.

MANUFACTURING PROCESS FOR READY VEGETABLES PULAV MIX

The process of making vegetable pulav using the ready mix involves adding appropriate quantity of water to the mix and mild heating. Due to the ease in cooking and the convenience it provides the ready vegetable pulav mix.

The ready vegetable pulav mix is prepared by cooking dehydrated rice, potato cubes or slices, peas or any other vegetables and frying and/or drying under well defined processing condition to avoid browning discolouration burning or scorching. The dry ingredients are mixed with edible fat or oil, salt and other optional ingredients in suitable proportion.

The essential Ingredients are pre-cooked and dehydrated rice-whole grains, broken rice shall not be used

- Edible fat or oil
- Salt
- Vegetables-Dried/fried potato cubes or slices, peas, onions and any other vegetable.

The following are the optional ingredients may be used for the preparation of ready vegetables pulav mix.

Dry fruit and nuts-such as spiced or roasted cashewnut, groundnuts, walnuts, raisins etc.

- Spices condiments and their extracts .

These shall be clean, freshly ground chillies, pepper, cumin seeds, coriander seads, cloves, ginger garlic, turmeric etc. either singly or in suitable combinations such as curry powder providing whole some flavour blends. These shall be free from any sign of infestation, foreign matter or any undesirable odour or taste.

The preservative added to the vegetable pulav mix is 0.06-0.1% potassium metabisulfite of finished product for longer shelf life.

MANUFACTURING PROCESS FOR READY UPMA MIX

The process of making upma using the ready mix, involves bringing to boil the appropriate quantity of water, adding the mix to it and lighty heating.

Ready upma mix may be prepared by dry blending of the roasted/cooked dried semolina, dehydrated vegetables, roasted/fried dals edible fat or oils mustard seeds salt and optional ingredients.

The essential, Ingredients are wheat semolina (Suji). Edible fat or oil salt, dried and fried vegetables, dals (roasted/fried) Mustard seed).

The optional Ingredients are :-

Spices, Condiments and their Extracts:- These shall be cleaned freshly ground chillies, pepper, cumin seeds coriander seeds, cloves, ginger garlic, turmeric etc. either singly or in suitable combination providing wholesome flavour blends.

Dry fruits and nuts, such as spiced or roasted cashewnuts groundnuts, walnuts raisins etc.

Permitted Flavouring.

Citric acid/Tartaric acid (0.3-0.5% of finished product).

PROCESS OF MANUFACTURE OF READY KHICHDI MIX

The process of making khichdi using the ready mix involves bringing to boil the appropriate quantity of water, adding the mix to it and lightly heating. Due to ease in cooking. Saving in time and labour and convenience it provides to consumers.

The ready khichdi mix may be prepared by separately cooking/roasting rice and dals and drying then under well defined condition to avoid browning, scorching and case hardening onions if added, are chopped and fried in edible fat or oil. The rice and Dals are dry mixed along with edible fat or salt and other optional ingredients in suitable proportions.

The Essential Ingredients are:-

Rice - Pre-cooked whole grain; broken rice shall not be used,

Dals - Pre-cooked, whole dals, broken dals shall not be used,

Edible Fat or oil

Salt and the optional ingredients are:-

Spices, condiments and their extracts, onions, fried vegetable, sugar dry fruits and nuts.

The preservative sodium Benzoate 0.05-0.1% is added to the finished product.

PROCESS OF MANUFACTURE OF INSTANT CURRIED DAL MIX

In the preparation of Instant curried dal mix, the dals are cooked under steam pressure and dried under well defined condition to avoid shrinkage and case hardening and subsequently blended with salt dry coriander leaves, edible fat or oil and other optional ingredients.

The process of making dals using the ready mix, involves adding appropriate quantity of water to the mix and mild heating, due to the case in cooking and the convenience it provides the ready mix.

The essential ingredients are precooked Dals, Edible Fat or Oil, Salts Dried Coriander Leaves and the optional ingredients are spices condiments and their extracts onions amchur, tomato powder, tamarind powder.

The preservative Sodium Benzoate 0.06-0.1% is added to the finished instant curried dal mix.

PREPARATION OF VEGETABLES FOR CANNING

The raw material to be processed for canning should be of good quality.

Sorting and Grading:-

If the raw material before processing results in greater uniformity of finished product and in standardisation and improvement in methods of preparation, processing and preservation vegetables that are too green, over ripe, spoiled or show serious insect damage should be discarded. Grading may be done manually or with the help of mechanical grader e.g. screen grade, roller grader etc.

Washing:-

Vegetables are washed manually or mechanically to remove dirt foreign matter and surface microorganisms washing can be made more effective by causing the product to roll during washing with high pressure water sprays. The most effective washer is a revolving spray washing machine used on tomatoes and root vegetables severe washing sometimes bruises the product or removes valuable juices.

Peeling & Slicing:-

The washed vegetables are next peeled by hand knife or machine.

Blanching:-

Blanching is done with live steam, which clear the vegetables from dirt and organisms, rids it of earthy flavours fexes some, of the colours and expels the respiratory gases from the food, care should be taken in the peeling and blanching steps to avoid cooking otherwise it may harm the flavour is appearance, or texture of the product. The period of exposure 42-10 minutes. Hard water should not be used for blanching as it toughens the tissue and destroy the natural texture. Blanching is done by treating with boiling water or steam.

OUTLINE OF THE CANNING PROCESS

The process of canning involves washing, filling, exhausting, closing heat treatment, cooling, labelling and storage of the cans. Exhausting is carried out either by a vacuum treatment or by passing the cans through a steam-heated chamber. The all important heat treatment commonly known as "retorting" may be continuous or a batch operation. The three methods of cooling usually employed are: (i) by immersion of the cans in running cold water, (ii) by spraying the cold water (iii) by treating the cans with cold water without first removing them from the retorts.

The manner of heat treatment and cooling adopted is largely dependent upon the kind of food being canned washing the cans before filling is a highly desirable and necessary operation it serve the purpose of reducing to a minimum contamination by dust which is likely to take place during the period of storage of the empty cans. It is undesirable to built up a stock of washed can but it may be necessary to wash slightly in advance of filling requirement. When this is the practice the washed, cans should be kept in an inverted position until they are fed to the filling machine.

DETAILS OF CANNING FOR READY TO EAT VEG.

Can Filling:-

From the washer the cans pass to the filling operation. The usual practice is to allow them to roll by gravity down a runway fitted with a device for righting than upon their base for filling. The can may flow down the centre of a filling table upon a second belt or conveyor for transfer to the seamer.

Now the required weight of curried vegetables is placed in the can the space between the filled surface and the can top known as the head space is of the utmost importance. If the space is too much it will tend to make the can collapse on cooling after retorting. If too little spice is allowed adequate provision is not made for inevitable expansion in retorting with the result that the can will bulge and leaks may be made in the seams, or the can will burst. When deciding on the level of the filled can allowance must be made for the countersink of the lid.

Clinching:-

The cans after filling proceed to the clinching machine in which the lids are partially secured by a single seam by this means the lid is left sufficiently loose to permit of the escape of air and water vapour but sufficiently tight to prevent spilling of the contents.

Exhausting:-

The next stage in the removal of the air in the headspace known as exhausting. The primary object of exhausting cans prior to hermetically closing them is to remove the air from the headspace. The principle adopted is that the can passes automatically into a closing machine in which it is vacuumised and closed in successive operation in a matter of seconds and the can passes out of the machine ready for retorting.

Retorting or Processing:-

This is a very important part of the manufacture of canned foods and therefore, it should be subjected to the closest possible scientific scruting.

The length of time of the heat treatment must be such that all possibility of bacterial growth in the material, after cooking must be removed, and at the same time over cooking has to be avoided.

These are three chief factor which control the operation.

1. Nature of the material
2. Variety of micro-organisms likely to be present and the temperature and time of heating required to inhibit their activity.

3. The cleanliness of the premises, and the freshness of the materials to be handled, curried vegetables are processed at temperature above 100°C (115° - 120°C) under steam pressure in a close retort.

Cooling:-

After processing, the cans are cooled rapidly to stop the cooking process and to prevent stock burning especially in cans at the centre of large-stacks, where they may remain hot for several hours, cooling is done by (a) immersing or passing the hot cans in tanks containing cold water (b) spraying with jits of cold water (c) turning cold water in the case of canned vegetables and (d) exposing the cans to air in small lots, when water supply is scarce.

Labelling and Storing:-

Labelling serves to identify the products by kind and make and also protect the cans from rusting canned foods though stable for substantial periods of time should be stored under dry condition to avoid rusting and leakage storage of cans at high temperature should be avoided as it shortens the shelf life.

FORMULATION OF CURRY POWDER

Commonly Used Curry Powders:-

The following are the combinations of some curry powders (masalas) commonly used.

CHAT MASALA

S.No.	Ingredient	Quantity (weight kg)
1.	Salt white	3
2.	Dry mango	2
3.	Salt black	1
4.	Cumin	2
5.	Black pepper	1`
6.	Chillies	1
7.	Pomegranate seeds	1

8.	Musk million	1
9.	Coriander	1
10.	Mini leaves	1
11.	Long pepper	1
12.	Bishop's seeds	1/2
13.	Asafoetida	1/2

SAMBHAR

S.No.	Ingredient	Quantity (Weight Kg)
1.	Coriander	1
2.	Pulse arhar	7.5
3.	Cumin	1.1
4.	Turmeric	1/2
5.	Fenugreek seeds	1
6.	Chilies	1
7.	Rai	1/2
8.	Black pepper	1/2
9.	Poppy seeds	1/2
10.	Mustard	1/2
11.	Cloves	1/4
12.	Nutmeg	1/4
13.	Mace	1/4
14.	Caraway	1/4
15.	Asafoetida	1/4
16.	Salt	1

PUNJABI CHOLA KA MASALA

S.No.	Ingredients	Quantity (Weight Kg)
1.	Coriander	1.2
2.	Dry Mango	1
3.	Pomegranate seeds	0.4
4.	Salt White	2
5.	Chillies	1
6.	Cumin	0.8
7.	Fenugreek	0.6
8.	Carsia	0.4
9.	Black pepper	0.8
10.	Dry ginger	0.8
11.	Cardamom seed	0.6

12.	Mini leaves	1
13.	Mustard	0.8
14.	Nutmeg	0.6
15.	Mace	0.4
16.	Cloves	0.6
17.	Chinnamon	0.5
18.	Caraway	0.5

CURRY POWDER

S.No.	Ingredients	Quantity (Weight Kg)
1.	Coriander	1.4
2.	Pulse	2.6
3.	Turmeric	1
4.	Chilies	1.2
5.	Cassia	0.6
6.	Cumin	1.0
7.	Poppy seeds	0.6
8.	Fenugreek	0.6
9.	Cardamon	0.8
10.	Black pepper	1
11.	Garlic	0.8
12.	Mustard	0.6
13.	Dry ginger	0.6
14.	Cloves	0.8
15.	Nutmeg	0.8
16.	Mace	0.3
17.	Salt white	2.2
18.	Asafoetida	0.5
19.	Caraway	0.5

MANUFACTURING PROCESS OF READY TO EAT VEGETABLES

Curried vegetables are prepared by admixing the vegetables in curry to prepare ready to serve canned vegetables in curried form.

Potatoes and cauliflowers and tomatoes, potatoes and peas potatoes, peas and cauliflower, peas and paneer are some of the suitable combination. The vegetables are prepared for canning in the same way as for cooking A special type of gravy is prepared or follows for one dozens of A 2/2 (450 gm) cans of curried vegetables

		(oz)	(gm.)
Mustard (Whole)	-	3/4	21
Coriander powder	-	3/4	21
Red Chilli powder	-	1/2 to 3/4	14 to 21
Turmeric Powder	-	1½ to - 13/9	40 to 49
Common salt	-	3¼	91
Vegetable oil (Hydrogenated)	-	14	400
Water	-	make up gravy for 12 cans.	

PREPARATION OF GRAVY OR CURRY

The fat is heated in a pan and the mustard (whole) fried in it for a few minutes till the seeds craks. The other ingredient are then added and frying continued for a few more minutes. The require quantity of water is then added and the whole mass is then brought to boil sixteen to twenty once of the vegetable depending upon the combination are filled in to each 450 gm plain can. Hot gravy is added to the can and the can closed and processed for 60 to 75 minutes at 10 psig (0.7 kgs/cm^2).

The preparation and cooking of the number of defferent combination of curried vegetables requires coordination of all of the preparation. Each operation must be so timed and coordinated with every other operation that each of the products progresses steadily through the plant with a minimum of delay anywhere along the line otherwise both the flavour and sanitary quanlities of the curried vegetables will be poor. The kitchens must have adequate cooking facilities and equipment which will included a battery of kettles ovens steam cookers grills and deep fat foyer. In addition ther must be a variity of specialized equipment such as vegetables dicers slicers and comminuting machine and also homogenizers, mixer and blenders. Large walk-in coolers must be provided not only for fresh vegetables but also to hold partially processed foods overnight and during short period when certain processing equipment may be shut down for repair.

Direction for use

Heating suggestion:- Empty the vegetable and thoroughly heat stirring well occasionally.

Microwave instruction:- After pouring the vegetable in a microwave dish cover & cook for 3 minute stir occasionally.

The preservative shall be added in the gravy or curry as 0.03-0.05% Potassium metabisulphite of finished product to maintain the shelf life for longer period.

DUM ALOO (POTATOES IN THICK GRAVY)

Potatoes	-	1.500 kgs.
Brown cardamonm peeled	-	2
Cloves	-	4
Cumin seeds	-	5 gms
Poppy seeds	-	10 gms
Onion	-	100 gms
Ginger	-	15 gms
Garlic	-	7 gms
Water	-	750 ml
Vegetable oil	-	200 ml
Whole dry red kashmiri chillies	-	2
Cinnamon	-	2.5 m stick
Bay leaves	-	2
Onions grated	-	250 gms
Tomatoes pureed	-	250 gms.
Salt	-	25 gms
Red chilli powder	-	5 gms.
Turmeric powder	-	5 gms.
Garam masala powder	-	3 gms.
Presvative (Potassium Metabisulphite	-	0.03-0.05%

PROCESS FLOW SHEET FOR READY TO EAT CURRIED VEGETABLES

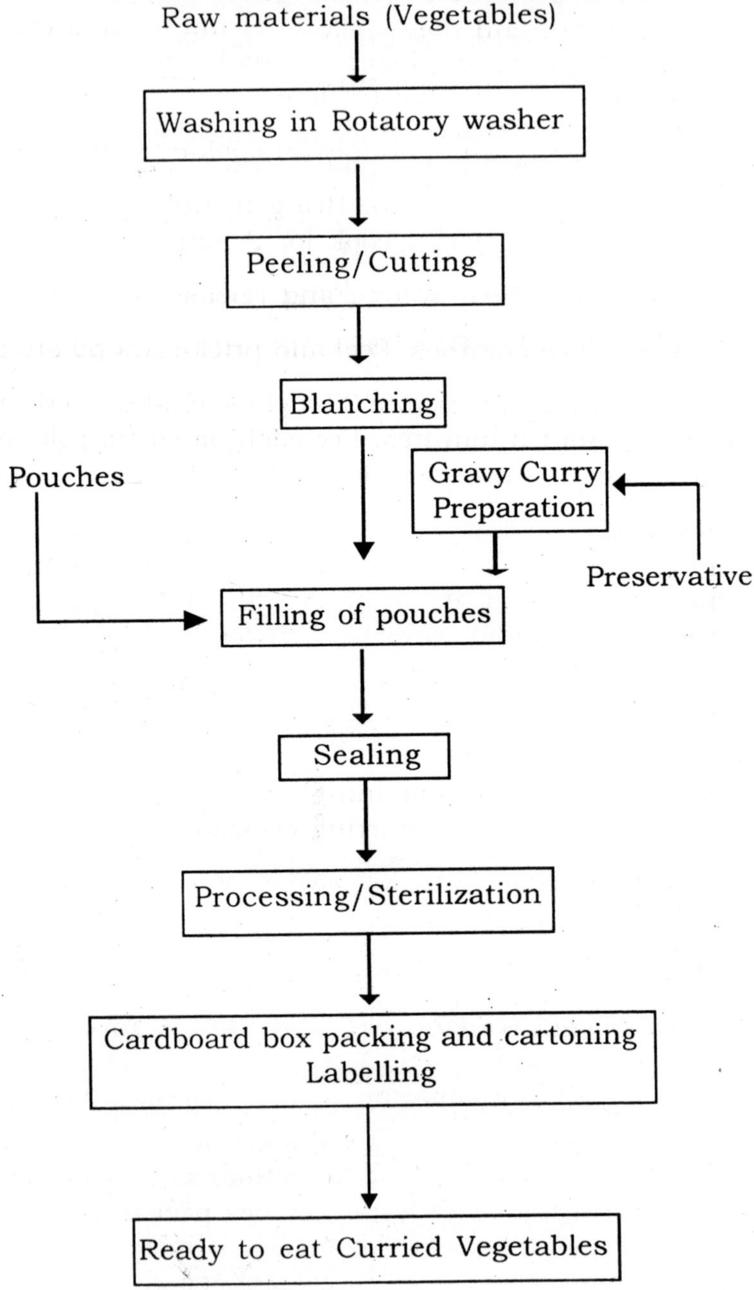

Process Steps

1. In a S.S. pan, roast together brown cardamoms, cloves, cumin and poppy seeds. Grind roasted ingredients together with onion, ginger and garlic into a paste, adding a little water from time to time.

2. Put water and potatoes in cooking pan.

3. Close cooking pan. Bring to full pressure on high heat. Reduce heat and cook for 2 minutes.

4. Remove heat source and release pressure.

5. Remove potatoes. Peel and prick each potato all over.

6. Group potatoes into 3 batches. Heat oil in deep-frying pan for about 3 minutes. Fry each batch till golden brown and remove. Strain oil cooking vessel.

7. Place cooking vessel on high heat. Add whole chillies, cinnamon and bay leaves. Stir for a few seconds. Add grated onions and fry till golden brown. Add ground paste, tomato puree, salt, chilli and turmeric powders. Stir for a few seconds.

8. Stir fry till oil shows separately (approximately 3 minutes). Add potatoes and stir gently to coat the potatoes with masala. Add remaining water. Simmer on low heat for about 5 minutes, stirring occasionally.

9. Add garam masala powder. Mix well.

10. Then fill in the cans (previously cleaned) and process like other curries.

MA KI DAL (WHOLE BLACK GRAM)

1 lit.	-	water
200 gms	-	whole black gram
50 gms	-	kidney beans soaked in water for 1 hour and drained
200 gms	-	tomatoes peeled and chopped
5 gms	-	ginger cut into thin strips
3 gms	-	garlic chopped

4	-	green chillies chopped
2	-	whole dry red Kashmiri chillies
15 gms	-	salt
5 gms	-	red chilli powder
5 gms	-	ghee
0.03-0.075	-	potassium metabisulphite (Preservative)

Tempering

2 tablespoons	-	ghee
1 small (50 gms.)	-	onion chopped
5 gms	-	ginger chopped
1/2 teaspoon	-	red chilli powder

1. Pour water into cooking vessel. Bring to boil on high heat. Add all other ingredients except those for termpering. Stir.

2. Close cooking vessel. Bring to full pressure on high heat. Reduce heat and cook for 30 minnutes.

3. Remove heat source. Allow to cool naturally.

4. Open cooking vessel. Partially mash dal with back of a ladle.

5. Placecooking vessel on low heat. Simmer to obtain a creamy consistency (approximately 5 minutes), stirring occasionally.

6. For tempering, heat ghee in a pan for about 1 minute. Add onion and fry till transparent. Add ginger and continue frying till onion is golden brown. Remove pan from heat. Add chilli powder and pour over dal. Mix thoroughly.

7. Fill in the cans and process like other curry.

PACKAGING OPERATION OF READY TO EAT CURRY

For flexible packaging of ready to eat curry, the flexible laminated pouches multilayer or Aluminium foil laminated plastic film material is used. The packaging operation is conducted by automatic form fill seal (FFS) machine. The detailed descriptions are as follow.

Form Fill Seal (FFS) Operation of Flexible Packaging

Description of Operation

Flexible packaging is one of fast developing packaging form in India. Form fill seal (FSS) is an automatic operation for this type of packaging.

For this operation various machineries are in use in Indian packaging industry. These machines ranges from semi-automatic to fully automatic with microprocessor based controls. These systems are used in place of several hard packaging systems like glass bottle, tin, cartons and other container packing system.

Form fill seal machine uses a reel of flexible material (paper, film or laminates) and either forms it into a tube and then seal at regular interval and fill it on regular intervals or fold it length wise and seal it at right angles to the fold to form a series of pockets which are filled and closed.

Machines of the first type form pouches or pillows with a seal at each end and down the center of one face. While second type of operation produces sachets with three or all four edge sealed.

Form fill and seal machinery may be conventionally grouped in three types.

A. Vertical Machine, in which material is formed into a circular section tube over a forming box; and

B. Horizontal machine, in which material is formed into a rectangular section tube through a forming box; and

C. Sachet forming machines which of themselves are of two types the first uses a single web folded in half and then cross sealed and second utilises two webs which are brought together and initially sealed on three side in each instance, after filling the remaining side is sealed to form the complete pack.

Operations involved in each type are given in subsequent sections.

FFS Operation Vertical

The opeation of vertical FFS, machine involves

1. Feeding and unwinding of film roll.

2. Conversion of the film in to a tube passing through the plate around the injection tube.

3. Effect the vertical seal by suitable vertical heat. Push in one side to creat base for standup pouch. Just opposite to vertical seal.

4. Pull the film down and effect top horizontal seal of preceding pouch and bottom seal of succeeding pouch.

5. Cut and detach the pouch after predetermine quantity is injected in preceding pouch, and pull down the former tube at predetermine level.

F. F. S. Operation Horizontal

Horizontal machine in FFS operation are as follows:

a. Feeding of film roll and unwinding.

b. Forming a rectangular section and inserting of product.

c. Tube sealing.

d. Side sealing cutting and pulling.

FFS Operation Horizontal: Sachet Forming

In case of FFS system of sachet packing. The operation is intermittent and mostly in horizontal form. The stages of operation are as follows.

1. Feeding and unwinding.

2. Folding the film in V or W (in case of gussated sachets). Shape and passed to the sealing stations or two saparate film are feed.

3. Vertical sealing is followed by horizontal sealing. The horizonetal sealing at this stage is optional. It is essential for tourside seal puch or standup pouch.

4. The web is drawn forward by a pair of roller and each pouch is separated from the wed. and transferred to filling staion.

Analysis of Norms

Norms considered for the evaluation of FFS technology level of FFS machiner are as follows:

- Type of Forming operation
- Type of filling operation
- Type of sealing operation
- Speed
- Manpower required
- Flexibility of handling material to be packed
- Flexibility of using packing material
- Packing Range
- Control System
- Counting System
- Checking system
- Other Features

In India, this technology was introduced about 12 years ago by couple of leading manufacturers of this type of machinery. These machines are available with various features like.

1. Filling Features

- Auger Filler for powder
- Volumetric filler for powder, granules and free flowing viscous liquid
- Weigh filler
- Liquid dosar
- Cup Filler

- Gravity Filler
- Counter Filler

2. Single or twin head system
3. Packing speed of 5000 bags/hr or 7200 sachets/hr.
4. Three side, four side and gussated and pillow type seals.
5. Photocell print registration.
   - No product no puch
   - Dry or ink type coding
   - Gusseting unit
   - Nitrogen gas flushing
   - Pouch counter
   - Digital pouch length or weigh control etc.

PACKING AND MARKING OF READY MIX FOOD

The ready mix food shall be packed in flexible food grade thermoplastic film of multilayer or monolayer construction or laminate with paper and/or aluminium foil so as to provide a high resistance to the passage of oxygen and water vapour and to produce an effective heat seal. The mix may also be packed in other conventional suitable rigid container such as tin, HDPE glass etc.

The materials may be packed in 100 gm, 250 gm, 400 gm, 500 gm, 2,000 gm pack or in sizes as egreed to between the purchaser and the vendor.

Marking

Each container shall be suitably marked so as to give the following information:-

A. Name of the material;
B. Indication of the source of manufacture;
C. Batch or code number;
D. Net mass;
E. List of ingredients used in descending order of composition;
F. Method of preparation;

G. Date of manufacture;

H. The words best before...........(the date to be given by the manufacture); and,

I. Any other details required under the Standard of Weights and Measures (Packaged Commodities) Rules 1977/Food Adulteration Rules, 1955;

The container may also be marked with the Standard Mark.

PLANT ECONOMICS

Rated Plant Capacity = 5000 CANS/Day

LAND & BUILDING

Land Area 2000 sq.mtrs. Rs. 44,00,000.00

PLANT & MACHINERY

1. Rotary vegetables washing machine,
2. Blanching Equipment
3. Pea Huller Equipped
4. Peas Grader
5. Potato Peeler
6. Carborandum
7. Vegetable Slicer
8. Potato Slicer
9. Rotary Diceing & Cubing machine
10. Reforming unit
11. Double Seaming machine
12. Can opener Table
13. Treadle lid embassing machine
14. Seam checking Gauge
15. Hand Can Tester
16. Vacuum Tester
17. Flange Rectifiers
18. Empty can washer
19. Working table
20. Aluminium Trays
21. Storage and Fixing Tanks
23. Canning retort
24. Gauge safety valve & Steam Pet Cock
26. Straight line exhaust box
27. Cover of aluminium
28. Curry filling machine
29. Material Handing Equipments
30. Misc. equipments
31. Laboratory Equipments
32. Steam Boiler
34. Tray Dryer

FIXED CAPITAL

1. Land & Building	Rs.	44,00,000.00
2. Plant & Machinery	Rs.	33,08,000.00
3. Other Fixed Assets	Rs.	20,80,000.00
TOTAL	Rs.	97,88,000.00

RAW MATERIALS

1. Fresh vegetables
2. Curry powder
3. Packaging materials
4. Misc. Labels cartons etc.
5. Wheat Samolina Sugar Flavour etc.

TOTAL WORKING CAPITAL/MONTH

1. Raw Material	Rs.	13,32,000.00
2. Salary & Wages	Rs.	2,07,000.00
3. Utilities & Overheads	Rs.	5,70,500.00
TOTAL	Rs.	21,09,500.00

TOTAL CAPITAL INVESTMENT

Total Fixed Capital	Rs.	97,88,000.00
Total Working Capital for 3 Months	Rs.	63,28,500.00
TOTAL	Rs.	1,61,16,500.00

TURN OVER/ANNUM

By sale of Ready to eat Food of Different Combination (15,00,000-Cans of 450 gm)	Rs.4,20,00,000.00

PROFIT SALES RATIO = Profit/Sales x 100 = 28.74%

RATE OF RETURN = Operating profit/T.C.I x 100 = 74.91%

BREAK EVEN POINT (B.E.P) = 40.87%

14

READY TO EAT MOONG HALWA, PANJEERI ETC.

Ready to eat food viz, ready Moong Halwa mix, Panjeeri etc. are gaining enormous eminence in modern era. It is consumed by the defence forces in an appreciable quantity. Apart from being consumed in bulk quantities by defence personnels. These "ready to eat" foods also serve the ease of their availability to people during outing, in picnics etc, where they relish these ready to eat food. The future scope of these ready to eat food is very bright.

There are various methods of preserving processed foods; canning is comparatively a modern technique. The principles of canning are to pack food in an impervious container e.g. metal can with or without coating which can prevent any contact between the atmosphere and the processed food; and to kill all natural micro-biological flora in the food and thus render it sterile. Foods canned under modern sanitary condition after processing are less likely to be infected be of fresher quality than those stored uncanned and their nutritional value is substantially the same as the fresh food.

REQUIREMENTS FOR READY TO EAT MOONGDAL HALWA

Requirements for Ready Moong Halwa Mix
Table

Sl.No.	Characteristic	Requirement	Method of Test, Ref to
(1)	(2)	(3)	(4)
1.	Moisture, perecent by mass, max	4	Annex B of IS 12569: 1989
2.	Total ash (on dry basis),percent by mass, Max	0.4	Appendix D of IS 4684: 1975
3.	Acid insoluble ash on dry basis, percent by mass, Max	0.1	Annex C of IS 12569: 1989
4.	Fat (on dry basis), percent by mass, Min	28	Annex D of IS 12569: 1989
5.	Sugar (on dry basis), percent by mass, Min	35	Clause 8 of IS 6287: 1986
6.	Acid value of extracted fat, Max	1.2	Clause 7 of IS 548 (Part 1) : 1964
7.	Protein (N x 6.25) on dry basis), percent by mass, Min	4.0	IS 7219 : 1973
8.	Uric acid, mg/100 g, Max	10	IS 4333 (Part 5): 1970

RAW MATERIALS

Moong dal, desi ghee, sugar, dry fruits, wheat flour, Ilaichi, flavour, sodium benzoates, green coriander/pudine leaves, ginger, spices, packaging materials, and others.

PROCESS OF MANUFACTURE OF READY MOONG HALWA

The process of making halwa from the ready mix, involves adding appropriate quantity of water to the mix and mild heating. Due to ease in cooking and the convenience it provides the ready mix is gradually gaining popularity.

Ready Moong Halwa mix is prepared by cooking the moong dal paste in desi ghee and subsequently dry mixing various ingredients so as to provide a homogenized mixture having a characteristic flavour of cooked halwa as light amber brown colour. Roasted dry fruits like cashewnuts, almonds, raisins and permitted flavour may also be used as optional ingredients. The product is then packed.

The essential ingredient of Ready Moongdal - Halwa Mix are wet moongdal paste, Edible fat or oil, sugar and the optional ingredients are dry fruits and nuts, flavour and cardamom.

Though preservative is generally not required as packaging condition is sterilized by irradiations to check the bacteria, yeast and mould growth. Still 0.05% of sodium Benzoate is added to the ready to eat moongdal Halwa mix to increase the shelf life without quality deterioration.

FORMULATION OF MOONGDAL HALWA

	(Parts by Wt.) (Kgs.)
Moong dall	30
Desi ghee	28
Sugar	35
Dry fruits	7
Ilaichi, Colour, Flavour	q.s (as required)
Sodium Benzoate	0.05%

Details of Process

1. Clean the dhoya moongdal to remove the foreign matters as stone, dust, ash, outer skin etc.

2. Wash the moongdall with clean water 3-4 times to remove surface polishes etc.

3. Soak the moong dal in clean water over night (12-14 hours approx.)

4. Wet grind the moong dal to prepare a paste of the same.

5. Then in hot aluminium pan or steel pan Roast/cook the dal paste with desi ghee till a light brown colour is obtained.

6. Then to it add the sugar and roasted dry fruits pieces (Almond Pist, Cashew nuts), elaichi powder etc. is reduced to 3-4%. Then to it, add the sodium benzoate 0.05% and lomogenise the same.

7. Then, cool the moong dal halwa to room temperature.

8. Then fill it in pouches (laminated multi layer polypropylene food grade) and seal the pouches. of sizes 250 gms, 500 gms., 750 gms., 1000 gms etc. by automatic vacuum pouch sealing machine.

9. The halwa pouches are now passed through radiation chamber for sterilisation of pouches by killing bacteria micro organisms etc.

10. Then, it is packed in card board paper packs.

11. The paper cardboard packs are further packed in corrugated paper cartons for storage and despatching purposes.

12. The finished product is marketed to the desired consumers.

MANUFACTURING PROCESS

PANJEERI

Panjeeri is generally prepared by mixing mildly roasted wheat flour, roasted cashewnuts, almonds, raisins, elaichi, sugar (powder) etc. Then, it is homogenisedly mixed for uniform distribution of all the ingredients. Then to it, Sodium Benzoate 0.05% of finished product is added.

The product is cooled to room temperature then it is hygienically packed in the laminated polythene pouches under nitrogen gas flushing systems by automatic form fill seal (FFS) pouch packing machine.

The pouches are now irradiated by radiation sterilisation technique to kill all the bacterial, micro organisms present in the pouches. Side by side without deterioration of any quality or loss of flavours etc.

The pouches are now packed in printed cardboard paper packs and sealed. These pouches are now further packed in corrugated paper cartons. Then, it is sealed by self adhesive tapes.

It is now stored and despatched for marketing.

FORMULATION FOR PANJEERI

	(% By Wt.)
Fine Coarse Flour (Wheat)	780
Sugar (Powdered)	18
Desi Ghee	2
Dry Fruits	2

MANUFACTURING PROCESS

1. Procure all the raw materials from the market.

2. Weigh it into desired quantity as specified in the formulation.

3. Now, roast the wheat flour in aluminium or S.S. Pan on light fire till a very light amber colour of flour is obtained.

4. Then, add Ghee to it and mix uniformly.

5. Then add the powdered sugar and roasted dry fruits pieces to it mix homogeneously.

6. Cool the panjeeri to room temperature.

7. Then, pack into the laminated polythene pouches with nitrogen gas flush automatic pouch weighing filling and sealing (FFS) machine.

8. The filled pouches are passed through radiation chambers for sterilisation and killing of bacteria and micro-organisms present in the pouches.

9. The panjeeri pouches are now packed in cardboard packs and then in corrugated cardboard boxes.

10. It is then sealed by self adhesive tapes and store for marketing to the desired customers.

PACKAGING OF RADIATION STABILIZED FOODS

One of the important considerations in radiation preservation of foods is packaging. If permanent preservation is to occur, food must be protected from recontamination. Therefore hermetically sealed containers are required for sterile products. Pasteurized products require special packaging, related to each food product specifically.

Flexible Containers

Radiation processing of foods permits the storage of perishable commodities of high moisture content in plastic containers at usual room temperatures. Flexible containers have been developed for foods. Functional, economical plastic containers are being developed and should find application in radiation sterilization and pasteurization

PAPER OR KULHAR PACKAGING MATERIAL

Paper and kulhar Packaging materials are not suitable for packaging of these food products. As the sterilisation process will not be efective and also the food products will be recontaminated in it within short period after sterilisation.

PACKAGING OPERATION OF READY TO EAT FOOD

For flexible packaging the flexible laminated pouches multilayer or Aluminium foil laminated plastic film material is used. The packaging operation is conducted by automatic form fill seal (FFS) machine. The detailed descriptions are as follow.

Form Fill Seal (FFS) Operation of Flexible Packaging

Description of Operation

Flexible packaging is one of fast developing packaging from in India. Form fill seal (FSS) is a automatic operation for this type of packaging.

Form this operation various machineries are in use in Indian packaging industry. These machines ranges from semi-automatic to fully automatic with microprocessor based controls. These systems are used in place of several hard packaging systems like glass bottle, tin, cartons and other container packing system.

Form fill seal machine uses a reel of flexible material (paper, film or laminates) and either forms it into a tube and then seal at regular interval and fill it on regular intervals or fold it length wise and seal it at right angles to the fold to form a series of pockets which are filled and closed.

Machines of the first type form pouches or pillows with a seal at each end and down the center of one face. While second type of operation produces sachets with three or all four edge sealed.

Form fill and seal machinery may be conventionally grouped in three types.

a. Vertical Machine, in which material is formed into a circular section tube over a forming box; and

b. Horizontal machine, in which material is formed into a rectangular section tube through a forming box; and

c. Sachet forming machines which of themselves are of two types the first uses a single web folded in half and then cross sealed and second utilises two webs which are brought together and initially sealed on three side in each instance, after filling the remaining side is sealed to form the complete pack.

Operations involved in each type are given in subsequent sections.

FFS Operation Vertical

The opeation of vertical FFS, machine involves

1. Feeding and unwinding of film roll.

2. Conversion of the film in to a tube passing through the plate around the injection tube.

3. Effect the vertical seal by suitable vertical heat. Push in one side to creat base for standup pouch. Just opposite to vertical seal.

4. Pull the film down and effect top horizontal seal of preceding pouch and bottom seal of succeeding pouch.

5. Cut and detach the pouch after predetermine quantity is injected in preceding pouch, and pull down the former tube at predetermine level.

F. F. S. Operation Horizontal

Horizontal machine in FFS operation are as follows:

a. Feeding of film roll and unwinding.

b. Forming a rectangular section and inserting of product.

c. Tube sealing.

d. Side sealing cutting and pulling.

PACKING AND MARKING OF READY FOOD

The ready food shall be packed in flexible food grade thermoplastic film of multilayer or monolayer construction or laminate with paper and/or aluminium foil so as to provide a high resistance to the passage of oxygen and water vapour and to produce an effective heat seal. The food may also be packed in other conventional suitable rigid container such as tin, HDPE glass etc.

The materials may be packed in 100 gm, 250 gm, 400 gm, 500 gm, 2,000 gm pack or in sizes as agreed to between the purchaser and the vendor.

Marking

Each container shall be suitably marked so as to give the following information:-

A. Name of the material;

B. Indication of the source of manufacture;

C. Batch or code number;

D. Net mass;

E. List of ingredients used in descending order of composition;

F. Method of preparation;

G. Date of manufacture;

H. The words best before..........(the date to be given by the manufacture); and,

I. Any other details required under the Standard of Weights and Measures (Packaged Commodities) Rules 1977/Food Adulteration Rules, 1955;

The container may also be marked with the Standard Mark.

PLANT ECONOMICS

Rated Plant Capacity = 1500.00 Kgs/Day

LAND & BUILDING

Land Area 1000 sq.mts = Rs. 38,15,000.00

PLANT & MACHINERY

1. Washing tank
2. Stainless steel soaking tank
3. Wet grinder
4. Aluminium Pan
5. Gas chulha
6. Ventilator fans
7. Automatic weighing, filling (FFS) Pouch sealing machine
8. Semi Automatic glass bottle weighing, filling & crown cap sealing unit
9. Autmatic labelling unit
10. Gamma-radiation sterilisation unit
11. Semi automatic carton sealing machine
12. Pipes pumps, fittings, structures & other Miscellaneous
13. PVC water storage tank
14. Laboratory testing equipment
15. Miscellaneous equipment

Wet Grinder

FIXED CAPITAL

1. Land & Building	Rs.	38,15,000.00
2. Plant & Machinery	Rs.	20,86,000.00
3. Other Fixed Assets	Rs.	5,45,000.00
TOTAL	Rs.	64,46,000.00

RAW MATERIALS

Moong dal, Desi ghee, Sugar, Dry fruits, Ilaichi, Colour, Flavour, Sodium Benzoate, Fine Coarse wheat flour, Desi ghee, Jeera, Onion, Red chilli powder, Green chillies, Ginger & Packaging materials etc.

TOTAL WORKING CAPITAL/MONTH

1. Raw Material	Rs.	17,52,270.00
2. Salary & Wages	Rs.	1,91,520.00
3. Utilities & Overheads	Rs.	1,95,900.00
TOTAL	Rs.	21,39,690.00

TOTAL CAPITAL INVESTMENT

Total Fixed Capital	Rs.	64,46,000.00
Total Working Capital for 3 Months	Rs.	64,19,070.00
TOTAL	Rs.	1,28,65,070.00

TURN OVER/ANNUM

Sale of moong dal halwa 300000 kgs & panjeeri 150000 kgs	Rs.3,60,00,000.00

PROFIT SALES RATIO = Profit/Sales x 100 = 21.24%

RATE OF RETURN = Operating profit/T.C.I x 100 = 59.45%

BREAK EVEN POINT (B.E.P) = 37.23%

15

RICE PUFF

Rice puff being one of the most nutritious food and is consumed as breakfast food not only in India but elsewhere in the world. Protein-calorie malnutrition (PCM) amongst children is prevalent in some parts of the country. Many efforts have been undertaken to ameliorate this socio-economic problem. One of these is the formulation of high protein foods. Rice puff is becoming increasingly popular in many states Rice contains high amounts of fat and proteins, although there are some difference in varieties popularizing Rice in the diet will help in combating protein-calorie malnutrition in children to a certain extent.

RAW MATERIALS

Rice is the chief raw material for a Rice Mill. Rice is a khariff crop like jawar, bajra, maize groundnut & cotton etc.

MANUFACTURING PROCESS

Usually rice is used as the raw material for the puffed rice. It is cleaned before puffing to reduce the amount of bran present on the finished product.

PUFFED RICE

General Considerations

Puffing process may be conveniently divided into two types (i) atmospheric pressure procedures which rely upon the sudden application of heat to obtain the necessary rapid vaporization of water and (ii) pressure - drop processes which involve suddenly transferring super-heated, moist particles into a space at lower pressure. In the latter case the pressure drop may be achieved by releasing the seal on a vessel containing a product which has been equilibrated with high temperature steam or it may be secured by transferring the hot material from the atmosphere into an evacuated chamber.

The puffing phenomenon results from the sudden expansion of water vapour (steam) in the interstice of the granule. The particle is fixed in its expanded state by the dehydration resulting from the rapid diffusion of the water vapour out of it. Gun puffing may result in an increase of apparent volume (bulk density decrease) of sixfold to eightfold for rice.

Puffed products must be maintained at about three percent moisture (or less) in order to have the desired crispness. Even at five percent moisture a definite toughness becomes evident. These levels are more critical and harder to maintain in foods which have been gun puffed.

DETAILS OF PROCESS

Generally, Rice puff can be manufactured by following two process.

1. Oven-puffed process, and
2. Gun-puffed process.

Oven-puffed process is most widely used for manufacturing of rice puff.

OVEN PUFFED PROCESS

Rice are used as the raw material for rice puff. After cleaning and classifying according to size, the rice is tempered with added moisture in steel bins of small diameter at approximately 85°F of 24 hours. The rice (tempered) is weight in requisite (say 1400 lbs.) quantity and fed to the toasted croker.

To secure the puffed effect, the cooled and tempered

Rice is passed through toasting ovens at 500° to 600°F. Transit time is about 45 to 60 seconds. The material is then visually inspected for colour and agglomeration and sent to the packing line.

PLANT ECONOMICS

Rated Plant Capacity = 1.00 Ton/Day

LAND & BUILDING

Land Area 1000 sq.ft. = Rental Based

PLANT & MACHINERY

1. Automatic Puffed Rice Making Machine
2. Bag stiching machine
3. Hot pouch sealing machine
4. Weighing balance

FIXED CAPITAL

1. Land & Building	Rs.	Rental
2. Plant & Machinery	Rs.	1,26,200.00
3. Other Fixed Assets	Rs.	25,000.00
TOTAL	Rs.	1,51,200.00

RAW MATERIALS

1. Rice
2. Salt
3. Jute bags
4. Polythene bags
5. Polypack

TOTAL WORKING CAPITAL/MONTH

1. Raw Material	Rs.	3,72,250.00
2. Salary & Wages	Rs.	25,935.00
3. Utilities & Overheads	Rs.	24,125.00
TOTAL	Rs.	4,22,310.00

TOTAL CAPITAL INVESTMENT

Total Fixed Capital	Rs.	1,51,200.00
Total Working Capital for 3 Months	Rs.	12,66,930.00
TOTAL	Rs.	14,18,130.00

TURN OVER/ANNUM

By sale of Puffed Rice 300 tons	Rs.	55,50,000.00

PROFIT SALES RATIO = Profit/Sales x 100 = 4.61%

RATE OF RETURN = Operating profit/T.C.I x 100 = 18.05%

BREAK EVEN POINT (B.E.P) = 64.58%

16

RICE FLAKES, CORN FLAKES & WHEAT FLAKES (INTEGRATED UNIT)

RAW MATERIALS

Corn

Maize is consumed as food in many ways, the simplest being in its natural form cooked on charcoal. Other ways include boiled cobs with chutney and baked cobs with butter. The corns are often popped and sold in packets.

Nutritive Value

Nutritive value of maize/100 gms.

Moisture	-	14.9 gm.
Protein	-	11.1 gm.
Fat	-	3.6 gm.
Minerals	-	1.5 gm.
Fibre	-	2.7 gm.
Carbohydrates	-	66.2 gm.
Calories	-	342
Calcium	-	10 gm.
Phosphorus	-	348 mg.
Iron	-	2.0 mg.
Vitamin A (Carotene)	-	90 mg.
Thiamine	-	.42 mg.
Riboflavin	-	.16 mg.
Niacin	-	1.8 mg.

Composition of Grains

The nature grain or paddy is botanically called caryopsis and consists of a loose outer husk enclosing the kernel. The husk varies in thickness as well as the case with which it separates from the kernal in different types of rice. It constitutes up to 23% of the paddy. The kernel itself is made up of three parts, viz. The outer layers which include the percarp (or seed coat) with the underlying aleurone layer the starchy endosperm, and the germ (or embryo), which on the average amount respectively to 6.0, 91.75 and 2.25% of the grain.

TABLE CHEMICAL COMPOSITION OF RICE, WHEAT AND MAIZE

	RICE		
	Husked	Milled	Maize
Protein, %	8.9	7.6	10.0
Fat, %	2.0	0.3	4.3
Carbohydrates, %	77.2	79.4	73.4
Fibre, %	1.0	0.2	2.3
Ash, %	1.9	0.4	1.5
Thiamine, g/g.	3-5	0.6-1.0	4.4
Riboflavin, g/g	0.8-1.0	0.28	1.3-1.5
Nicotinic acid g/g	55	15-20	21 ±
Pantothenic acid, g./g.	17	6.4	8 ±
Pyridoxine, g/g.	10.3	4.5	--
Choline Chloride, g/g.	--	880	370 ±

* FAO nutr. Stud., No. 1,1954, 65

± Yellow Corn.

Distribution of B-Vitamins in The Structural Part of Wheat kernel

	% of Total			
	Thiamine	Niacin	Riboflavin	Pentotheric acid
Pericarp, testa and hyaline	1	4	5	8
Aleurone	31	84	37	39
Endosperm	3	11.5	32	41
Scutellum	62.5	1	14	4
Embryo	2	1	12	3.5

Distribution of Carbohydrates in Commercial Wheat Fraction

	% of Total		
	Endosperm	Germ	Bran
Starelo	95.8	31.5	14.1
Sugar	1.5	36.4	7.6
Cellulose	0.3	16.8	35.2
Hemi Cellulose	2.4	15.3	43.1

MANUFACTURING PROCESS

Hybrid yellow and white corn can be used for the manufacture of corn flakes. The corn grains are first cleaned and polished to remove dirt, dust and bran etc. Large size of grains which generally can be retained on a No.6 mesh screen are preferred. The polished grains are milled so as to remove the germ and bran. The broken pieces, which are comparatively big in size are cooked under pressure in rotary steam cooker, which generally handles a batch of about 500 kg. at a time. The hominy is weighed into the cooker where it is subjected to the live steam for about 2 hours and mixed with flavouring material. The flavouring syrup which usually confirm sugar, malt, salt and water to have specified test of the finished products. The cooked material i.e. grits pick up moisture which rises to about 33 percent. A uniform translucency in the grifts indicates on adequate cook. The cooked material carried to an agitator or lump breaker and then is discharged into a man cooler or may be sent to suitable drier where the preheated air is blown to reduce the moisture content to the desired degree about 15 percent to 20 percent. The dried material is kept in tempering tanks for few hours to permit the residual moisture to become equally distributed. This is very essential to have uniform pressing in the flakes. It is also nece-temperature of the cooked hominy for giving to rollers for pressing, otherwise, the uniformity in thickness can necessary and carefully control the moisture contents and not be maintained. With more moisture flakes are expected to be thick. The tempered material is next passed through a heavy duty flaking machine (with a pair of water cooled rolls 20 inches diameter and about 24 inches-long). The flakes are then immediately transferred to rotary or suitable ovens for roasting. The ovens are usually gas fired and consist of slightly conical, rotating cylinder with per metal screen enclosed in a well insulated outer jacket, which is exhausted to the atmosphere for removal of moisture and fumes. In rotating the flakes are continuously carried forward until they are dropped into conveyer, when the propper degree of roasting has been accomplished. The roasted flakes are subjected to inspection preferably on conveyers or tables. Then properly roasted flakes are screened or graded and transferred to the packing bins immediately because flakes are hygroscopic. It is necessary to pack in water resistant packages generally polythene containers or with those waxed paper.

PROCESS FLOW SHEET FOR CORN FLAKES

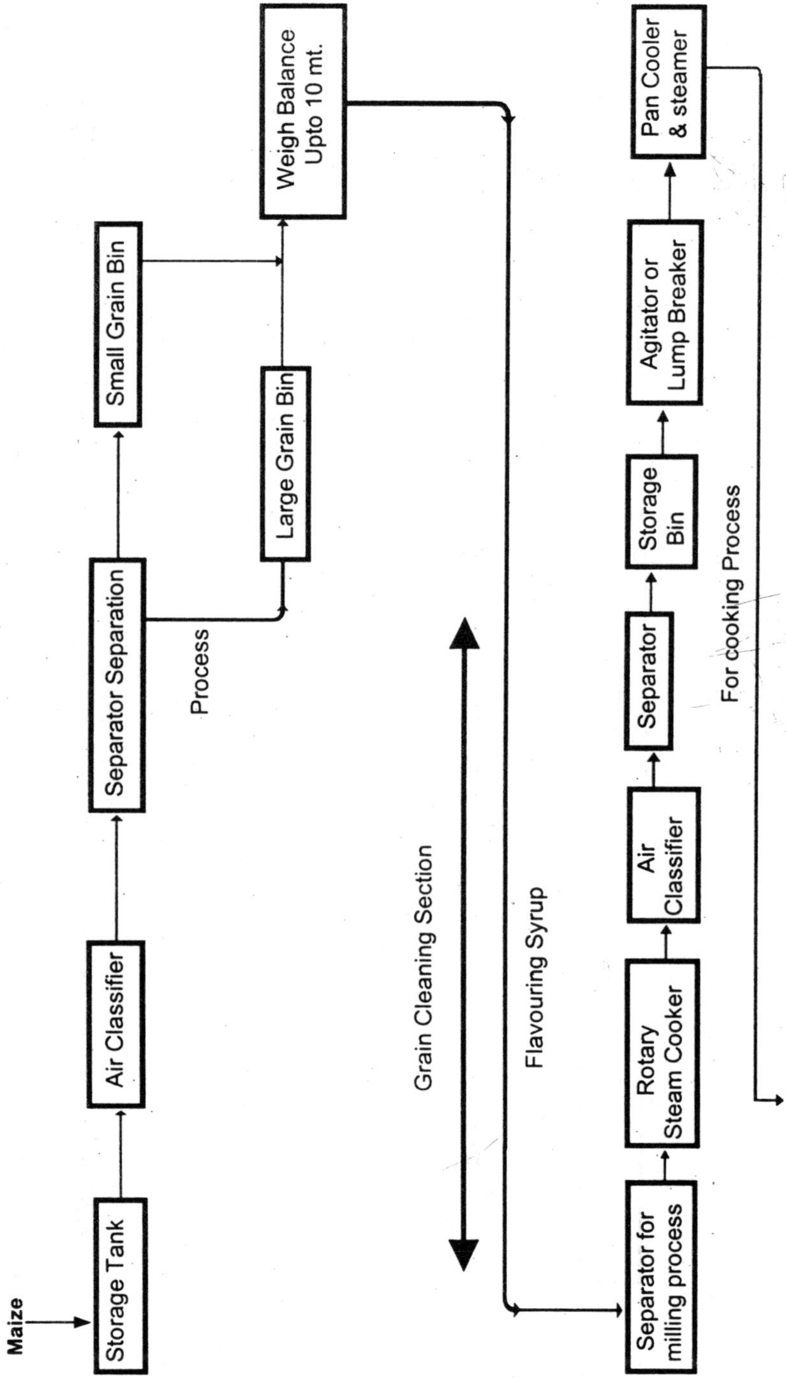

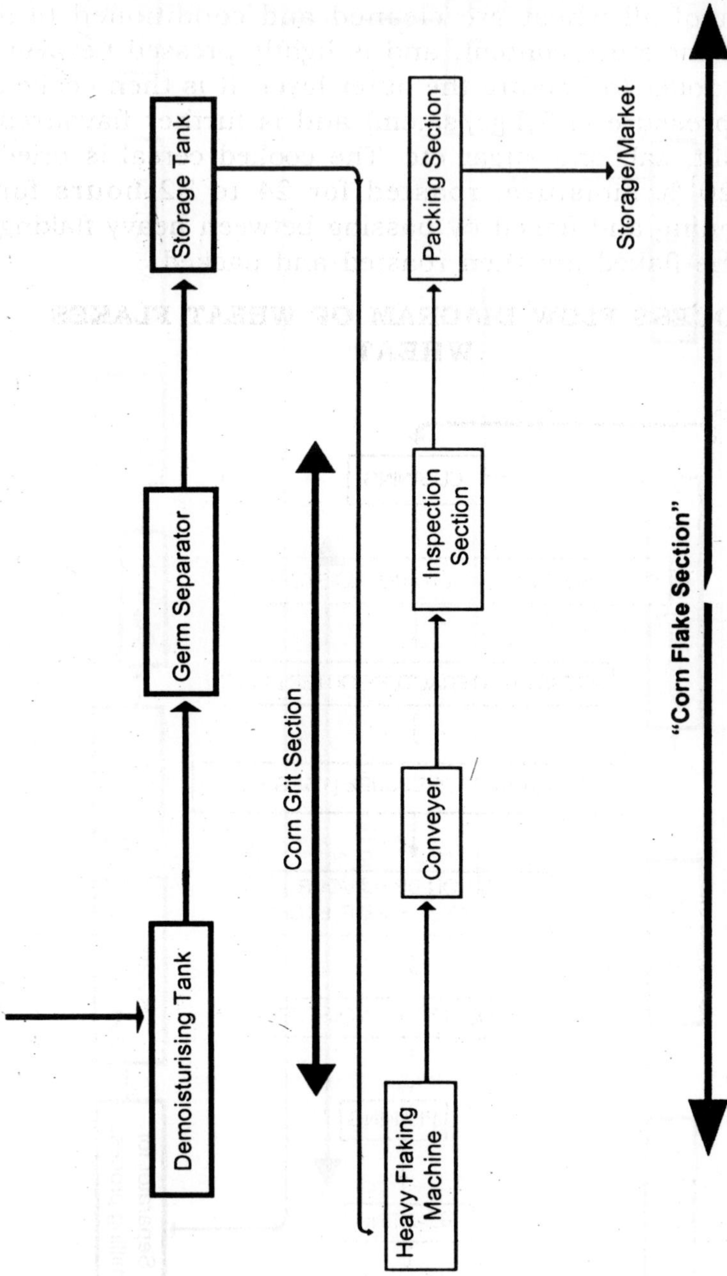
Demoisturising Tank
Germ Separator
Storage Tank
Corn Grit Section
Heavy Flaking Machine
Conveyer
Inspection Section
Packing Section
Storage/Market
"Corn Flake Section"

MANUFACTURING PROCESS OF WHEAT FLAKES

First of all wheat are cleaned and conditioned to a suitable moisture content, and is lightly pressed between smooth roller to fracture the outer layer. It is then cooked under pressure (1.5 kgs/sq.cm) and is further flavoured with malt, salt and sugar etc. The cooked cereal is dried to 15-20 % moisture, roasted for 24 to 72 hours for conditioning and flaked by passing between heavy flaking rolls. The flaked are then roasted and packed.

PROCESS FLOW DIAGRAM OF WHEAT FLAKES

WHEAT

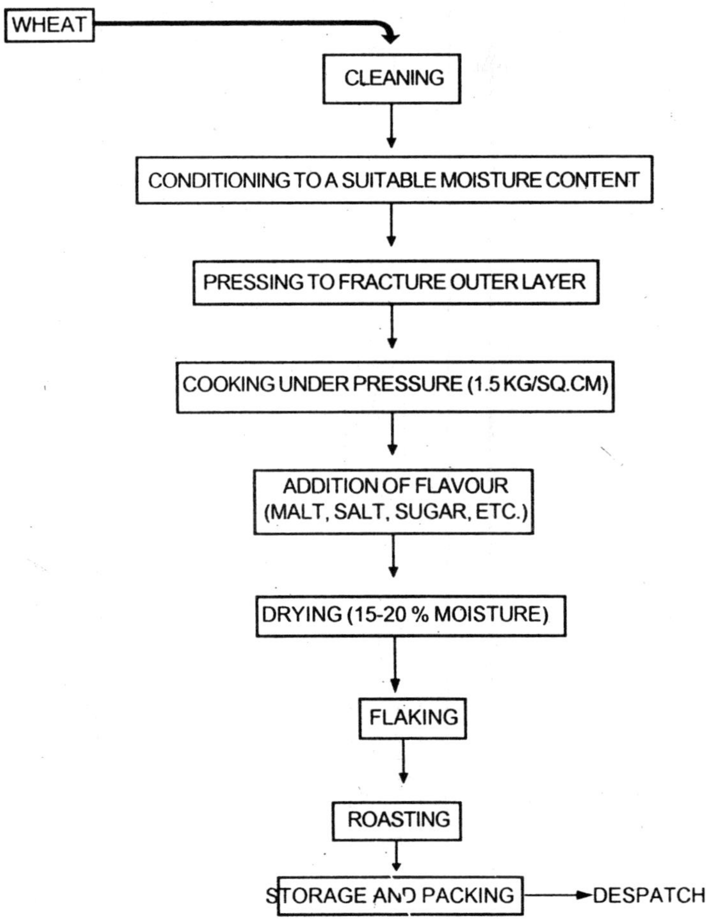

PLANT ECONOMICS

Rated Plant Capacity = 6.00 Tons/Day

LAND & BUILDING

Land Required 1 Acre. = Rs. 68,00,000.00

PLANT & MACHINERY

1. Boiler
2. Abrasion Machine
3. Carter disc separator
4. Dicky sifter
5. Blocking Machine
6. Rotary steam cookers tank
7. Mixer for cooled corn
8. Agitator
9. Cooler
10. Sweet Drier
11. Tempering Tanks
12. Rotary oven
13. Flaking Machine
14. Screening and cooling equipment
15. Automatic weighing, filling and sealing machine
16. Curning machine
17. Elevator or Conveyer
18. Inspection Table
19. Furnace
20. Compression Roller
21. Coating Reel
22. Pipe lines fittings valves etc.
23. Storage water tank
24. Laboratory testing equipment

FIXED CAPITAL

1. Land & Building	Rs. 68,00,000.00
2. Plant & Machinery	Rs. 76,85,000.00
3. Other Fixed Assets	Rs. 34,25,000.00
TOTAL	Rs. 1,79,10,000.00

RAW MATERIALS

1. Rice
2. Corn like maize etc.
3. Wheat
4. Vitamins
5. Disodium phosphate
6. Sugar
7. Malt syrup
8. Packaging material

TOTAL WORKING CAPITAL/MONTH

1. Raw Material	Rs. 19,28,000.00
2. Salary & Wages	Rs. 1,81,545.00
3. Utilities & Overheads	Rs. 3,36,000.00
TOTAL	Rs. 24,45,545.00

TOTAL CAPITAL INVESTMENT

Total Fixed Capital	Rs. 1,79,10,000.00
Total Working Capital for 3 Months	Rs. 73,36,635.00
TOTAL	Rs. 2,52,46,635.00

TURN OVER/ANNUM

By sale of Rice flakes 600 tons
By sale of Corn flakes 600 tons
By sale of Wheat flakes 600 tons Rs.4,08,00,000.00

PROFIT SALES RATIO = Profit/Sales x 100 = 12.67%
RATE OF RETURN = Operating profit/T.C.I x 100 = 20.48%
BREAK EVEN POINT (B.E.P) = 62.91%

17

SNACK FOOD

Today, a whole new generation of food products floods the market, catering to entirely new breed of consumers. Rapid industrialization and rising standards of living have not only pushed the boundings of the market but have also brought about general changes in the profile of Indian consumer. Snack foods have got tremendous demand in throughout India and also having bright future demand.

The average composition of a properly fired rice snack is as follows:-

Moisture	-	3 %
Protein	-	6.7 %
Fat	-	37.1 %
Carbohydrates	-	51.2 %
Minerals	-	3.0 %

MANUFACTURING PROCESS

Cereal grits are used as raw material for making snacks. Initially, it is ground into a paste and after the treatment of steaming, this is kneaded to produce dough containing about 15% moisture. The remaining process is un-operational sequence, as follows:-

Humidification

While corn grits or rice grits, which form the raw material, contain generally between 13% to 15% moisture, the appropriate moisture content of the raw material for the manufacture of snack ranges between 14% to 16%. Humidifier consists of tumbler which uniformly and

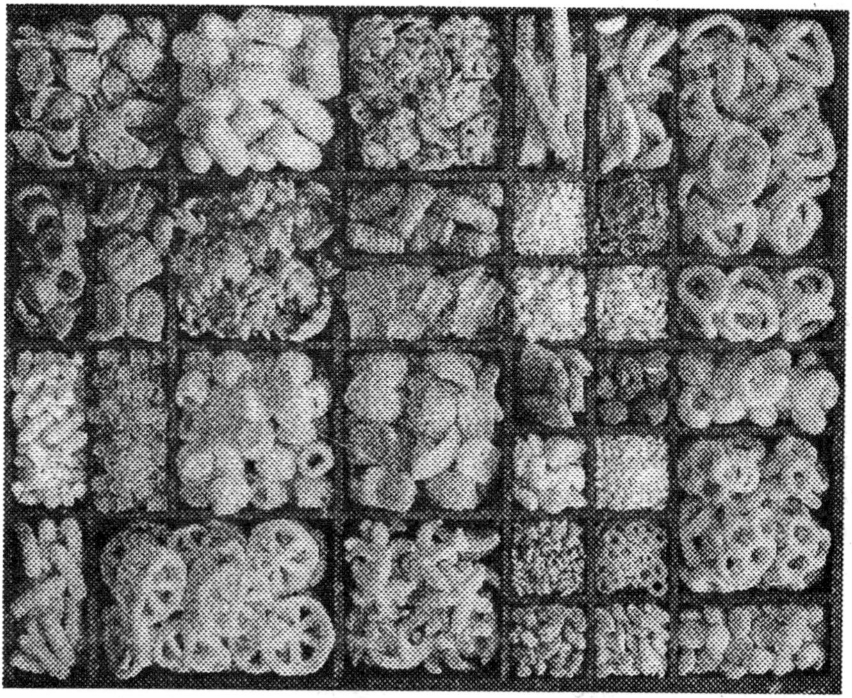

appropriately applies moisture to the grits. The meshes of the grits range between 14 to 16, and after being humidified are inserted into a container or receptacle where they are left quietly for a period of about twenty minutes to enable the moisture to penetrate and saturate the grits uniformly.

Puffing

After humidification, the grits are fed into the cylinder of puff machine by means of a screw, carried in a forward direction, and as the cereal grits move ahead, the space between the cylinder and the screw is narrowed. High pressure is generated and, at the same time, because of friction heat, the temperature of the raw-material reaches as high as 180°C more or less.

The raw material, which is sufficiently gelated by the generation of this high temperature and pressure, is forced out into the atmosphere through tiny holes in the die where upon, as a result of the large pressure difference, moisture is instantaneously evaporated and, including bubbles, is inflated to form and produce expanded material (puffed product).

Cutting

The inflated material, which has been extruded, is cut into requisite length by a rotary cutter.

Roasting

As moisture still remains in the expanded material which has been cut up into requisite lengths, it is slightly roasted in a rotary oven, and simultaneously with drying, the flavouring of the cereals are drawn out.

Seasoning (By rotary seasoning machine)

The surface of the expanded material (puffed product) which comes out of the rotary oven is flavoured and seasoned by a spraying of vegetable oil and seasoning. By the rotation of a slightly slanted drum, the expanded material is uniformly flavored and seasoned as it moves forward.

Finishing & Drying

The puff snack, which has been flavoured and seasoned with oil and seasoning powder, possess little moisture, and therefore needs no finishing and drying. However, in the event that the seasoning, juices are watery, the puff snack is dried by a finishing and drying machine. Drying is adequately performed by the passage of air at a temperature of about 80°C.

Packaging

Snack foods deteriorate due to moisture and oxygen, a film is utilized which prevents permeation of moisture and gases. Packing and packaging are both performed by an automatic bag making, filling and packaging machine. Before packing and packaging weighing is undertaken either manually or automatically as the case may be.

Protein Snack

Ingredients		*(Kgs)*
Cracker Meal	-	125
Bread Flour	-	85
Sunflower Meal	-	85
Promine D	-	15
Gum Arabic	-	3
Onion Salt	-	2
Celery Salt	-	1
Water	-	80

Process

Mix all dry ingredients and add sufficient water to make a paste that will just flow. Extrude into desired shape into deep fat at 375°F and fry until light brown. Drain dry. Add salt as desired.

Protein Crackers

Promine - D	-	40 gms
Wheat Flour (General purpose)	-	360 gms
Salt	-	20 gms
Ammonium Bicarbonate	-	15 gms
Hydrogenated Vegetable shortening	-	100 gms
Water	-	240 gms

Process

Mix dry ingredients, add water, and knead. Then pass through extruder and puffing machine then pack into desired packaging materials.

PROCESS DETAILS

The manufacture of a composite cereal by the gun puffing method is described as follow.

Corn cones, oat flour, and a flavour pre-mix consisting of salt coloring substances, flavoring compounds, etc. are combined in a screw conveyor with interrupted flights. The homogenous mixture is dumped through a rotary valve into a continuous steam-jacketed cooker. Water is added

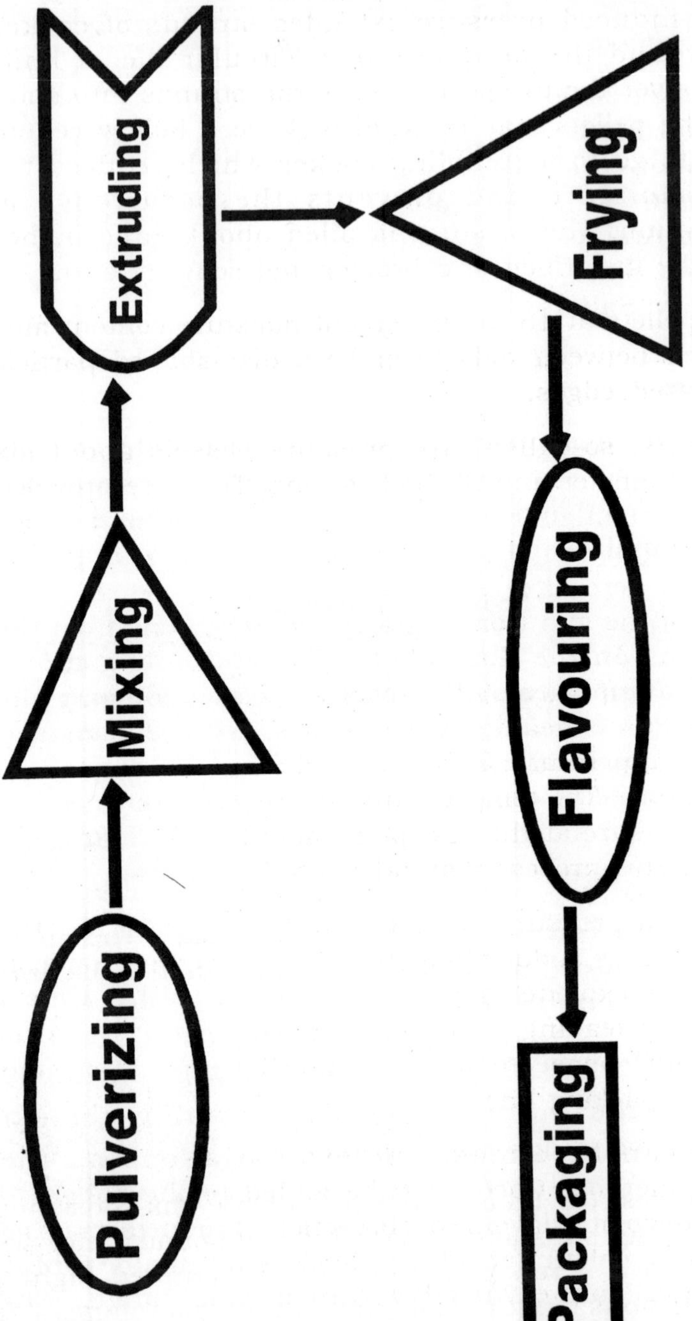

PROCESS FLOW CHART FOR NAMKEEN SNACKS

by a metering device so that the product going to the extruder is at 38 to 40 percent moisture content.

Auger-induced pressure extrudes strands of cooked dough around the periphery of a circular die. A knife travelling over the die surface cuts the strands into short pellets. The pellets may be solid or have a hollow center. The pellets go to a tumbling cooker which reduces the surface moisture and prevents the occurrence of agglomeration. The product is piled about three inches deep on the metal belt of a proctor and sehwarz oven.

Solid pellets at 15 to 16 percent moisture content may be bumped between rolls to make a disc-shaped particle with serrated edges.

The guns, so-called, are pressure vessels about six inches in diameter and 30 inches long. They are provided with a steam inlet, a bleed-off valve, and a means for heating the gun-usually by a gas flame. A charge of pellets at 11 to 12 percent moisture content is dropped into the open end of the gun from a gravity chute leading from the storage bins on the floor above. The end of the gun is sealed by a trip-valve. All valves are closed, sealing the gun. If the gun is heated by gas flames, it is slowly rotated while the temperature, and consequently the pressure, is slowly built up. The temperature may reach 500° to 800°F, and the pressure at the end point may be 100 to 200 lb. per sq. in. This process may take 5 to 7 minutes.

When the pressure reaches the necessary level, the end of the gun is suddenly opened by a trigger mechanism. The contents explode into a cage or bin provided with a floor opening leading to a conveyor belt. The material is then visually inspected for color and agglomeration and sent to the packing line.

There can be almost endless variations on the preceding method. Cocoa can be added to the dough to make a chocolate flavoured confection. Products may be made of any colour for which there is a suitable edible dye. Shapes canbe varied within a wide range. Raw materials may be almost any combination of cereals.

Some composite-dough, gun-puffed cereals are the trade-marked Mix, Coco-Puffs, Jets, Trix, Cheerious etc.

Details of Snacks Food Plant

The solid design of all parts, precision & extremely accurate manufacturing methods ensure in combination of minimum maintenance requirements & trouble free operation. The machine is precisely designed to ensure minimum power consumption. The extruder is so versable that by just replacing sets of nozzles the user has the advantage of changing the shape of the final product.

The versability of the extruder can be gauged from the fact that the user can make use of either of the following raw materials. Corn grit rice grit, wheat samolina, sabudana etc.

SNACKS FOOD PLANT

TECHNICAL SPECIFICATIONS

	CAPACITY (In KG/hr)	BARREL LENGTH (In mm)	SCREW DIA (In mm)	MAIN MOTOR DRIVE (H.P.)	CUTTER MOTOR DRIVE (H.P.)	FEEDER MOTOR DRIVE (H.P.)	COOLING SYSTEM	MIXER MOTOR DRIVE (H.P.)	CONMORISED OVEN DRIER TOTAL ELECTRIC (H.P.)
SNACKS FOOD PLANT	80 TO 100	458	70	25	1/2 D.C.	1/2 D.C.	1/2 H.P. A.C. BLOWER	3 A.C.	—

DETAILS OF PLANT & MACHINES

Cap: 150 kgs/hour Puff Snack Making Plant.

Sl.No.	Machine or Equipment	Unit	Power Rating
1.	Humidifier made of S.S.-320	2 No.	1.2 KW
2.	Screw Conveyor	1 No.	1.5 KW
3.	Grain puff machine	3 No.	52 KW
4.	Conveyor	1 No.	0.4 KW
5.	Conveyor	1 No.	0.4 KW
6.	Rotary oven, gas fired, L.P.G. gas consumption 8 kgs/hour	1 No.	0.75 KW
7.	Conveyor	1 No.	0.4 KW
8.	Seasoning service tank, gas fired, L.P.G. Gas consumption 2 kgs/hour	1 No.	0.4 KW
9.	Rotary seasoning machine	1 Nos.	0.4 KW
10.	Powder spraying system	1 Nos.	1.6 KW
11.	Conveyor	1 No.	0.4 KW
12.	Bucket Type Conveyor	1 No.	1.5 KW
13.	Automatic weighing machine	3 No.	
14.	Automatic packing machine	1 No.	0.4 KW
15.	Conveyor	1 No.	0.2 KW
16.	Compressor	3 No.	17.1 KW

PLANT ECONOMICS

Rated Plant Capacity = 1300.00 Kgs./Day

LAND & BUILDING

Land Area 2000 sq.mt. = Rs. 21,50,000.00

FIXED CAPITAL

1. Land & Building	Rs.	21,50,000.00
2. Plant & Machinery	Rs.	26,50,000.00
3. Other Fixed Assets	Rs.	5,00,000.00
TOTAL	Rs.	53,00,000.00

RAW MATERIALS

1. Proamine D
2. Wheat Flour
3. Salt
4. Ammonium Bicarbonate
5. Hydrogenated Vegetable shortening
6. Packaging materials

TOTAL WORKING CAPITAL/MONTH

1. Raw Material	Rs.	10,76,500.00
2. Salary & Wages	Rs.	1,22,360.00
3. Utilities & Overheads	Rs.	1,85,000.00
TOTAL	Rs.	13,83,860.00

TOTAL CAPITAL INVESTMENT

Total Fixed Capital	Rs.	53,00,000.00
Total Working Capital for 3 Months	Rs.	41,51,580.00
TOTAL	Rs.	94,51,580.00

TURN OVER/ANNUM

By sale of 390000 kgs. Rs.2,34,00,000.00

PROFIT SALES RATIO = Profit/Sales x 100 = 18.98%

RATE OF RETURN = Operating profit/T.C.I x 100 = 46.99%

BREAK EVEN POINT (B.E.P) = 46.29%

18

PACKAGING OF SNACK FOODS

INTRODUCTION

Food products categorized as snacks differ not only from country to country but are also perceived differently bt the industries that manufacture them as well as the consumers who enjoy them. Therefore for the purpose of this article, they are taken to mean rather narrowly as ready to eat ambient, shelf stable (6 to 12 weeks) savory products, prepacked and offered through a variety of outlets including supermarkets and other food retailers as well as catering establishments. These include potato crisps, other reformed products based no potato powder such as potato sticks, extruded savory snacks and roasted nuts. In countries where potato is a less popular raw material, products based on yam, sweet potato or other tubers can also be classified as snacks if they are manufactured using largely similar technology since of the packaging requirements will be the same. The increasingly popular products such as Chinese dim sum and Indian samosas, bhajjis and the like, which may loosely be called snacks and whose packaging requirements are quite different from those of conventional snack foods, are therefore outside the scope this article.

THE PRODUCT GROUP

Broadly speaking, snack food products may be divided into the following categories based on the process technology associated with their manufacture.

1. **Deep fat fried.** This includes potato crisps and potato strips/sticks/rings, and represents by far the major portion of the snack food business.

2. **Quick fried.** Pre-formed partly cooked pellets derived from potato, potato starch and/or other cereal materials are fried at high temperature (i.e. of the order of 200°C) for a short time (10-15 seconds) giving expanded. light-textured products.

3. **Extrusion-cooked.** Cereal/potato powder mixes are extruded through dies at high pressure and temperature to give an expanded base which, after further drying, is enrobed with oil and flavour. A large number of products are available in this category and they display varying sizes, shapes, textures and flavours.

4. **Roasted.** This generally represented by nuts, particularly in the form of dry roasted peanuts.

5. **Baked.** This generally produces snacks of much lower oil content as well as offers an opportunity for different flavour development. An example is savory mini biscuits.

The primary raw materials for snacks are potato, either fresh or dehydrated, cereals (maize, rice, wheat etc.) and nuts. Notwithstanding the important influence these raw materials have on the quality of the final products, by far the most important ingredient that can affect product shelf life is the oil used, either in frying or as a carrier for seasoning. Snack products as a group, can be said to be consumed principally for pleasure, Whilst many relevant factors undoubtedly have their influence on the shelf life of a snack product, some like the packaging materials and the system employed do have major effects. Recent years have seen an explosive introduction of a huge variety of flavours, with a particular emphasis on the use of flavours derived from natural sources. This development, which although has helped to meet the ever increasing consumers demand for interesting texture and new flavours, has also brought along unusual shelf life problems for the manufacturers. Incidents of premature termination of shelf life as a result of microbiological soilage due to the use of less than hygienic herbs and spices have been reported. Care in the choice of flavours for snack foods of the right microbiological quality is therefore recommended.

PACKAGING MATERIALS FOR SNACK FOODS

One of the most important functions of food packaging is the protection of the product from environmental factors such as light, water vapour, gases and odours during its shelf life. The actual protection required, however, depends on the nature of the product. In respect of the shelf life of snacks, the following are the main properties of flexible packaging materials (e.g. co-extruded oriented polypropylene (OPP), which can affect the storage quality of a product.

(a) Water vapour transmission rate (WVTR): For a given material such as co-extruded OPP, this is primarily a function of film thickness (figure 1). The lower the WVTR of a film, the better is the moisture barrier of a packaging film, of course, may be further enhanced by various

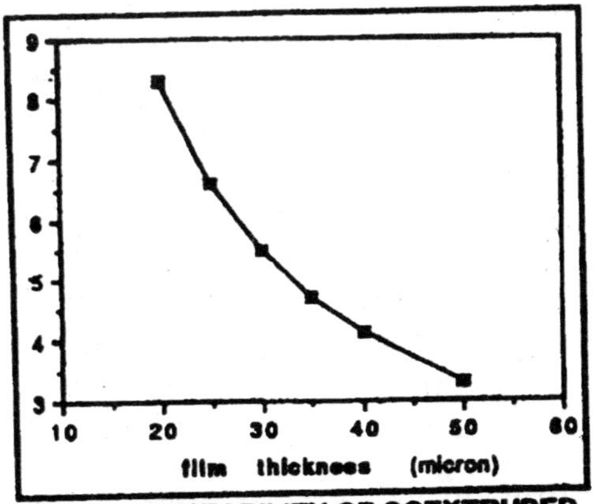

FIG. 1 PERMEABILITY OF COEXTRUDED OPP FILMS TO WATER VAPOUR.

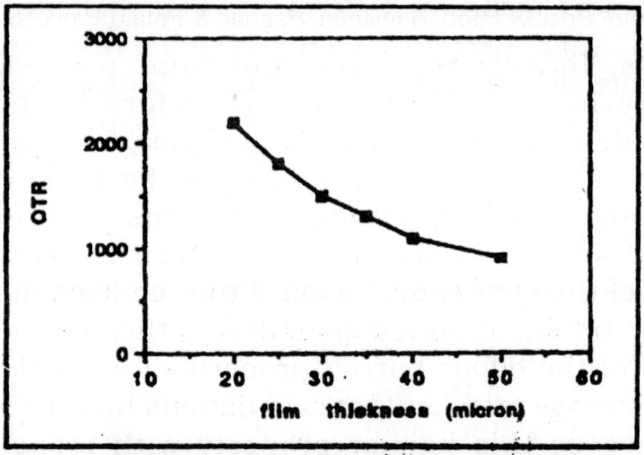

FIG. 2 PERMEABILITY OF COEXTRUDED OPP FILMS TO OXYGEN.

processes such as coating with an additional barrier material, lamination and metallisation (Table 1).

(b) Oxygen transmission rate (OTR): Similar to WVTR, OTR of clear OPP decreases as the thickness of the film increases (Figure 2). Permeability to oxygen is substantially reduced by coating with a suitable barrier material (e.g. acrylic) and by metallisation (Table 1).

(c) Optical density (OD): This is defined as OD = Log 10 (incident light/transmitted light). Determined using a suitable densitiometer (at 23 + 2°C, 50+5% RH), it is a measure of the light barrier property of a film (Figure 3).

The greater the OD of a film, the better is the light barrier and hence protection against light-induced changes (e.g. oxidation and bleaching).

(d) Flavour/odour barrier property: The significance of flavour/odour barrier performance of a packaging film lies in its practical importance in relation to the flavour retention of packaged to the flavour retention of packaged foods such as snack, and also with respect to protection against tainting by extraneous sources. Snack products are usually highly flavoured and contain an appreciable amount of oil, making them susceptible to contamination by taints, flavour retention and taint protection over relatively long shelf lives are therefore an important consideration. The odour barrier performance of coextruded OPP films should not be assessed on the basis of oxygen performance of coextruded OPP films should not be assessed on the basis of oxygen permeability, indeed because of the very many flavours that be used and odours that may be encountered potentially, there is no general measure of the odour barrier property of a packaging film. Specific storage tests and/or calculations have to be carried out to assess this barrier property with respect to the flavour/odour in question.

Work carried out by BCL resulted in the derivation of a simple equation based on Fix law of diffusion, which can be used to estimate the likely permeation coefficients of a wide range of chemical substances through coextruded OPP as well as polyethylene, at low odourant concentrations. In the SI system, permeation coefficients have the unit-g mm-2 Pa-1 S-1, which represents the weight of flavourant/odourant permeating a polymer specimen one meter thick, one require meter in area, per second, with a vapour pressure deference across the specimen of one Pascal (=10 ppm vol/vol). The permeation data, together with information relating to the pack contents and storage / display environment, provide a convenient method for estimating the estimating the transfer rates of flavours or contaminants through commercial flexible packs. Expert has shown that the rate of transmission (R in g s-1) of flavourant (e.g. vinegar flavour measured as acetic acid through a packaging film is given by the following formula:

$$R=(PC \times VP \times A)/L$$

Where PC=pereation coefficient ($g\ m\ m^{-2}\ Pa^{-1}\ S^{-1}$)

VP=vapour pressure of flavourant (Pa)

A=area of film (m^2)

L=thickness of film (m)

Strictly speaking, VP should be the difference in vapour

pressure of flavourant between the inside and the outside of the pack: but for practical purposes, the inside pack vapour pressure, as measured by headspace gas chromatography, will suffice. Using this formula, it is possible in the event that highly flavoured snacks are being packaged, to conduct flavour loss calculations, thereby providing the reassurance that the chosen OPP film, for example, will give an adequate barrier.

During the shelf life of a snack, besides possible flavour loss, two main deterioration processes take place together, one being texture loss due to moisture pick up, the other being rancidity development which requires oxygen and may be light-induced. Although both need to be controlled, relatively speaking and depending on the prevailing environmental conditions such as temperature and relative humidity, in the UK, the former is more important to potato crisps and related snacks and the latter, to nuts because of their compositional different, Thus currently biaxially oriented polypropylene (OPP) films are the most commonly used packaging materials for crisps and snacks within Europe, while nuts are usually packaged in, for example, PVDC coat OPP/LDPE laminate of metallised polyester LDPE laminate, depending on the value of the product. OPP has qualities of toughness (against punchure and abrasion) and clarity and is rendered heat sealable

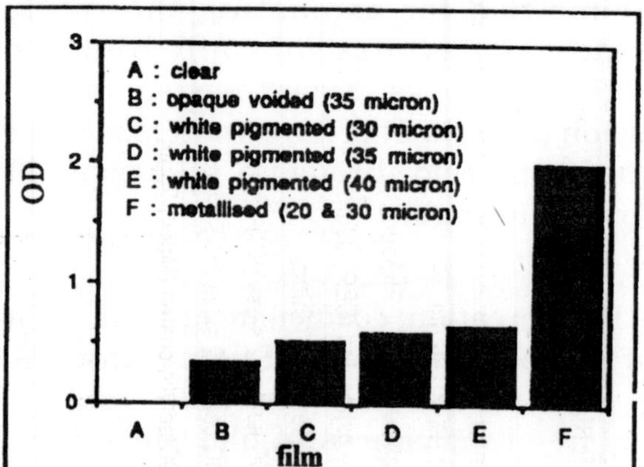

FIG. 3 OPTICAL DENSITIES OF SOME COEXTRUDED OPP FILMS.

by coextrusion with polyolefin copolymers (polypropylene co-ethylene) or by off-line coating (e.g. with PVDC).

Table 1 lists typical WVTRs and OTRs of some OPP films used for crisps and snacks packaging. It must be stressed that these values are flat sheet permeability values; the protection of the product depends on the total barrier provided by the film pack. The sheet barrier properties may be altered by bad conversion techniques, or by mishandling such as scratching by poorly maintained packaging leakage during the shelf life of the product. Pack barrier for snacks is thus a combination of:

film barrier

TABLE 1

TYPICAL WATER VAPOUR TRANMISSION RATES AND OXYGEN TRANSMISSION RATESOF SOME BIAXIALLY ORIENTED POLYPROPYLENE FILMS USED FOR SNACKS.

MATERIAL TYPE	OTR ($cm^3/m^2/24h/atm$ at $23+2°C$ and 90% RH)	WVTR ($g/m^2/24h$ at 38°C and 90% RH)
clear (CEP)- 30 µm	<1500	<5.5
opaque voided (CEP)-35µm	1550	5.2
white pigmented (CEP)-30µm	<1500	<5.5
metallised (CEP)-30µm	<120	<0.8
PVDC coated 2 sides (ICI)-28µm	16	5.0
PVDC coated 2 sides (ICI)-39µm	5	2.3
PVDC/acrylic coated (Mobil)-26µm	23	4.2
acrylic coated 2 sides (Mobil)-30µm	650	4.0
metallised/acrylic coated (Mobil)-21µm	1-2	1.0-1.5

(Source: Various technical data sheets. Courtaulds Films Polyproylene (CFP), ICI 'Propafilms', and Mobil Plastics Europe).

- maintenance of film barrier
- seal integrity.

In practice, to achieve the required level of protection of a snack, it does not necessarily follow that the highest barrier material is the choice of packaging. The packaging material that is chosen will be a compromise between protective requirements, shelf life, aesthetics and cost. In the crisps sector, until recently, a 30 micron clear OPP film has been the most cost effective form of packaging for commodity products with short shelf life (12 weeks or less) while metallised OPP laminates have found use in larger family packs, sensitive products and high added value products. With snack manufacturers having to put pressure on costs to counter the effect of any increase in materials cost, the latest trend is towards downgauging but not at the expense of either product protection or machine performance. In the nuts sector, commodity products with short shelf life requirements are packed in nitrogen gas flushed PVDC coated OPP/LDPE laminates while higher added value products and those with longer shelf life requirements are packed in nitrogen gas flushed metallised polyester/LDPE laminates. The principal spoilage mechanism, in this case-oxidative rancidity, is very long achievable shelf lives in MAP for snack foods. MAP materials must have very high moisture and gas barrier properties and metallised films and laminates possess these necessary properties.

The popularity of multipacks, both of single and mixed varieties of standard packs, has been increasing over the years, Multipacks provide variety and economy to the consumer and a means of sales promotion to the manufacturer. The packaging of multipacks is more involved and there are many variations. In the UK, the most popular system uses a heatsealed outside bag, usually of OPP, that takes 6, 8, 10, or 12 standard packs. A varying amount of manual operation is usually involved. The permeability of a multipacks may be estimated by treating the different layers of film as resistances in series, analogous to the resistance of electrical elements in series.

$$\frac{l_t}{P_t} = \frac{I_1}{P_1} + \frac{I_2}{P_2} + \frac{I_n}{P_n}$$

where P_t=permeability of the composite
I_t. = total thickness
P=permeabilites of the individual layers 1, 2,....n
l=thicknesses of layers 1.2....n

In practice, putting smaller packs into a bigger multipacks bag gives a marginal laminating effect, resulting in extra protection of the products again environmental factors. Recent studies have demonstrated that, for products like potato crisps and related snacks, long-term moisture-gain experiments are no longer required to predict product shelf life and package performance in respect of water vapour transfer. The data required are:

- the moisture-sorption isotherm data
- the pack properties i.e. WVTR of the film/laminate
- the external/storage conditions.

The stability of the product and its shelf life may be modelled using readily available computer spreadsheet software.

Within the European Community, the need to achieve harmonisation of legislation in member states in respect of materials and articles destined for use in contact with foods and the need to product the consumer from risks associated with the migration of barmful substances from packaging materials, have meant that food packaging migration is now under the control of the relevant legislation. The EC plastics directive 90/128/EEC as amended by directive 92/39/EEC, sets an overall migration limit for all plastics food contact materials and articles of 10 kg/dm_2 (or 60 mg/kg of food), and lists monomers and other starting substances approved for use in the manufacture of plastics with restrictions where necessary. In the UK, the implementation of this directive and two other directive, i,e,82/711/EEC on test condition and Articles in Contact with Food Regulations. This piece of legislation applies to all in the chain from the plastics manufacturer, through the plastics converter, the food packer/manufacturer, to the food retailer. All have a definite role to play in the compliance of the overall migration and where appropriate, specific migration limits, though each may have a slightly different responsibility to bear. Regarding overall (global) migration values from co-extruded OPP films, the following are typical results:

(a) <1 using distilled water of equivalent quality
(b) <1 mg/dm^2 using 3% acid (w/v) in aqurous solution
(c) <1 mg/dm^2 using rectified olive oil

The snack manufacturer obviously has a responsibility to ensure that all the information supplied to him by the packaging film supplier in respect of migration into food simulants is appropriate to his actual snack product, and this does not take into consideration any sensory analysis required additionally. Furthermore, since the snack manufacturer may also be expected to supply the retailer with compliance statements, it seems therefore some migration testing by the former cannot be avoided. This is particularly relevant in the case of new/novel product and film combination, where migration testing can well be an important part of the shelf life evaluation programme.

Rigid cylindrical containers made of plastics (e.g. HDPE) or metal (either tinplate or aluminium) as well as printed spirally wound composite tubes with resealable plastics or metal lids are also used to package snack foods. The former, flushed with nitrogen, have been used for high quality products such as nuts while the latter have been used for fabricated moulded potato crisps that can be stacked like biscuits, These packaging formats are in general less popular and they provide similar protection of the product from environmental factors as their more-widely used flexible counterparts.

PACKAGING SYSTEMS

Snack foods manufacture is a high volume business and computerized weighing machines have become commonplace. One such system is made up of ten heads arranged readily and the crisps or other products are fed into these via a central feed, coming from the conveyer belt supplying the whole line. A required weight is set for the machine and a computer scans the heads some 500 times every minute to decide which of the heads together would give the nearest to the desired weight, resulting in very precise control of pack weight. Wrapping machines used are commonly of the vertical form fill seal (VFFS) type (Figure 4): the speed at which they operate is best expressed in meters of film pulled per minute rather than number of packs per minute.

From the wrapping machines the packs, ready date-coded and priced, are fed on rotary tables for packing into card board distribution cartons. Modern designs have meant that the cartons can be easily opened and used to aid display in supermarkets as well as smaller outlets.

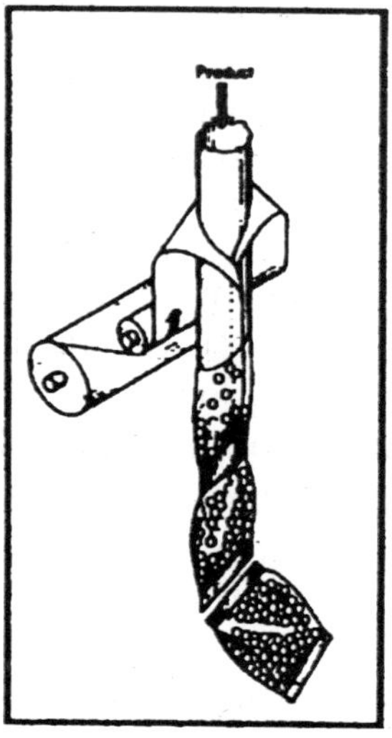

Fig. 4 Pouch Packvertical-from-Fill-Seal (VFFS) Operation

As regards the use of modified atmosphere, there are generally two techniques employed to replace the air within modified atmosphere packages.

1. Gas flushing

In this technique, the replacement of air inside the package is performed by a continuous gas stream e.g. nitrogen, which dilutes the air surrounding the food product before the package is sealed. The great advantage of this technique is the speed of the machine. As the dilution of air is continuous, the product packaging rate can be very high. Gas flushing is normally arrived out, for snack products, on vertical form fill seal machines. Since the replacement of air inside the packages is achieved by dilution, there is a limit to the efficiency of this technique. Typical residual oxygen levels in gas flushed packages are 25%. Therefore, if the food product to be packaged is particularly oxygen sensitive and/or a long shelf life required, then the gas flushing technique is not normally suitable.

2. Compensated vacuum

In this technique, air is removed by pulling a vacuum on the air within the package and then breaking the vacuum with the desired gas e.g. nitrogen. Since the replacement of air is completed by a two step process, the speed of operation of the equipment is slower than equipment using the gas flushing technique. Also the pulling of a vacuum means that this technique is unsuitable for fragile products such as potato crisps packaged in flexible packaging materials. However, as the air is removed by vacuum and not simply diluted the efficiency of the unit with respect to residual oxygen level is better than gas flushing. Therefore, a compensated machine is usually used for packaging snack products that are particularly oxygen sensitive.

19

CEREAL & LEGUME BASED FOODS-RAW MATERIAL, PREPARATION, PACKAGING

INTRODUCTION

The rice and wheat are the major cereals of the state. Punjab contributes around 54% of its rice production and 43% of its wheat production ton the central grain resqurces pool. Majority of the food grains produced in the country are consumed in the form of traditional foods while only a small amount is processed into convenience foods.

Despite such a large consumption of traditional foods and a great potential for their commercial production and marketing these products is have received very little attention form the industry.

- Their high perishability and lack of appropriate technology for large scale mechanized production and marketing of such products.
- Lack of involvement of women in food processing industry.
- Conservative outlook of the consumer towards processed foods.
- High cost of preparation and low purchasing power of consumers.
- Lack of organized marketing channels in rural areas.

Presently due to increased operations of MNC's urbanization industrialisation & women going into jobs there is an increased demand for shelf stable foods of Indian culinary. This demand is likely to increase in coming years. If low cost technologies for large scale mechanized production along with suitable preservation and packaging method are devised this would go a long way to appease the palate of Indian household. The present effort of listing some of the North India traditional foods their recipes and method of preparation would help industry to consider mechanized production of such products.

WHEAT PRODUCTS

Wheat is one of the most important cereal in India contributing one third to the total food grain basket of the country. In term of area (25.4 million hectares) as well as production India ranks 4th in the world.

Under All India Coordinated Programmes and state/ local programmes of the Agricultural Universities a large number of varieties have been identified/recommended for cultivation by farmers and to reach various processing through marketing channels. The important varieties recommended and identified for cultivation in different zones of the country are as follows.

NORTHERN HILL ZONE

1. Irrigated timely sown	HS 240 UP 1109 HD 2380
2. Rainfed timely sown	VL 421 HS 240 DH 2380 UP 1109 DT 4600
3. Rainfed timely sown high attitude	HPW 42
4. Rainfed very early sown	VL 616 HS 277
5. Rainfed late sown	HS 295

NORTHERN WESTERN PLAINS ZONE

1. Irrigated timely sown	HD 2329 HD 2204 HD 2428 WH 542 WH 283 WH 416 CPAN 3004 RAJ 3077 PBW 154 PBW 343 UP 2338 PDW 2159DO PBW 34 (d) PDW 233 (d 1) WH 896 (d)
2. Rainfed timely sown	C 3306 KUNDAN PBW 65 PBW 175 PBW 299
3. Irrigated late sown	HD 2285 HD 2270 PBW 226 RAJ 2184 RAJ 3077 WH 2191 UP 2338 RAJ 3765 PBW 373 (I)
iv) Saline soil	KRL 11-4 RAJ 3077

NORTHERN EASTERN PLAINS ZONE

1. Irrigated timely sown	HD 1102 UP 262 HUW 206 K.7410 K 8804 HD 2402 DL 784-3 K 9107 9DEWAO HP 1731 (RAJLUXMI)
2. Rainfed timely sown	C 306 K 8027
3. Irrigated late sown	HD 2307 HUW 234 HP 1633 (I) PBW 373 (I)
4. Rainfed late sown	HDR 77 K 8962 (INDRA)
5. Saline soil	KRL1-4 RAJ 3077

CENTRAL ZONE

1. Irrigated timely sown	LOK 1 WH 147 WD 2236 HI 1077 GW 190 RAJ 1555 (D) HI 8381 (D) DL 803-3 (KANCHAN)
2. Rainfed timely sown	C 306 JU 12 (D) MEGDOOT (D) A 930-1 (D) SUJATA NARBADA 4 HYB 65 HW 2004 (I)
3. Irrigated late sown	LOK 1 J 405 SWATI HD 23227 GW 173 KRL 1-4 RAJ 3077
4. Saline soil	KRL 1-4 RAJ 3077

PENINSULAR ZONE

1. Irrigated timely sown	HD 2189 DWR 39 HD 4502 (D) HD 2380 DWR 162 MACS 2496 DDK 1001 (DIC I)
2. Rainfed timely sown	NI 5439 N 59 (D) BIJAGA YELLOW (D) MACS 1967 (D)
3. Irrigated late sown	HI 977 HD 2501 DWAR 195 ANUIRADHA D) NIAW 34 (I)

SOUTHERN HILLS ZONE

1. Restricted irrigation	HW 741 HW 971 HUW 318m NP 200
2. Rainfed	(Dic) NP 200 (Dic)

The coverage of post green revolution wheat varieties

is as follows.

Maximum coverage of major post green revolution wheat varieties.

>0.5	>0.1	>0.2	>0.4
WG 357	HD 2009	WL 711	HD 2329
WG 357	HD 2285	HUW 234	
RAJ 1555	HD 2204	UP 262	
HP 1102	WH 147		
BW 11	WH 283		
HW 2189	PBW 154		
VL 616	RAJ 3077		
HUW 206	WL 1562		
LOK-1	LOK-1		

Out of the total production of 62.47 million tonnes hardly about 9 million tonnes is processed by roller flour milling industry for maida suji and resultant atta. Out of this only about 2.8 million tonnes is used by baking industry for bread biscuits and noodles. Thus around 85% of wheat and a substantial quantity of milled product are consumed in the form of traditional products listed here with.

CHAPATIES (ROTIS): Wheat is consumed in different form of chapaties like Tandoori Khamiri(fermented) Missi Roomali etc. Rotis are mostly consumed during lunch and dinner. Medium Strong elastic doughs are suitable for tawe waali and tandoori roties while a strong and elastic dough is suited for miss (with besan) & Khamiri roti. Chapaties are mostly prepared fresh and highly pliable soft and had a mild baked aroma. Most of the wheat varieties having medium string characteristics and amber colour have been found to be suitable for chapati baking. Varieties having high molecular weight glutenins and phospholipids have been found to be superior for chapati baking because of simplicity of method of chapati baking and very short shelf life of chapaties no organised sale of chapaties has taken place though the need for ready to bake or ready to serve chapaties has been felt in cosmopolitan cities and in large industrial canteens. One of the major constraint in the large scale production and marketing of chapaties seems to be the non availability of automatic rolling and baking machines. A semi mechanised leg operated chapati flattening unit and associated baking unit having a production capacity of 400 chapaties per hour with five person has been designed by DFRL Mysore CFTRI has also attempted a chapati making system that resembles more with corn tortilla machines available in Mexico.

Chapaties prepared in fully mechanised units crumble during storage in chain stores. They are also susceptible to stalling ropiness and mold growth. Chapaties within few hours of preparation tends to develop brittle texture as a result of starch retrogradation and losse aroma and moisture. During subsequent storage, chapaties develop ropiness followed by fungal growth and fermentative odours. Though it has not been possible be completely arrest the brittleness development ropiness fungal growth and bacterial spoilage could be arrested by hurdle technology involving in pack processing use of antimycotic agents and pH control. Use of stable flavour based on curnene oleoresin and milk powder has been found to considerably reduce the perception of stalling. Process developed by arya et at has been found to keep chapaties in safe condition for more than six month and preserved chapaties are claimed to be liked by troops and members of various mountaineering and rowing expeditions.

PACKAGED CHAPATIES FOR GENERAL MARKETING

Chapaties preserved by the process developed by arya et. al. are said to have a shelf life of more than six months. This much shelf life though essential for pack rations of armed forces due to logistic reasons is neither necessary nor desirable for commercial marketing. To attain this much shelf life highly costly moisture proof aluminium foil laminate packaging and in pack processing are necessary which make the process highly costly. Chapaties being a staple food for daily consumption a shelf life of 5 days should be more than adequate for commercial marketing. In fact a process has been developed successfully for the short term preservations of chapaties by using only antimycotic agents in the dough and packing baked chapaties in plastic pouches. This method has also been extensively tried and has been found highly effective.

PUFF AND SERVE CHAPATIES

As already stated earlier chapaties are mostly prepared fresh and served hot. The consumer highly like fresh puffed chapaties. In order to meet this requirement DFRL mysore has developed a process for preservation of partially chapaties which consumers can puff on an open gas flame or on an open coil heater at the time of consumption. The process enables preservation for 5-7n day and retention of puffing characteristics even after storage. Since puff and serve chapaties meet consumers expectations in respect of fresh baking and reasonable shelf life for marketing these are expected to be highly successful in commercial marketing. However, the product has yet to be test marketed.

POORIS

Poories are prepared from stiff dough and are deep fried at high temperature using poori aag (full flame). Poories are traditionally prepared during festivities or on sundays by halwa is and consumed for breakfast/brunch/lunch. Pithi wali pooris (will dal stuffing) are also popular.

PARATHAS

Parathas are shallow fried on tawa (hot plate). A simple as well as wallan waala paratha are the breakfast delights in northern india. These are consumed with subzi (vegetable curry) or fried eggs omelette etc. in the morning.

SPICED POTATO PARATHAS

Besides plain chapaties processes have also been developed for the preservation of sliced potato chapaties and parathhas. These are prepared by mixed spices and boiled vegetables in the dough or by giving spices and seasoned vegetables in between two chapaties and subsequently baking them on a hot plate with application of oil/vanaspati on the surface. The spiced parathas can be prepared layers to impart crispness and more uniform baking. Incorporation of vegetables helps in retention of soft texture during storages the moisture content in spiced potato chapaties varied between 30-35% as compared to 28-33% in plain chapaties. Antimycotic agents are required to be incorporated in both flour and vegetable and use of milk solids is not desirable because of tendency of spiced vegetable to brown during storage. The process developed by DFRL Mysore permit a shelf life of one year under ambient conditions. Spiced potato parathas when subjected to large scale consumer acceptance trials involving more than 300 troops were graded highly acceptable in taste texture and aroma. The type of oil used during baking has been found to considerably influence the keeping quality of spiced potato parathas. While unsaturated vegetables oils like ground nut oil sunflower oil etc. are suitable for fresh chapaties these tend to impart stored taste and undesirable aroma after few weeks of storage. Considering the high acceptance of stuffed parathas throughout the country and excellent keeping quality of the spiced vegetable chapaties and parathas, these have excellent potential for marketing though tortal mechanization of the product manufacture is yet to be achieved it is possible to atomize some of the unit operations which will keep total investment on machineries and plants within reasonable limits.

FLAT/PITA BREAD

Flat breads with upto 10 days shelf life in polyethylene bags have been produced. The hard wheats like PBW 34 PDW 215 WL 1562 PBW 154 & wg 357 with about 10-12% protein 64-68% WA 4 minute dough development time and about 7% Da produced excellent results in experiments conducted at FST.

MAKKI DI ROTI TE SARSON DA SAG

Maize chapaties with mustard leave curry are consumed very frequently in winters in norhtern India especially in Punjab. PAU has recently introduced winter maize. The crop is harvested in summers. Maize has a very active lipase enzyme. In summers, if finds optimum temperature for its active lipase enzyme. In summers, it finds optimum temperature for its activity. Hence maize atta turns bitter in summers. In Mexico, where maize is consumed the year around masa (by treating with time) is prepared and converted into chapaties in automatic lines.

MANNS (SWEET ROTI)

Consumed by people baisakhi and at special occasions. Apparel version Gordita in Mexico is prepared mechanically in automatic lines and is available in chain stores.

DALIA (PORRIDGE)

Wheat as such or after toasting is milted to grits using hands chakkis. The hard wheat or durum wheat are most suited for this product. A oarboiled or lyepeeled wheat product called Bulgar/whirled wheat is popular in the west. The product is boiled in water sugar added to taste and served in breakfast as such or with milk.

KARAH (HALWA)

The halwa prepared from either flour or semolina. form a part of parsad and ritual servings. It is prepared and served in sacred shrings gruduwaras temples and during several religious ceremonies. The consumption of halwa is thus enormous. It is prepared by toasting semolina/flour in ghee to a peculiar browning and aroma to which a thin syrup of sugar and water is added and then it is cooked to the required consistency. It may be enriched and garnished with dry fruits. A quick cooking mixture for this can be prepared after dry toasting of semolina to which fat and water may be added at the time of consumption.

INSTANT MIX FOR HALWA

It is prepared by roasting/cooking and drying of individual ingredients and blending in suitable proportions. The mixes are generally packed in pollyethylene. pollyethylene of metallised polyester packs. Because all the ingredients under go heat treatment during cooking drying operation infestation during storage is not a serious problem but case should be taken to avoid chances of contamination during packaging. Uniform distribution of ingredients in the manufacture of instant imxes is a major technological constraint. Loss of volatile during storage and resulting charger in flavour vis off flavours resulting from oxidation of lipids is one of the limiting factor in shelf life determination. Use of oleoresin and microencapsulatee flours is likely to prove useful in proper blending of flavour and in minimizing losses of volatile during storage. Recently some of microencapsulated cardamom oil has tried in halwa mix by DFRL. About 8 0% of the added flavour was retained in microencapsulated flavour incorporated halwa mix as compared to 50% retention in powdered cardamom added product.

Degree of saturation and fatty acid composition of oil used during roasting or seasoning mainly determines the stability of the mix. Generally, vanaspati has been found most suitable in imparting longest shelf life to Halwa is compared to refined ground nut oil, palmolein and cottonseed oil. Despite very good quality of instant mixes, their market share among Indian dietary and their demand is expected to increase in the coming years.

SHELF STABLE HALWA

Besides instant halwa mixes processes have also been developed for preservation of Halwa in ready to eat state by using either Hurdle Technology or thermal processing in retort pouches by DFRL. Thermally processed halwa is regularly supplied to *Department of Ocean Development* for members of America Expeditions. Except slight fading of colour and brown discolouration no spoilage has been observed in retort pouched processed Halwa. The know how for retort pouch processing of Halwa is available from DFRL Mysore through NDRC. However due to high cost of cans and retort pouches thermally processed Halwa is relatively costly in comparison to instant mixes. Ready to eat Halwa has also been preserved by Hurdle Technology using antimycotic agents and original taste. Because of lower cost on packaging and machineries. cost of finished products processed by Hurdle Technology is much less as compared to retort pouched processed Halwa.

CHOORMA/PANJIRI

These are prepared and consumed in winters. Panjiri is consumed by women in abundance after child birth.

PINNIS

These are prepared by roasting wheat flour/powdered dals (moong sabut and mashdhuli) in lots of pure ghee. The taste of pinnies prepared by grand mother still lingers in tounges. These are invariably prepared in winters with lots of desi ghee and dry fruits. Grand mother notion says that these sharpen brain and provides takat (mental strength) to school/collage going generation. product is very popular in north.

JOLES (SEVIAN)

These were prepared in homes by housewives or by skill artisans. During the last two decades their regular mechanised production has been established along with small and cottage scale sector. Vermicelli are relatively lower priced than instant noodles and and other extrude products. One of the reason for their popularity is their long usage in various forms. Process of manufacture of vermicelli is relatively simple and involves preparation of stiff dough from wheat flour or semolina and extruding the dough through fine orifices followed by drying under controlled humidity and temperature. In small scale sector vermicelli are dried in sun which preferred for vermicalli production in our country provided smaller machines are designed for cottage and small scale sector.

ROASTED WHEAT/MAIZE

In winter consumption of toasted wheat/ maize with Jaggery in villages and hostels by students is a common practice.

FRIED PRODUCTS

Fried products form the largest group of snack products in our country prepared either in homes or by small scale confections. Frying not only aids in cooking it helps in destruction of antinutitive factors aids in moisture evaporation and thereby imparts shelf stability and above all it imparts most acceptable flavour. Both sweet and salty fried wheat snacks are prepared by frying wheat flour dough after sheeting and cutting into different shapes at oil temperature ranging from 140-1600°C. Inclusion of oil in dough impart crispness and using frying temperature above 1700°C invariably darkens the product causes decisive fragility. The moisture content in fried wheat products ranges from 2-6% equilibrate to 0.20-0.35 water activity. As a result of low was the product does not support microbial activity and have long life if packed in moisture proof packaging. The shelf life of the products governed by the rate of antioxidation of fat which in turn is determined by the type of oil used during frying. Products fried in unsaturated oils develop rancidify faster than those fried in vanaspati or palm oil.

Despite high popularity of sweet and salty fried wheat snacks these are mostly marketed by small scale confectioner their large scale production and marketing has not taken place appreciably shelf life nad packaging. Viewed from different angles it may also be argued tha since their preparation is quite simple not requiring any sophisticated processing equipments consumers fined it easier to prepare in their home rather than purchasing from market at a higher price. Whatever may be the reason these products are widely consumed and have considerable market potential. Some of these are as follows.

GOLGAPPAS (PANI PURI)

These are a delicacy and are preferred by ladies and children. Golgappas prepared from atta are large or more crisp contain less fat and are preferred more. The small golgappas prepared from maida/semolina are less crisp and contain more fat. These are prepared by deep frying. During serving a hole is punched at the top by thumb and the hollow is filled with potato mesal and chilled sweet or salty water. During outings in the evening families guzzle the golgappas with a relish.

MATHIS

Mathis are prepared from stiff dough on mathi aag (slow fire). These are salty snack which are deep fat fried. Khasta mathis are generally more preferred. Sometimes fenugreek leaves (dry) are also added to the dough. To make them more nutritious soybean flour can also be added.

MATTAR

Mattar are salty snack which are cut like pea pods from stiff salty dough and are keep fat fried to a golden colour and pleasant aroma.

GULABJAMUN/RASGULLAS

Are common sweets that contain what flour and are consumed enormously in the north. Instant Gulab jamun mix, jalebi mix and rasgulla mix. Such mixes based on chemical leavening are prepared by blending wheat flour milk flour milk powder vegetable oil and leavening agents in suitable proportions and are marketed mostly by packing them in plastic film pouches followed by duplex board cartons. Among these, Instant Gulab Jamun mix is most popular and has highest sales. Since only one unit operation of dry blending of ingredients is involved these are no major constraints faced during the manufacture of instant mixes except occasional problem of uneven mixing of chemical leavening. During storage however all the mixed lend to develop infestation. Heating of wheat flour and/ or low dose (50-100 krads) irrdation of packaged mixes have been found to be effective. Control granularity moisture land adequate missing are other essential requirements for adequate product acceptability.

CHAAMP, KALEJI, KEEMA

Prepared from wheat gluten are being sold in Paharganj since decades. Sales are enormous.

RICE PRODUCTS

The predominant varieties of rice recommended for cultivation in Punjab are PR 106 PR 111 (superfine) IR 8 and Jaya (coarse) and Basmati 370 386 and Pusa Basmati 1 (Basmati). Rice is being consumed in the form of traditional products which are listed as follows.

MARUNDA

Is prepared from rice and sugar. A product resermbling marunda in mechanised units (Grain slices) prepared a from broken or whole rice is becoming popular in Europe.

PHIRNI

Rice paste is cooked with milk. Chilled and served as sweet dish.

KHEER

Is a variation sweet dish. The rice is cooked in milk and served hor or cold after addition of wager (dry fruit).

GUR WAALE CHAWAL

Are prepared by mixing cooked rice jaggery and ghee and are served steaming hot as a sweet dish.

BHELPURI

Contains expanded rice mixed with spices. It is a variation snack in homes or off day outing treat.

CHIRVA

Chirva with makhane form part of prasad in many shrines. It is also used to prepare sweet salty salty and sour evening snacks.

MURMURA/KHEEL

Puffed and expanded products. Forms part of rajasthani bhujia or fried salty snacks.

PULAV

Rice pulav with precooked vegetables or meat is called biryani. It is consumed to quite an extent in the north.

KHICHRI

Rice and split channe ki daal is a common easily digestible meal for people with weak stomach. It is also used with curd forms as a part of ritual for people going to attend important job.

PHULWARIAN

Are like extruded rice pallets which expand on frying and are consumed as snacks. In India many extruded products are prepared by housewives themselves or by skilled artisans from rice and legumes and served after frying as snacks. With the advent of cooker extruders a few companies have started marketing extruded pellets (fryums) which need frying before use and ready to eat expanded and spiced snacks in attractive packs. Both these type products are prepared from wheat flour with or without potato or corn flour.

Extruded pellets are prepared from wheat rice or maize flours or from their blends. After proper conditioning and equilibration the ingredients are cooked in a primary extruder. The cooked material is then cooled and densified in a secondary extruder. In the secondary stage the temperature of the extrudate is kept below 100°C to eliminate product expansion. Immediately after expansion the moisture content is around 20-25 5 which is brought down to 7-8% by hot air drying in tunnel dryer. The dried pellets are packed in attractive plastic film packs. These pellets equilibrate to 0.45-0.60 a and remain stable for more than six months at room temperature. Before consumption, these have to be fried in oil which imparts crispness softness and about 4-6 times volume expansion,. The products have excellent storage stability and impart resistance and can be transported easily. These are also relatively less costly to expanded ready to eat snacks.

EXPANDED EXTRUDED SNACKS

Ready to eat expanded products are prepared by using high pressure cooking and mixing equipments where enough work and heat are applied to the cereal base having appropriate moisture to thoroughly gelatinise or cook all the ingredients. The temperature during extrusion is about 1000 C and as materials are continuously compressed during working extrudate expands when allowed to pass through die due to sudden fall of pressure and release of steam. The shape and size of the product are dependent on the die design and the cutter speed. The products processed by this method are rarely toasted or dried and coated with flavours either by dusting or by spraying with spice oil mixtures. Advantages of this method are the products are ready to eat requiring no processing and can be produced from a combination of cereals pulses and starches. The products are produced and marketed in different shape and sizes and level of fat roasted and fried products. On the other hand since the material is expanded and fragile and flavours are applied at the surface the packing requirements are stringent and shelf life is relatively shorter than pellets.

Both pellet and expanded extruded products are commercially marketed and are quite popular among children. Mostly these are produced from cereals like wheat rice and corn and invariably contain low protein. In order to make them nutritionally balanced processing conditions for manufacturing expanded ready to eat snacks from sorghum plus defatted soy flour and rice plus defatted soy flour have been optimised at DFRL Mysore. The products are highly crisp and tasty and protein content range from 15-20% thus making then highly useful for school going children.

POPCORNS

Plain salty popcorn are popular among children. No variations of popcorn are available in India whereas in eastern countries popcorn in chocolate orange lemon flavours are available. Cheese coated salty products in the country.

WINTER PRODUCTS

1. MARUNDA : Is a sweet product prepared from puffed rice. Sugar with water is heated to desire consistency and puffed rice rolled into it to a sheet of uniform thickness and cut to pieces of desired sizes and shapes.

2. GACCHAK: Is a product prepared from jaggery and groundnut. Peanuts are dry roasted and jaggery heated and modified to desired consistency. Both are mixed and moulded into desired sizes and shapes.

3. REORIAN: Is a product prepared by heating sugar till they could be drawn into single thread. Now on they are pulled on or off a wooden speck for quite some time (Process is quite labour intensive). Now, it is cut into pieces and at higher temperatures coated with sesame seeds (oilseeds) which get fixed on sugar balls resulting into an attractive candy.

All the above products are consumed to a considerable extent during winters in India. These products have markets worth millions of rupees. Unfortunately there exists no quality control & no standards have been laid down for such products. These products are prepared and sold very unhygenically. They have a number of problems of getting soggy sugar sticking to hand when they absorb moisture. With variation in market batches of rice sesame and peanuts quality of these products vary considerably. There are also wide batch to batch variations due to uncontrolled conditions.

Hence work on such products standardization of recipes development of machinery and technology would go a long way in encouraging trade between countries. Food processing industry though in infancy in India is expanding at a rapid pace and would welcome international collaboration with foreign companies in production and export of such traditional products.

SUMMER DRINKS

1. SATTU (BARLEY WATER): Is a very popular summer drink and is supposed to have a medicinal value and safeguards against sunstroke as per popular belief amongst people. It is prepared by soaking toasting grinding barley and preparing drink with sugar or jaggery With increase in working couples in India and families going nuclear such products are waning off and are difficult to prepare at home. A ready beverage thus will have a great scope. It would help integrated use of rice milling machinery that operates seasonally.

2. GANNE KA RAS (CANE JUICE): People prefer to consume it fresh. On heat sterilization sugars and flavours change character. A cheap product in pouches of 200 ml with freshness and reasonable pricing would capture mass markets and would compete with carbonated beverages.

3. KANKI: Is a saltish fermented drink prepared from black carrots and a mix of condiments. It is tasty and highly preferred traditional drink in summers.

Unfortunately no work by any institution in India on the standardization of these products have been done despite the fact that they are the major consumables of the masses in different weather. It is also evident that there are a large number of grain based convenience foods which are traditionally prepared and marketed either by small scale artisans or by cottage and small scale industry. Many of the products are also prepared in homes or served in food service establishment. The technology of their production has remained more of an art and little emphasis has been laid in infusing in new technological developments in their production and marketing. Though some information has been generated in laboratories and research institutions in scientific evaluation of processing parameters and physicochemical aspects of products R & D efforts in design of equipments and machineries for up scaling of technologies of their production has not made much headway. Also, whatever information has been generated in research institution has not percolated to industries mainly because of poor technological absorption capacity of industries and lack of adequate interaction between research institutes. It is, therefore, suggested be laid on design/fabrication of indigenous machineries to upgrade the technological base of convenience food industry.

SOME SELECTED RECIPES OF TRADITIONAL FOODS

MATHI

Ingredients.

Maida	:	100 gm
Salt	:	pinch
Ghee (melted)	:	20 gm
Ajwain	:	2-3 gm (1/2 tsp)
Oil	:	for frying

Method

Mix maida salt and ajwain thoroughly. Rub in ghee till grainy even texture is obtained. Use water to make a very stiff dough. Keep covered with wet cloth and leave for 15-20 minutes. Divide into 10 portions. Heat oil in a frying pan and when hot lower the time. Roll each ball thin prick with a fork and fry till golden brown.

MATRI

Ingredients.

Flour	:	100 gms
Chillies	:	1/2 tip
Salt	:	to taste
Oil	:	for frying

Method

1. Knead flour with salt and chilies to make the dough.
2. Make small balls and rolls them into 2 long strips.
3. Deep fry on slow fire till golden brown.

SEVIAN

Ingredients

Vermicelli	:	1 cup
Sugar	:	1½ cup
Ghee	:	1 cup
Cashewnut broken	:	25 mg
Milk	:	3 cups

Method.

Heat ghee in a pan and fry vermicelli in ghee till golden brown. Then, add boiled milk in and cook it for 15-10 minutes till the vermicelli are done.

SUJI HALWA

Ingredients

Suji semolina (suji)	:	100 gm
Sugar	:	100 gm
Ghee	:	100 gm
Water	:	300 gm
Almonds	:	optional
Raisins	:	optional
Cardamum (green elaichi)	:	optional

Method.

Heat the ghee add semolina and stir on a slow fire till the mixture becomes light creamy in colour and the ghee leaves the sides of the pan. Mix sugar in water and make a sugar syrup. And add to the syrup and stir briskly till it is absorbed in the semolina. Mix the crushed cardamon almonds. Serve hot.

PINNIS

Ingredients

Wheat flour/urad flour	:	1 kg
Ghee	:	750 gms
Powdered sugar	:	850 gms
Dry fruits		

Method.

1. Heat ghee in a large pan
2. Add flour and roast it till golden brown
3. Add dry fruits and roast for 2-3 minutes
4. Add sugar remove from five and mix well

MALL PURA

Ingredients

Wheat flour	:	50 gm
Maida	:	50 gm
Suji	:	50 gm
Powdered Milk	:	25 gm
Powdered sugar	:	10 gm
Sugar	:	100 gm
Baking Powder	:	9 Pinch
Ghee	:	for frying
Water	:	for making syrup

Method

1. Mix wheat flour suji maida together and add powdered milk powdered sugar and pinch of baking powder in it and make into a thick paste with water.

2. Heat ghee in a deep vessel and add spoon full to mixture and fry till golden brown.

3. Then make a syrup of 2 thread consistency with sugar and water and put the fried malpoora in the syrup for 5-10 minutes and then serve hot.

GULAB JAMUN

Ingredients

Khoya	:	200 gm
Paneer	:	50 gm
Maida	:	60 gm
Soda bicarbonate	:	1/4 tsp
Sugar	:	750 gm
Ghee	:	for frying

Method

Mix khoya chenna maida soda bicarbonate and knead to a very smooth dough. Make small balls and fry them till golden brown. Ad water to the sugar and make sugar syrup. Add the fried balls to the sugar and keep them for sometimes so that sugar syrup penetrates in the balls. Serve hot or cold. It can be garnished with coconut powder.

POORIES

Ingredients

Wheat flour	:	375 gm
Ghee or oil	:	20 gm
Salt	:	to taste

Method

1. Prepare a stiff dough with above mentioned ingredients using water and keep it for some time.

2. Divide into small balls and roll out to 3-4 inch diameter puris.

3. Deep fry on both sided in oil or ghee till puffed and brownish in colour.

4. Serve hot.

JALEBI

Ingredients

Wheat flour	:	1/2 kg
Gram dal flour	:	124 gm
Ghee	:	1¼ kg
Sugar	:	2 kg
Water	:	10 cups

Method

1. Prepare a batter by mixing and nicely beating wheat flour and gram dal flour.

2. Make a thick syrup by boiling sugar in about 7-8 cups of water.

3. Remove the pan from fire and keep it on boiling water so that it may not get cooled.

4. Boil ghee in deep karahi.

5. Fill in jalebi mould batter and let down the better through the hole of the mould into the ghee so as the form circular jalebi 3 or 5 continuous inner circles.

6. Fry till done on both sides.

7. Remove each jalebi dip it in the hot syrup for about a minute and drain.

8. Serve hot.

Note : Jalebi mould can be made out of any vessel with a hole in the centre.

SAMOSA

Ingredients

For covering.

Flour	:	2 cups
Oil or fat	:	3 tsp

For jelling.

Boiled and cooked potatoes along with onions and peas.

Method

1. Prepare a hard dough with water. Knead well till soft.
2. Divide it into eight portions.
3. Roll each one into a round roti 15 cmin diameter.
4. Cut each into half.
5. Stiff each roti with prepared strffing and shape into samosa.
6. Deep fry in hot oil or medium heat till golden brown.
7. Serve hot.

DALIA (BROKEN WHEAT PORRIDGE)

Ingredients

Broken wheat	:	50 gm
Sugar	:	50 gm
Milk	:	500 ml

Method

Boil the milk and add broken wheat into it and pressure cook it on a slow fire for 5-10 minutes and then remove from the fire and add sugar in and cook for 2 minutes and serve hot.

PHULAVARIAN

Ingredients

Rice	:	100 gm
Water	:	for boiling rice
Salt	:	to taste
Chillies	:	to taste
Cumin powder	:	to taste

Method

1. Boil the rice
2. Mash the boiled rice and add the spices
3. Make a cone with hole and pur the mixture to it.
4. Pipe the phylvarian and dry then in sun.
5. Deep fry in oil serve hot.

RICE KHICHRI

Ingredients

Rice	:	150 gm
Moong Dal (Washed)	:	30 gm
Vegetable oil	:	1½ tsp
Salt	:	1 tsp.
Cumin	:	2 gm

Method

1. Clean and wash the rice and washed moong dal.
2. Add about 3 cups of water and salt.
3. Pressure cook it for 5 minutes.
4. Fry cumin seeds in ghee add to the khicnri.

SWEET RICE

Ingredients

Rice	:	240 gm
Jaggery	:	150 gm
Water	:	450 ml
Saunf	:	15 gm
Ghee	:	30 gm

Method

Wash the rice and soak in water for 1-2 hrs. Make syrup of water and jaggery and strain. Put rice ghee Saunf in syrup and cook on fire till rice is ready.

SUGARCANE JUICE KHEER

Ingredients

Juice	:	200 ml
Rice	:	25 gm
Water	:	60 ml

Method

1. Clean and wash the rice.
2. Cook in water until half done.
3. Add sugarcane juice and keep on stirring. When the consistency becomes thick remove it form fire.
4. Serve hot garnished with coconut and dry fruits.

PHIRNI

Ingredients

Milk	:	1 lt.
Sugar	:	150 gm
Almonds	:	30 gm
Rice	:	40 gm

Method

Soak rice of good quality for about an hour and then grind very fine with 4 to 5 tsp. Full of cold water. Mix the rice paste with the milk cook on a medium heat and stir till the mixture is of creamy consistency. Remove from fire add sugar and stir. Simmer till it fully dissolved and then boil for 1 minutes. Add the shredded branched almond and serve.

PUFFED RICE LADDOO

Ingredients

Puffed rice	:	100 gm
Jaggery	:	200 gm
Ghee or Oil	:	30 gm

Method

1. Make syrup of one string consistency with jaggery and one cup of water.
2. Remove from fire.
3. Mix in puffed rice and fat.
4. Form into small balls.
5. For making marunda spread the mixture on a flat greased tray.

MARUNDA

Ingredients

Puffed rice	:	50 gm
Roasted Bengal Gram	:	25 gm
Roasted Peanut Kernels	:	25 gm
Jaggery	:	25 gm

Method

1. Make the thread syrup of jaggery

2. Add rice grams and peanuts
3. Prepare balls of mixture.

BLACK GRAM : (URAD) PAPPADS

Ingredients

Powdered dal	:	1 kg
Chillies	:	100 gm
Salt	:	to taste

asafoetida dissolved in water

Method

1. Knead the flour with water.
2. Take a little and roll it in dry flour to form thin pappads.
3. Dry them in sun for 1 or 2 days.
4. Deep fry or roast them before serving.

VADIAN

Ingredients

Green gram dal (split)	:	1 kg
Salt	:	to taste

Black Pepper & cumin coarsely ground asafoetida dissolved in water.

Method

1. Soak dal for 4-5 hours.
2. Remove the husk and grind the dal.
3. Add salt asafoetida pepper and cumin and mix well.
4. Keep it over nigh for fermentation.
5. In the morning make small portions from the mixture and dry them in sun for 3-4 days.

BESAN POORA

Ingredients

Besan	:	50 gm
Onion	:	10 gm
Green	:	5 gm
Salt	:	1/2 tsp
Coriander leaves	:	5 gm
Water	:	for making batter

Method

1. Sift the besan and salt.
2. Chop the onion green chillies and coriander finely. Add the sieved ingredients.
3. Make a batter with water.
4. Spread the batter on a greased tavato form a round of about 12 cm diameter cook for 3 minutes turn over.
5. Add the melted fat around the edges and little on top. Fry till crisp.

BESAN LADDOOS

Ingredients

Besan	:	100 gm
Fat	:	100 gm
Sugar powder	:	100 gm
Cardamum	:	3.5 gm

Method

1. Roast besan in fat cream colour.
2. Remove pan from fire. Add powdered sugar and well.
3. Add crushed cardamum. Form into even shaped balls with wet hands.

PAKORAS

Ingredients

Besan	:	
Salt	:	Finely chopped on
Green Chillies	:	granted
Spinach	:	
Carrote	:	
Potatoes	:	
Onion	:	
Oil for frying	:	

Method

1. Take besan in a bowl and add all spices.
2. Add vegetables.
3. Add water to make thick batter.
4. Heat oil in a deep pan.
5. Fry pakoras.

BHUGA

Ingredients

Khoa	:	200 gm
Sesame	:	200 gm
Sugar	:	200 gm

Method

1. Grind sesame and sugar together.
2. Add khoa to it and mix well.
3. Make small balls and serve.

SESAME GACHAK

Ingredients

Sesame	:	125 gm
Roasted peanuts	:	50 gm
Cardamon kernels	:	10 gm
Dry coconut powder	:	1/4 cups
Sugar/jaggery	:	250 gm

Method

1. Roast sesame to light brown colour.
2. Cool and powder together with peanuts.
3. Prepare syrup of 1 strand consistency with one cup of water.
4. Mix all ingredients except coconut and keep stirring till the mixture.
5. Grease a plate of spread mixture on it.

CHIKKI

Ingredients

Jaggery	:	100 gm
Peanut kernels	:	30 gm
Water	:	1-2 tsp.

Method

1. Prepare two strand syrupof jaggery and water.
2. Add peanut kernels.
3. Grease a plate and pour syrup in it.
4. Keep it to eat. Cut into pieces.

GULGULAS

Ingredients

Wheat flour	:	100 gm
Jaggery	:	100 gm
Water	:	Pinch
Oil for frying	:	Pinch
Metha Soda	:	Pinch

Method

1. Make thin syrup of jaggery with water.
2. Add soda to flour and make dough with syrup.
3. Serve it for some time.
4. Make small balls of the dough and deep fry then.

20

PRESENT MANUFACTURERS OF SNACK FOOD

Chheda Specialities Foods Pvt. Ltd.
Mr. Ashok Chedda
Chheda House, Plot No. 7,
B.M.C Industrial Estate,
Sai Nagar,
Near Tata Wasan Service Centre,
Kandivali (W), Mumbai-400067
Phone: +(91)-8447562124
+(91)-(22)-28632323
61330800/64574243
Fax: +(91)-(22)-28634141

Ginger Food Products Pvt. Ltd.
A-104, GLG Complex,
Dr. Shurveer Singh Marg,
Fatehpura, Udaipur-313001,
Rajasthan, India
Mobile: +91 9929559666

Savour India Private Limited
Contact Person: Mr. Jatin Girdhar
23-24 DDA Market, Jail Road,
Shiv NagarNew Delhi-110 058,
India
Phone: +(91)-(11)-65499544
Mobile: +(91)-9810585553
Fax: +(91)-(11)-25571894
E-mail: info@savourindia.com

Bhikharams Food Products Pvt. Ltd
Mr. Om Prakash Agarwal
Mr. Shiv Agarwal
251, Chandani Chowk,
Near Fateh Puri,
Delhi, India - 110006
Phone: +91-11-28833158
9899216037
Web: www.bhikharamsfood.com

CavinKare Pvt. Ltd.,
Cavinville, No. 12,
Cenotaph Road,
Chennai - 600 018.
Phone: 044-66317560
Fax: 044-24362879
Email: corpcomm@cavinkare.com
exports@cavinkare.com
sales@cavinkare.com

Laxmi Snacks Pvt. Ltd.
11, 12, Anand Industrial Estate,
Borsad Chokdi, Anand-388 001
Ta. & Dist: Anand Gujarat.
INDIA
Phone: +91-2692-262814
+91-2692-262849
Fax: + 91-2692-262039
Email: info@realnamkeen.com
sampark@realnamkeen.com

MTR Foods Pvt. Ltd.
No.1, 2nd & 3rd floor
100 feet inner Ring Road,
Ejipura, Bangalore-560047
Ph: +9180-40812100

DFM Foods Ltd.
Regd. and Corporate Office
8377, Roshanara Road,
Delhi-110007
Tel: +91-11-23826445
Fax: +91-11-23822409
E-mail: info@dfmfoods.com

Jabsons Foods
(A Division of Jabsons
Cottonseed Ind. Pvt. Ltd.)
A-2, Bholav Udyog Nagar,
Bharuch (Gujarat) 392 002.
INDIA
Tel.: +91-2642-246727
247721, 228255
Fax: +91-2642-246826
E-mail: sales@jabsons.com
Website: www.jabsons.com

AFP Manufacturing Co. Private Limited
Shikha Soni
Mobile: +91-9650597309
+91-11-45626356
+91-11-45626357
A-1/22, Janak Puri,
New Delhi -110058 Delhi, India

Deepak Foods
Sachin Sharma
1885/3, Near Asthal Mandir,
Sangam Vihar,
New Delhi-110062 Delhi, India
Phone: 08042903780

Bellanzo
Vansh & Reyansh Foods 108,
Clusture-d, Sector-3, Bawana
Delhi-110039 Delhi, India
Mobile: +91-9953144180

Ashokasha Exim Pvt Limited
Avinash Agarwal
Phone: +91-9871271186
+91-11-47080771
+91-11-47080772
Office No. 604, 6th Floor,
Ring Road Mall,
Mangalam Place,
Rohini, Sector No. 3
New Delhi-110 085 Delhi, India

Ashoka Namkeen Pvt Limited
Phone: +91-9313131000
+91-11-47123333
A-281, Okhla Ph-I
New Delhi-110020 Delhi, India

SKB Food Products Pvt Ltd.
Sudhir Gupta
Phone: 08043256598
D-4, SMA Industrial Estate,
G.T. Karnal Road
New Delhi-110033 Delhi, India

21

MANUFACTURERS OF POTATO CHIPS/WAFERS AND NAMKEENS

Patco Foods Private Limited
N. H. 8, Near Kosamba,
At & Post Dhamdod,
TA. Mangrol
Surat-394125, Gujarat, India
Mobile: +(91)-9904809663
+(91)-9737060666
Fax: +(91)-(261)-2407610

Jay Laxmi Food Processing Pvt. Ltd.
SR No. 135/1, Dhayari,
Nanded Phata, Sinhgad Road
Pune-411041, Maharashtra, India
Mobile: +(91)-9850161033
+(91)-9860057094
Phone: +(91)-(20)-24390939

Sonal Foods
Chandrakant Compound,
Singh Estate,
Opposite Thakur College,
Gate No. 6,
Kandivali East,
Mumbai-400101,
Maharashtra, India
Mobile: +(91)-9323553617
+(91)-9819897317
+(91)-8652748724
+(91)-9768437911
Phone: +(91)-(22)-28461581
+(91)-(22)-28853591

Delight Products
Office No. 7, 2nd Floor,
Near RDC Bank,
Mavdi Main Road
Rajkot-360004,
Gujarat, India
Mobile: +(91)-9979098112
+(91)-9712999916
Phone: +(91)-(281)-2366966
Fax: +(91)-(281)-2366966

Guddy Wafers
Ramdev Nagar,
Opp. Water Tank,
Navsari Nagar Palika,
Ghelakhadi
Navsari-396445, Gujarat, India
Mobile: +(91)-9825083993
+(91)-9137304303
Phone: +(91)-(2637)-292250
+(91)-(2637)-323931

Narayanji Gajakwale Pvt Ltd
344, Johari Bazar
Jaipur-302001, Rajasthan, India
Mobile: +(91)-9414052088
+(91)-9950248998
Phone: +(91)-(141)-2574390

Maa Laxmi Namkeen
A-183, Sector A- 4, UPSIDC,
Tronica City,
Loni, Ghaziabad-201301,
Uttar Pradesh, India
Mobile: +(91)-9250903779
+(91)-9999792449

Durva Exports
Rohit Rabadiya
Phone: 08046072085
Rohit Plot No. 20,
Silver Sand-1,
Opposite Big Bazaar,
Rajkot-360005 Gujarat, India

Mali Agro Traders
NB Mali
No. 265, Rameshwar,
Sola Road Ahmedabad-380063,
Gujarat, India
Mobile: +91-9998490000

HK Oil Refinery
Junaid Khan
Mobile: +91-9372065727
+91-240-2370069
Gut No. 2/2, Bhavsing Pura,
Power House Road
Aurangabad-431001,
Maharashtra, India

Dhoomley Wafers
Santosh Dhumal
Phone: 08049187050
Plot No. G-30, M.I.D.C.,
Manmad Road,
Ahmadnagar-414111
Maharashtra, India

Kas Namkeen
Akila Rathod
Phone: 08045358942
Vijayraj Nagar, Plot No. 19,
Satya-Vijay,
Near Panchratna Building
Bhavnagar-364006,
Gujarat, India

B. G. Foods
Arun B. Ghatage
Mobile: +91-9422414252
Gat No. 196/2,
Near Jirge Petrol Pump, Shirol,
Tal.-Shirol, Kolhapur-416103
Maharashtra, India

Raghuvanshi Khaman & Farsan Mart
Mahesh J Chandarana
Phone: 08045136878
Shop No. 3, Nalanda Datta
Mandir Road,
Malad East, Mumbai-400097
Maharashtra, India

Rajpurohit Food Processor
Dineshsingh Rajpurohit
Phone: 08042537112
No. 56/5, Near Bijali Mitra Mandal,
Karvenagar, Pune-411038
Maharashtra, India

Shree Ram Gruh Udyog
Kishor Patel
Phone: 09582085028
G-2151, Natoda G.I.D.C.,
Kisan Gate,
Palawar Road, Rajkot-360021
Gujarat, India

Accure8 Products
Chirag Gajjar
Phone: 08045388645
Atika industrial area,
Dheber Road South
Rajkot-360002 Gujarat, India

Jeeyo Natural Fresh
Jagmohan Vijay
Phone: 08042907813
D-84, Janpath, Shyam Nagar,
New Sanganer Road, Sodala
Jaipur-302 006 Rajasthan, India

Frontier Biscuit Factory Private Limited
Mobile: +91-9810144594
C-35/10, Lawrence, Road
Industrial Area
New Delhi-110035 Delhi, India

Pragati Snacks Pvt Limited
Netrapal Singh Rawat
Phone: 08046056685
No. 4672/21,
Ansari Road,
Darya Ganj,
New Delhi-110002
Delhi, India

Kuber Group
Ravi
Phone: 08043043572
No. 10/58,
Kirti Nagar Industrial Area
Delhi-110 015, Delhi, India

NSEC Technical Services Center
Nitika Anand
Mobile: +91-9810832329
+91-11-26921562
Okhla , Phase -2
New Delhi-110001, Delhi, India

Yadav Matthi Wale
Monu Yadav
Phone: +91-11-27347077
N. U. 24- A,
Opposite Sadashiv Mandir,
Pitam Pura,
Delhi-110088
Delhi, India

22

MANUFACTURERS OF PAPADS

Jainson Food Works
Ankit Shyamsukha
Phone: 08042972709
F-5/27-28, 1st Floor,
Krishna Nagar, Delhi-110006
Delhi, India

Sweet N Juicy
Mandeep Singh Sawhney
Mobile: +91-9899990479
E-3, Greater Kailash Part -1
New Delhi-110048
Delhi, India

Jaivik Haat
Mobile: +91-9811017311
+91-11-47597091
Shop Number 127 & 128,
First Floor,
R. G. Mall, Near Dharamkunj Apartments,
Sector- 9, Rohini,
Delhi-110085
Delhi, India

Aditya Stores
Rajesh Jha
Mobile: +91-8588864500
G-54/55, 2nd Floor,
School Road Uttam Nagar East
New Delhi-110059
Delhi, India

Karan Trading Company
Mobile: +91-9810836943
+91-11-22353050
J-406, Old Seema Puri,
Near Old Seema Puri Police Station
Delhi-110095, Delhi, India

Everybody Food Products Private Limited
Sajjad Husain
Phone: 08042952605
F-148, Shaheen Bagh,
Abulfazal Enclave, Part- II,
Okhla
New Delhi – 110025,
Delhi, India

Port Indus Trading Company Private Limited
Saurabh Jain
Phone: 08045357543
C-2-15, SDA, Aurbindo Marg
New Delhi-110016, Delhi, India

Life-Fit Health Foods
Phone: +91-11-26349525
4, Ring Road,
Opp. Maharani Bagh
New Delhi-110065, Delhi, India

Shakti Bhog Food's Limited
Kewal Krishan Kumar
Phone: +91-11-27694037
+91-11-27694060
24, SSI, Industrial Area, G.T. Karnal Road
New Delhi-110033, Delhi, India

Victoria Foods Private Limited
Udit Jain
Phone: 08043259868
No. B-32, Lawrence Road, Industrial Area
New Delhi-110035, Delhi, India

Garg Snacks
Pankaj Garg
Phone: 08046080758
592/1 Rishinagar,
Ranibagh, Manish Foods
Delhi-110034
Delhi, India

Kabir Foods Private Limited
Suneer Jain
Phone: 08049591815
No. 1109, D Mall, Netaji Subhash Place, Pitampura,
Delhi – 110034, Delhi, India

Shri Pashupati Mahila Grih Udyog
Ram Kishor Thakur
Phone: 08043258629
Xg-2, Shiva Enclave,
Paschim Vihar, Delhi-110063
Delhi, India

Dristi Organics
Sandeep Upreti
Phone: 08046075290
No. 244, Ground Flour,
DDA Flat, Bindapur, Uttam Nagar
New Delhi-110059, Delhi, India

Kaleva India
Sushil Aggarwal
Phone: 08045336113
No. 109, Gole Market
New Delhi-110001
Delhi, India

Sushma Gram Udyog, Delhi
Sushma Mittal
Naveen Mittal
Phone: 08049442936
801/C, Sukhdev Nagar,
Kotla Mubarakpur,
Opposite Defence Colony,
New Delhi – 110003, India

Saraswati Agroproducts Limited
Satyanand Giri
Phone: 09953356642
B-228, Budh Nagar,
Inderpuri
New Delhi – 110012,
Delhi, India

23

POTATO CHIPS/WAFERS MACHINERIES SUPPLIERS

Koyka Electronics Pvt. Ltd.
F 121, Tirkha Colony,
Tigaon Road,
Ballabhgarh, Faridabad-121006,
Haryana, India
Mobile: +(91)-9810501205
Phone: +(91)-(129)-2210991
Fax: +(91)-(129)-4062533
+(91)-(129)-4063206
Email: harsh@koykagroup.co.in
info@koykagroup.co.in

Jas Enterprises
No. 60, Shreenathji Estate,
Panna Estate Road,
Rakhial, Ahmedabad-380023,
Gujarat, India
Mobile: +(91)-9426180142
+(91)-9427417384
+(91)-9426088680
Phone: +(91)-(79)-22743454
+(91)-(79)-22745062
Fax: +(91)-(79)-22745062
Email: shethjas@gmail.com
info@jasenterprise.com
admin@pulveriser.co.in

Ramdev Engineers
150 Feet Ring Road,
Punit Chwkadi,
50 Feet Road,
Near Vrundavan Gau-Shala,
Ramdev Estate, Vavdi,
Survey No. 43
Rajkot-360003, Gujarat, India
Mobile: +(91)-9825299685
+(91)-9825858202
Email: ramdevengineers@gmail.com

Honey Combb Products
A-14, Mahalaxmi Industrial
Estate, B/h.
Maruti & Shiv shakti Estate,
Opposite Kirti Tools, Phase-1,
G I D C, Vatva
Ahmedabad-382445,
Gujarat, India
Mobile: +(91)-9426496342
+(91)-9825096342
Phone: +(91)-(79)-25830342
Email: info@honeycombb.com
sales@honeycombb.com

Tinytech Plants
Tagore Road
Rajkot-360002, Gujarat, India
Mobile: +(91)-9227606264
+(91)-9227606570
+(91)-9227909294
+(91)-9227505254
Phone: +(91)-(281)-2480166
Fax: +(91)-(281)-2467552
Email: tinytech@tinytechindia.com

Paras Engineers
Jivraj Park Industrial Area,
Street No. 2,
Plot No.17, Near Falcon
Submersible Pump,
Behind Hotel Krishna Park,
Survey No. 47,
Gondal Road, Vavdi,
Rajkot-360004, Gujarat, India
Mobile: +(91)-9377684888
+(91)-9825210019

J. K. Machine Tools
ShreeJi Industrial Estate, Morvi
Rajkot Highway,
Near Ajanta Clock,
Village- Sanala
Morvi-363641, Gujarat, India
Mobile: +(91)-9825419919
+(91)-9825258177
+(91)-9879492345
Phone: +(91)-(2822)-226933

Yash Food Equipment
B-207, Riddhi Siddhi,
Sector-20, Nerul
Mumbai-400706,
Maharashtra, India
Mobile: +(91)-8097256346
Phone: +(91)-(22)-65690020

Galaxy Enterprise
Shed No. 2, Plot No. 1,
Sahajanand Industrial Area,
B/h. Murlidhar Weigh Bridge,
Street No. 1, Aji Ring Road
Rajkot-360003, Gujarat, India
Mobile: +(91)-9723130630
+(91)-9909961149
+(91)-9925618976

Mod Tech Machinery
No. 234, Banwari Lal Compound,
Opp. Accurate Transformer Co.,
Sihani Chungi, Meerut Road
Ghaziabad-201001, Uttar
Pradesh, India
Mobile: +(91)-9971565666

National Engg. Works
B-61, Sector 8, Noida-201301,
Uttar Pradesh, India
Mobile: +(91)-9810901495
+(91)-9212367001

Zoya Food Processing & Packaging Machine
C- 358, Sector-10,
Noida-201301,
Uttar Pradesh, India
Mobile: +(91)-9717440236
+(91)-8800960146

Khushi Engineering
C-70, Sector-8
Noida-201301,
Uttar Pradesh, India
Mobile: +(91)-9810658565
+(91)-9250404001
+(91)-9990658565
Phone: +(91)-(120)-2425086
(91)-(120)-4325086

Deokali Engineering Works WZ-15 A, G.F., Bindra Market, Sant Pura, Tilak Nagar, New Delhi-110018, Delhi, India	Mobile: +(91)-9871123748 +(91)-8826708473 +(91)-9873085843 Phone: +(91)-(11)-25144733 +(91)-(11)-64645843 +(91)-(11)-64596712

24

SNACKS FOOD MACHINERIES SUPPLIERS

Grace Food Processing & Packaging Machinery
Nambardar Estate, A-92C,
Basement,
Taimoor Nagar,
New Friends Colony
New Delhi 110065,
Delhi, India
Mobile: +(91)-9015294680
+(91)-9213489019
+(91)-9654282680
+(91)-9811073680
Phone: +(91)-(11)-26841331
+(91)-(11)-26984713
Fax: +(91)-(11)-26841331
Email: gtlpacking@gmail.com
info@gracepackagingmachine.com

Koyka Electronics Pvt. Ltd.
F 121, Tirkha Colony,
Tigaon Road,
Ballabhgarh, Faridabad 121006,
Haryana, India
Mobile: +(91)-9810501205
Phone: +(91)-(129)-2210991
Fax: +(91)-(129)-4062533
+(91)-(129)-4063206
Email: harsh@koykagroup.co.in
info@koykagroup.co.in

Mac Well Machinery
B-65, Sector-8, Noida 201301,
Uttar Pradesh, India
Mobile: +(91)-9289267176
+(91)-9810906659
+(91)-9654735459
Phone: +(91)-(120)-6500533
Email: macwellmachinery@gmail.com
hemraj@mac-wellmachinery.com
macwellmachinery.jagjit@gmail.com

Noida Fabcon Machines Pvt. Ltd.
C150, Sector 63
Noida 201307,
Uttar Pradesh, India
Mobile: +(91)-9811209769
+(91)-8510077833
+(91)-8510077834
+(91)-9910490196
Fax: +(91)-(120)-4225551

Email: sales.nfm@fabcon.co.in
sales3.nfm@fabcon.co.in
sales2.nfm@fabcon.co.in

Aarzoo Engineering Works
C-319, Sector-10,
Noida 201301,
Uttar Pradesh, India
Mobile: +(91)-9810546591
+(91)-9211977522
Email: parvezalam8852@gmail.com
aarzooenggworks@gmail.com
info@aarzooengineering.com

Super Engineering Works
B 36, Sector No. 10
Noida 201301,
Uttar Pradesh, India
Mobile: +(91)-9911000588
+(91)-9811011770
Phone: +(91)-(120)-4155481
Email: ahsanali9810@gmail.com
ahsanali991100@gmail.com

Zia Engineering & Consultancy Services
C-27, Sector-10, Noida 201301,
Uttar Pradesh, India
Mobile: +(91)-9555338515
+(91)-9212884877
+(91)-9278620374
+(91)-9868585504

National Engg. Works
B-61, Sector 8, Noida 201301,
Uttar Pradesh, India
Mobile: +(91)-9810901495
+(91)-9212367001

Zoya Food Processing & Packaging Machine
C- 358, Sector-10
Noida 201301,
Uttar Pradesh, India
Mobile: +(91)-9717440236
+(91)-8800960146

S S & Associates
B- 38, LGF, South Extension,
Part- 2, Delhi 110049, India
Mobile: +(91)-9560539977
+(91)-9278868804
Phone: +(91)-(11)-65025222
+(91)-(11)-41349761
+(91)-(11)-41321341

A. S. Engineering Works, Noida
No. B- 33, Sector- 8,
Near Power House
Noida 201301, Uttar Pradesh,
India
Mobile: +(91)-9811059544
Phone: +(91)-(120)-4356803
+(91)-(120)-2425386

S. K. Engineering Works
B-28, Sector-10
Noida 201301,
Uttar Pradesh, India
Mobile: +(91)-9311098837
+(91)-9811098837
Phone: +(91)-(120)-4354881
+(91)-(120)-3248457
+(91)-(120)-3248587
Fax: +(91)-(120)-4354881

Sara Udyog
No. C-167, Sector-10
Noida 201301,
Uttar Pradesh, India
Mobile: +(91)-9871321622
+(91)-9868385709
+(91)-9810137891
Phone: +(91)-(120)-2521878
Fax: +(91)-(129)-2537786

Innovative Packtech Machines Pvt. Ltd.
G-196, Sector-63 Noida 201307,
Uttar Pradesh, India
Mobile: +(91)-9871374601
+(91)-9540945514
Phone: +(91)-(120)-2406214

SVM Engineering Works
D-305, Sector-10
Noida 201301,
Uttar Pradesh, India
Mobile: +(91)-9810744954
+(91)-9990724928

Syam Engineers Food Process
F-376, Sector-63
Noida 201301,
Uttar Pradesh, India
Mobile: +(91)-9971321727
+(91)-8527185133
+(91)-9711487316
Phone: +(91)-(120)-4210292

Shri Balaji Engineering Works, New Delhi
Khasra No. 40/7, Street No. 1,
Industrial Area,
Samay Pur, New Delhi 110042,
Delhi, India
Mobile: +(91)-9910191816
+(91)-9999640680
Phone: +(91)-(11)-32602747
+(91)-(11)-27830695

Sunil Machine Tools
L 131, Krishan Vihar,
Nr Bharat Shakti Public School
New Delhi 110086, Delhi, India
Mobile: +(91)-9911405225
+(91)-9810405225
+(91)-9911462022

Bharti Machinery Tools, New Delhi
Plot No. 871, Firni Road,
Pooth Khurd,
Near Sector 3, Bawana
Delhi 110039, India
Mobile: +(91)-9811456608
+(91)-8010141364
+(91)-7404445203
+(91)-8750179707

Indu Engineering Works
A-48, 1st Floor,
Wazirpur Industrial Area
New Delhi 110052, Delhi, India
Mobile: +(91)-9873217164
+(91)-9350876315
+(91)-9873903686
+(91)-9213263686
Phone: +(91)-(11)-27375054

Deokali Engineering Works
WZ-15 A, G.F.,
Bindra Market, Sant Pura,
Tilak Nagar. New Delhi 110018,
Delhi, India
Mobile: +(91)-9871123748
+(91)-8826708473
+(91)-9873085843
Phone: +(91)-(11)-25144733
+(91)-(11)-64645843
+(91)-(11)-64596712

25

PAPPAD MAKING MACHINERIES SUPPLIERS

Super Metal & Company
No. 3/33, L.I.G. Colony, L.I.G. Chouraha,
Behind Maya Medical Store,
A. B. Road
Indore-452008, Madhya Pradesh, India
Mobile: +(91)-9827212950
+(91)-9406630066
Phone: +(91)-(731)-2554272
+(91)-(731)-2557517
Email: india@supermetalcompany.com
info@omshrisaiseva.org

Jas Enterprises
No. 60, Shreenathji Estate,
Panna Estate Road,
Rakhial, Ahmedabad-380023,
Gujarat, India
Mobile: +(91)-9426180142
+(91)-9427417384
+(91)-9426088680
Phone: +(91)-(79)-22743454
+(91)-(79)-22745062
Fax: +(91)-(79)-22745062
Email: shethjas@gmail.com
info@jasenterprise.com
admin@pulveriser.co.in

Honey Combb Products
A-14, Mahalaxmi Industrial Estate,
B/h, Maruti & Shiv Shakti Estate,
Opposite Kirti Tools,
Phase-1, G I D C,
Vatva, Ahmedabad-382445,
Gujarat, India
Mobile: +(91)-9426496342
+(91)-9825096342
Phone: +(91)-(79)-25830342
Email: info@honeycombb.com
sales@honeycombb.com\

Vijay Engineering
No. 207, Manish Chamber,
Above Axis Bank,
Sonawala Road, Goregaon East
Mumbai-400063,
Maharashtra, India
Mobile: +(91)-9967130022
+(91)-9320267508
Phone: +(91)-(22)-26850232

+(91)-(22)-26859220
+(91)-(22)-32960232

R. K. Enterprises
Shop No. A-11, A-12, A-16,
NIT Complex,
Ganeshpeth, Near Rahul Hotel,
Opposite S.T. Bus Stand,
Nagpur-440018,
Maharashtra, India
Mobile: +(91)-9860347910
+(91)-9765320786
Phone: +(91)-(712)-2735216

Shankar Engineering Corporation
21, Parsee Church Street,
Business Communication
Centre, 1st Floor,
Room No. 12, Near Tea-Board of India
Kolkata-700001, West Bengal, India
Mobile: +(91)-8017117627
+(91)-8001771047

Meeta Food Technology
Plot No. I/97, Phase 4, GIDC,
Vitthal Udyognagar,
Anand-388121,
Gujarat, India
Mobile: +(91)-8905222002

Kirtiraj Trading Corporation
Capital Compound, Loteshwar
Bhagol
Anand-388001, Gujarat, India
Mobile: +(91)-9427610551
+(91)-9824011873
Phone: +(91)-(2692)-249370
+(91)-(2692)-248677
Fax: +(91)-(2692)-248677

Royal Engineering Works
No. 64, Sri Ram Nagar,
Opposite Sudarshan Dal Mill,
Palda
Indore-452001,
Madhya Pradesh, India
Mobile: +(91)-9630138433
+(91)-9827225886

Integrated Engineers
Plot No. 45 & 46, Sanjay
Industrial Estate,
Co-Operative Society Limited,
Madhav Nagar,
Taluka Miraj, Sangli-416416,
Maharashtra, India
Mobile: +(91)-9860161015
+(91)-7588866745
Phone: +(91)-(233)-2310295

Gaurang Enterprise
No. 29, Gopinath Estate,
Part- 1,
Near Soni- Ni-Chawl, N. H. No.
8, Odhav Ahmedabad-382415,
Gujarat, India
Mobile: +(91)-9904375157

Saini Engg. Works
Plot No. 359, Industrial Area,
Phase-IX,
S. A. S. Nagar, Mohali-160 062,
Punjab, India
Mobile: +(91)-9316450028
+(91)-9023568366

Gurpreet Engineering Works
Guru Nanak Nagar,
Nalas Road,Near Gurudwara
Sahib & Sargam Palace,
Rajpura, Patiala-140401,
Punjab, India

Mobile: +(91)-9256291102
+(91)-9878974460
+(91)-9464952354
+(91)-8427336971

A. V. Engineering Works
No. 12-A, Near Hira Automobile
Factory Area
Patiala-147001, Punjab, India
Mobile: +(91)-9876534921
Phone: +(91)-(175)-2361178
+(91)-(175)-2360935
Fax: +(91)-(175)-2361604

Gayatri Engineering Works
Plot No. I -114, Sab Chem,
Phase 4th,
G. I. D. C., Estate, VU Nagar,
Anand-388121, Gujarat, India
Mobile: +(91)-9898036760
+(91)-9825594145
Phone: +(91)-(2692)-230727

A. P. Industries
No. 30, Abhinav Arcade,
Between Manmohan Cross Road
To S. P. 150 Ring Road, Odhav
Ahmedabad-382415,
Gujarat, India
Mobile: +(91)-9409150555
+(91)-8238550555

Sunrise Marketing Co.
A-3/1, Shop No. 1,
Mohan Garden,
Hastsal Road, Uttam Nagar
New Delhi-110059, Delhi, India
Mobile: +(91)-9990544806
+(91)-9997234045
+(91)-9454330307
+(91)-8826623408

26

NAMKEEN, SNACKS, PAPPAD PACKAGING MACHINERIES SUPPLIERS

Bhalani Industries
No. 83, Karnavati Industrial Estate,
Odhav-Vastral S. P. Ring Road, Odhav
Ahmedabad-382415,
Gujarat, India
Mobile: +(91)-9825118008
Phone: +(91)-(79)-65258008
Email: info@bhalanigroup.com
bhalani8008@gmail.com

Aarzoo Engineering Works
C-319, Sector-10,
Noida-201301,
Uttar Pradesh, India
Mobile: +(91)-9810546591
+(91)-9211977522
Email: parvezalam8852@gmail.com
aarzooenggworks@gmail.com
info@aarzooengineering.com

Chamunda Engineering Works
No. 21, Parshva Corporation,
Behind Canara Bank, F-Road,
Phase-1, G. I. D. C., Vatva
Ahmedabad-382415,
Gujarat, India
Mobile: +(91)-9825111508
+(91)-7698508908
+(91)-9898874931
Email: cewmachinery@yahoo.com

Grace Food Processing & Packaging Machinery
Nambardar Estate, A-92C,
Basement,
Taimoor Nagar,
New Friends Colony
New Delhi-110065, Delhi, India
Mobile: +(91)-9015294680
+(91)-9213489019
+(91)-9654282680
+(91)-9811073680
Phone: +(91)-(11)-26841331

+(91)-(11)-26984713
Fax: +(91)-(11)-26841331
Email: gtlpacking@gmail.com
info@gracepackagingmachine.com

Kanishk Intertrade
399 A, 2nd Floor, Chirag Dilli
New Delhi-110017, Delhi, India
Mobile: +(91)-9958192946
+(91)-8860203889
+(91)-9873164064
Phone: +(91)-(11)-46134021

TRS International
Plot No. 93,
HUDDA Industrial Area,
Sector-59, Faridabad-121004,
Haryana, India
Mobile: +(91)-9312201682
+(91)-8882201682
Phone: +(91)-(129)-2245769
Email: trsmachines@gmail.com

Saurabh International
No. 6, Pritam Good Will
Apartment, Bhandara Road,
Near Haldiram Factory, East
Wardhaman Nagar
Nagpur-440008,
Maharashtra, India
Mobile: +(91)-9326755930
+(91)-9822278367
+(91)-9326793270
Phone: +(91)-(712)-2681682

Khushi Engineering
C- 70, Sector- 8
Noida-201301,
Uttar Pradesh, India
Mobile: +(91)-9810658565
+(91)-9250404001
+(91)-9990658565

Phone: +(91)-(120)-2425086
+(91)-(120)-4325086

Delight Fabricators
A-45, Bileshwar Estate,
Opposite G.V.M.M,
GIDC, Kathwada Road, Odhav
Ahmedabad-382415,
Gujarat, India
Mobile: +(91)-9824065713
+(91)-9924105713

Jawla Engineering Private Limited
Ankit Jawla
Mobile: +91-9312215225
Plot No. 51, Road No. 1,
Near Gounchi Drain,
Sarupur Industrial Area,
4 KM. Sohna Road, Ballabgarh
Faridabad-121004
Haryana, India

Balaji Plast Pack
Bharat Kadecha
Phone: 08376805366
Rajkot-Jamnagar Highway,
Behind Murlidhar Hotal, Village,
Naranka, Rajkot-360 110
Gujarat, India

Super-Tech Packing
Vishal Kumar
Mobile: +91-9873993184
+91-129-2233777
Plot No. 179, Friends Colony
Faridabad-121001
Haryana, India

World Pack Solution
Idress Khan
Mobile: +91-9711266196
+91-129-3228798

Plot No. 964,
Shiv Colony, Sector-19
Faridabad-121003
Haryana, India

Maruti Auto Mac Engineers
Haresh Patel
Phone: 08045136933
Plot No. 95, Road No. 8,
Opposite Water Tank,
G. I. D. C.,
Kathwada, Ahmedabad-382430
Gujarat, India

Shriji Traders, Rajkot
Nishant Kanabar
Call Us: 08042957013
No. 2/10, Bhakti Nagar,
Station Road,
Office No. 109 -110,
Opposite Gajanan Road,
Lines, Rajkot-360002,
Gujarat, India

Elite Industries
Sanjay Sharma
Mobile: +91-9993359359
+91-731-2720792
523/1, Sunder Nagar,
Sanwer Road, Sector 'A',
Industrial Area,
Indore-452015, Madhya
Pradesh, India

27

SUPPLIERS OF PACKAGING MATERIALS

Ayush Flexipack Pvt Limited
Mr. Aditya Kumar Ojha (Director)
J-88, Site-V, UPSIDC,
Kasna Industrial Area
Greater Noida-201306,
Uttar Pradesh, India
Mobile: +(91)-9312209417
+(91)-8744098090
+(91)-8744098094
+(91)-8744098093
Phone: +(91)-(120)-2341009

Poysha Packaging Pvt. Ltd.
N-29 & 30, National Steel Compound,
Patel Marg, Meerut Road
Ghaziabad-249403
Uttar Pradesh, India
Phone: 08045358227

Holymen Packaging Industries
Mr. Pintoo Ghosh (CEO)
No. C-56, Sector-4
Noida-201301,
Uttar Pradesh, India
Mobile: +(91)-9811311654
Phone: +(91)-(120)-3096000

Proactive Plast Pvt Limited
Senthil Kumar
Mobile: +91-9871374455
+91-120-4202819
C-261, Sector 44
Noida-201301
Uttar Pradesh, India

S. B. Packagings Ltd.
Mr. Puneet Mittal
(Manager)
3rd Floor, Vardhman Plaza Corner,
Inder Enclave, Paschim Vihar
New Delhi-110 087,
Delhi, India
Mobile: +(91)-9811772905
+(91)-9811779730
Phone: +(91)-(11)-25279191
Fax: +(91)-(11)-25272501

ISOE Printpack Industries Private Limited
Amit Sood
Phone: 08049473896
Bliss Impex Compound,
Opposite Flucksur India,
Behrampur Road, Khandsa
Gurgaon-122001 Haryana, India

S. R. G. Packaging Pvt. Ltd.
Sunil Gandhi
Phone: 08041947247
I-28, Site C, UPSIDC,
Industrial Area, Surajpur
Greater Noida-201306
Uttar Pradesh, India

Chirag Enterprises
Mr. Brij Gopal Taparia
No. 1967, Gali No. 15,
Shalimar Park,
Bhola Nath Nagar,
Near Farsh Bazar Thana,
Shahdara
Delhi-110032, India
Mobile: +(91)-9810188545
+(91)-9968895515
Phone: +(91)-(11)-22003083

Packman Industries
Mr. Ankit Khanna
(Managing Director)
No. 289, Udyog Kendra-II,
Ecotech-III
Greater Noida-201308,
Uttar Pradesh, India
Mobile: +(91)-9910110911

Jagannath Industries Pvt Ltd
Mr. Mukul Agrawal
Mr. Piyush Singhal
(Managing Director)
Plot No. 222, JDA Industrial
Area, Jaitpura
Jaipur-303704, Rajasthan, India
Mobile: +(91)-9413340012
+(91)-9413252200
+(91)-9314040012
Phone: +(91)-(1423)-224500
+(91)-(1423)-225100
Fax: +(91)-(1423)-225100

FlexiPack
Hiren Patel
Mobile: +91-9825803180
+91-2764-268273
No. 813, Kothari Estate,
Vilage Santej, Taluk Kalol
Ahmedabad-382721
Gujarat, India

Pelican Poly Film Pvt. Ltd.
Hiren Shah
Phone: 08049471370
P-212 / B, Gate No. 2,
Opposite Ravi Metal GIDC,
Metoda
Rajkot – 360021, Gujarat, India

Vishwakarma Health Care Private Limited
M. K. Sharma
Phone: 08046066243
Mangliyawas Nasirabaad Road,
Village, Bidikchiyawas
Ajmer-305001
Rajasthan, India

Purity Flexpack Limited
Mr. Kunal Patel
(Director & Head of Marketing)
Vanseti, PO-Tajpura, Near Halol,
District Panchmahal
Halol-389350, Gujarat, India

Mobile: +(91)-9979522244
+(91)-9879508744
+(91)-9904269108
Fax: +(91)-(265)-2427734
Email: seema@purityflexpack.com
kunal@purityflexpack.com
anil@purityflexpack.com
account@purityflexpack.com

R K Polybags
Mr. Prabaharan
No. 68, Indira Gandhi Street,
Ayanambakkam
Chennai-600095,
Tamil Nadu, India
Mobile: +(91)-9841999444
+(91)-9445203359
Phone: +(91)-(44)-64500653

Ocean League
Vicky Chugh
Phone: 09953364322
Shed No. 1, Building No. A/2,
Shree Ganesh Commercial & Industrial Complex,
Behind Gupta Compound,
Dapoda,
Gundavali Village, Bhiwandi
Thane-421302,
Maharashtra, India

Vee Dee Enterprises
Mr. Viral Shah (Proprietor)
No. 802, Gold Crest Business Center,
Opposite manubhai Jewellers,
L. T. Road,
Borivali West, Mumbai-400092,
Maharashtra, India
Mobile: +(91)-9820185984
+(91)-9821068531
+(91)-9324085984
Phone: +(91)-(22)-28903974
+(91)-(22)-28913984

Galaxy Industries
Vikesh K. Manchhani
Mobile: +91-9327918153
+91-79-22822530
+91-79-29093603
Plot No. 603, Phase-4,
G. I. D. C. Estate, Naroda
Ahmedabad – 382330,
Gujarat, India

28

NAMKEEN, SNACKS, PAPPAD RAW MATERIAL SUPPLIERS

Rishipal Gupta & Sons (Pawanjee Masala)
Ankur Gupta
Phone: 08045137564
!- 92, Sector-1,
Bawana Industrial Area
Delhi – 110039,
Delhi, India

Joshi Masala Company
Ramjas Joshi
Phone: 08447560702
No. 211 - B, Gali No. 4,
Padam Nagar, Kishan Ganj,
Nr Shastri Nagar,
Metro Station
Delhi – 110007, India

Shalimar Food Products
Mr. Gaurav Jagtap (Proprietor)
Off. Add. - Shalimar Complex,
Plot 13/2 W.B. Road
Deopur Dhule Dhule - 424002,
Maharashtra, India
Mobile: +(91)-9225644155
+(91)-9881171571
+(91)-9823414149
Phone: +(91)-(2562)-239799
Fax: +(91)-(2562)-239799

Janak Dehydration
Dilip N Mehta
Phone: 08042966453
Vazira Naka, Ashok Nagar,
D-5 Mumbai - 400092
Maharashtra, India

EIRI PROCESS TECHNOLOGY BOOKS

CHEMICAL/ DYES/ PETROCHEMICALS/ LUBRICANT/ ELECTROPLATING

01 Small Medium & Large Chemical Industries
02 Industrial Chemicals Technology Hand Book
03 Modern Technology of Organic & Inorganic Chemicals
04 Hand Book of Electroplating Anodizing & Surface Finishing Technology
05 Hand Book of Agro Chemical Industries (Insecticides & Pesticides)
06 Technology of Synthetic Dyes, Pigments Intermediates
07 Petrochemicals, Lubricants, Greases & Petroleum Refining
08 Hand Book of Lubricants, Greases & Petrochemicals Technology

GUMS, ADHESIVES AND SEALANTS

01 Technology Of Gums, Adhesives & Sealants With Formulations
02 Hand Book Of Adhesives With Their Formulaes
03 Adhesives Technology & Formulations Hand Book (Hand Book of Adhesives)
04 Technology of Glue and Adhesives with Adhesives Bonding and Formulations

SMALL SCALE INDUSTRIES/ STATIONERY/PAPER/ INKS/ CANDLES & EXPORT BUSINESS

01 Start Your Own Export Business (How To Export)
02 Start Your Own Small Business And Industry
03 Candle Making Processes & Formulations Hand Book
04 Stationery, Paper Converting & Packaging Industries
05 Modern Inks Formulations & Manufacturing Industries
06 Profitable Businesses To Start For Entrepreneurs
07 Modern Small & Cottage Scale Industries
08 Profitable Small Cottage Tiny & Home Industries

BIO FUEL & BIOPROCESSING

01 Technology Of Bio-Fules (Ethanol & Biodiesel)
02 Modern Technology Of Bioprocessing

PRINTING, SCREEN PRINTING & PACKAGING

01 Hand Book of Printing Processes Technologies & Industries
02 Hand Book Of Printing Technology (Offset, Screen, Flexo, Gravure, Inkjet & Digital)
03 Hand Book Of Offset Printing Technology
04 Screen Printing With Processes & Tech.
05 Hand Book Of Prepress
06 Hand Book Of Packaging Technology
07 Modern Packaging Technology for Processed Food, Bakery, Snack Foods, Spices and Allied Food Products
08 Hand Book Of Food Packaging Technology
09 Modern Technology of Printing Inks

PAINT, VARNISH, SOLVENTS, COATING & LACQUERS, POWDER COATING

01 Paint Pigment Varnish & Lacquer Manufacturing
02 Paint Varnish Solvents & Coating Technology

EIRI PROCESS TECHNOLOGY BOOKS

03 Paint, Pigment, Solvent, Coating Emulsion, Paint Additives & Formulations
04 Technology Of Coating, Resins, Pigments & Inks Industries
05 Manufacturing Technology & Formulations Hand Book On Thinners, Putty, Wall & Industrial Finishes And Synthetic Resins
06 Technology of Synthetic Resins and Emulsion Polymers
07 Technology of Paints and Coatings with Formulations
08 Powder Coating Technology Hand Book

PLASTIC/POLYMER PROCESS, COMPOUNDING, INJECTION MOULDING, ROTATIONAL MOULDING, PLASTIC FILM, FIBRE GLASS, PLASTIC WASTE RECYCLING, MOULDS, PET & RESINS INDUSTRIES

01 Moulds Design & Processing Hand Book
02 Hand Book Of Plastic Materials & Processing Technology
03 Injection Moulding Of Plastics
04 Plastic Processing and Packaging Industries
05 Plastic Waste Recycling Technology
06 Technology Of Plastic Films
07 Rotational Moulding Technology Hand Book
08 Plastic Compounding, Master Batches, Pet & Other Plastics
09 Synthetic Resins Technology With Formulations
10 Technology Of PVC Compounding And Its Applications
11 Hand Book of Polymer And Plastic Technology
12 Hand Book of Fibre Glass Moulding
13 Technology of Reinforced Plastics
14 Plastic Additives Technology Hand Book
15 Technology of Pet Bottles, Preform and Pet Recycling
16 Modern Technology of Extrusion & Extruded Products
17 Technology of Synthetic Resins & Emulsion Polymers
18 Technology of Plastic Additives with Processes and Packaging
19 Technology of Disposable Medical Products

BAKERY, CONFECTIONERY & BREAKFAST, PASTA & CEREALS

01 Hand Book Of Bakery Industries
02 Hand Book Of Confectionery With Formulations
03 Breakfast, Dietary Food, Pasta & Cereal Products Technology
04 Hand Book Of Modern Bakery Products
05 Modern Bakery Technology & Fermented Cereal Products With Formulae
06 Technology of Confectionery, Chocolates, Toffee, Candy, Chewing & Bubble Gums, Lollipop and Jelly Products with Formulations

AGRO CULTIVATION, ANIMAL FARMING, AGRO PLANTATION & AGRO CHEMICAL/ PESTICIDES/ FLORICULTURE & BEE KEEPING

01 Poultry Farming & Feed Formulations
02 Hand Book of Pig Farming
03 Agro Based Hand Book of Plantation, Cultivation & Farming
04 Agro Based Plantation Cultivation & Farming
05 Agro Chemical Industries (Insecticide & Pesticides)
06 Modern Bee Keeping & Honey Processing

EIRI PROCESS TECHNOLOGY BOOKS

07 Technology Of Modern Rice Milling And Basmati Rice
08 Hand Book Of Goat Farming
09 Floriculture Hand Book (Flowers Growing Technology)
10 Aloe Vera Cultivation, Processings, Formulations And Manufacturing Technology
11 Poultry Farming, Hatchery and Broiler Production

DAIRY FARM, MILK PROCESSING AND ICE CREAM

01 Hand Book of Dairy Formulations, Processes & Milk Processing Industries
02 Milk Processing And Dairy Products Industries
03 Hand Book Of Dairy Farming to Produce Milk with Packaging
04 Hand Book Of Ice Cream Technology And Formulae
05 Hand Book Of Milk Processing Dairy Products And Packaging Technology
06 Dairy Farming for Milk Production Technology
07 Commercial Dairy Farming with Project Profiles

HERBS & MEDICINAL CULTIVATION

01 Herbs, Medicinal & Aromatic Plants Cultivation
02 Aushidhi And Sungndhit Paudho Ka Vaysayik (Hindi)
03 Hand Book Of Aromatic & Medicinal Plants And Biodiesel (Jatropha)
04 Hand Book Of Medicinal & Aromatic Plants (Cultivation, Utilisation & Extraction Processed)

FOOD & AGRO PROCESSING, PRESERVATION, SNACK FOOD, DEHYDRATION, FRUIT BEVERAGE, POTATO, MAIZE, MEAT PROCESS

01 Fruits & Vegetables Processing Hand Book
02 Fruit Beverage & Processing With Mango
03 Food Processing & Agro Based Industries
04 Manufacturing Technology of Snacks Food, Namkeen, Pappad & Potato Products
05 Preservation & Canning Of Fruits and Vegetables
06 Hand Book of Food Dehydration & Drying
07 Meat Processing & Meat Products Hand Book
08 Technology of Food Preservation & Processing
09 Hand Book of Food Packaging Technology
10 Agro Based & Processed Food Products
11 Potato & Potato Processing Technology
12 Technology of Maize & Allied Com. Products
13 Technology of Food Processing Industries
14 Technology of Sweets (Mithai) with Formulae
15 Modern Technology of Frozen Food Products
16 Technology of Water and Packaged Drinking water
17 Complete Hand Book on Frozen Food Processing and Freeze Drying Technology
18 Technology of Sweets (Mithai), Namkeen and Snacks food with Formulae
19 Complete Book on Banana Cultivation, Dehydration, Ripening, Processing, Products and Packaging Technology

EIRI PROCESS TECHNOLOGY BOOKS

20 Technology of Chicken Meat and Poultry Products
21 Agro Food Processing and Packaging Technology
22 Modern Technology of Tomato Processing and Dehydration (Ketchup, Juice, Paste, Puree, Soup and Drying)
23 Modern Technology of Agro Processing and Food Packaging Products with Project Profiles
24 Start Your Own Coffee and Coffee Processing

SOAPS & DETERGENTS

01 Household Soap. Toilet Soap & Other Soap
02 Profitable Small Scale Manufacture Of Soaps & Detergents
03 Synthetic Detergents With Formulations
04 Modern Technology of Acid Slurry, Surfactants, Soap and Detergents with Formulae

ORGANIC FARMING AND FOOD

01 Hand Book Of Organic Farming And Organic Foods With Vermi-Composting And Neem Products

FISH FARMING & FISHERY PRODUCTS

01 Hand Book Of Fish Farming And Fishery Products

COSMETIC (SYNTHETIC & HERBAL)

01 Cosmetics Processes & Formulations
02 Herbal Cosmetics & Beauty Products With Formulations
03 Profitable Small Scale Manufacture Of Cosmetics (Synthetic & Herbal)
04 Hand Book Of Synthetic & Herbal Cosmetics (How to Make Beauty Products)
05 Technology Of Herbal Cosmetics & Toiletries Products With Formulae

OIL AND FATS

01 Hand Book of Oils, Fats And Derivatives With Refining & Packaging Technology
02 Technology of Oilseeds Processing, Oils & Fats and Refining

ESSENTIAL OILS & AROMATIC

01 Essential Oils Manufacturing & Aromatic Plants
02 Modern Technology Of Essential Oils
03 Technology Of Perfumes, Flavours & Essential Oils
04 Essential Oils Processes & Formulations

PERFUMES AND FLAVOURS

01 Hand Book Of Flavours & Food Colourants Technology
02 Hand Book Of Perfumes & Flavours
03 Hand Book of Perfumes With Formulations
04 Technology Of Perfumes, Flavours & Essential Oils
05 Hand Book Of Flavours Technology

BUILDING MATERIALS & CHEMICALS

01 Technology Of Building Materials & Chemicals With Processes

ALL FOLLOWING PROJECT REPORTS ARE READILY AVAILABLE

PAINT, ENAMEL, SOLVENTS, THINNERS, INKS & VARNISH
PAINT, ENAMEL, SOLVENTS, THINNERS, INKS & VARNISH

- Acrylic Emulsion Paints
- Acrylic Cement Paint (Dry Powder)
- Aluminium Paint
- Automobile Paints
- Ball Point Pen Refill Ink
- Bituminious Road Emulsion
- Bitumen
- Bituminious Felts For Water & Damp Proofing
- Bituminious Road Emulsion Rapid Medium & Slow Setting
- Buffing & Polishing
- Cement Paint For White & Grey Cement
- Dispersant
- Dry Distemper
- Dry Distemper & Cement Paint
- Duplicating Ink Black For Gestner Duplicator
- Emulsion Paints (Water Based)
- Hammertone Paint
- Insulating Varnish & Wire Enamel
- Iron Oxide Pigments
- Insulating Varnish (Poly Vinyl Butyral Based, Ffc Grade)
- Lime Colour (Cement Colour)
- Synthetic Red Oxide For Floorings
- Solvent & Thinners
- Marking Inks (Water Proof)
- Metal Naphthanate (As Drier For Paints)
- N.C.Putty
- Offset Printing Ink
- Oil Bound Distemper Paint
- Paint Brushes
- Paint Manufacture For Rolling Coating Of Aluminium And Steel Coil
- Paint Removers
- Paint Industry
- Paint & Varnish
- Picture Varnish
- Powder Coating Paint
- Printing Inks (Offset,Flexo & Roto Gravure)
- Primer Paint & Enamel Paint
- Putty & Water Proofing Paint
- Printing Inks (Flexo-Graphic Ink)
- Putty (Metal Casement)
- Red Oxide Primer (Anti Corrosive)
- Refrectory Paint (Graphite Based)
- Screen Printing Inks
- Silk Screen Printing Ink Formulation For Plastic, Paper, Cloth
- Stamp & Pad Ink
- Stoving Paint
- Spirit Soluble Maleic Resin
- Texture Paint
- Thinners And Its Allied Products
- Toner Ink
- Varnish Thinner (Solvent)
- Vacuum Metallizing Lacquers
- Wood Primer

PHARMACEUTICAL, DRUGS, AYURVEDIC/HERBAL COSMETICS & MEDICINES, HOMOEOPATHIC MEDICINES, HOMOEOPATHIC MEDICINES, DISPOSABLE SYRINGE, DENTAL COLLEGE & FINE CHEMICALS ETC.
MEDICINES, HOMOEOPATHIC MEDICINES, DISPOSABLE SYRINGE, DENTAL COLLEGE & FINE CHEMICALS ETC.

- Aromatic Pills
- Alumina From Bauxite
- Aspirin
- Ayurvedic Pain Balm Ointments
- Ayurvedic Churan And Tablets
- Ayurvedic Tablets (Hajmola Type)
- Ayurvedic/Herbalpharmacy
- Ayurvedic Sherbats
- Ayurvedic Products
- Bulk Drugs (E.O.U)
- Blood Bags
- Calcium Gluconate
- Capsule, Tablet & Injection With Modern Instruments
- Cashew Feni
- Chloroquinone Phosphate (Bulk Drugs)
- Clinical Thermometer
- Dental Clinic
- Dental College
- Dental Grade Eugenol
- Dextrose Monohydrate, Liquid Glucose
- Dehydrated Onion & Onion Powder
- Dextrose Powder (Anhydrous From Starch)
- Dextrose Saline Solution
- Distillery (I.M.F.L)
- Disposable Needles For Syringes
- Disprin
- Distilled Water
- Empty Hard Gelatine Capsules
- Fairness Cream
- Filling & Packing Of Capsules
- Glucose - D - Powder
- Glycerine
- Hair Colour Mate (Formulations And Process Only)
- Herbal Cosmetics
- Herbal Shampoo
- Herbal Shampoo And Cream
- Herbal Hair Oils (Ayurvedic)
- Homoe & Bio-Medicines With Mother Tincture
- Homoepathic Medicines
- Hypodermic Needles
- I.V. Fluids
- Ibuprofen
- Infusion & Transfusion Sets (I.V. Set)
- Injectable For Pharmaceuticals
- Injection Ampoules Packaging Box
- Integerated Surgical Cotton
- Ice Making Plant
- Ice & Cold Storage
- Lactose & By Products Processing From Milk
- Lichen (Jatamansi Charila)
- Liquid Glucose And Its By-Products
- L-Lysine Monohydro Chloride
- Liquid Glucose From Potatoes
- Medical College
- Methanol (Hpcl Grade)
- Nicotine From Tobacco Waste
- Ointment-Ayurvedic (Yellow & White)
- Pharmaceutical And Food Grade Gelatine
- Pharmaceutical Industry (Tablets, Capsules, Liquid, Gel, Ointment Powder Injectable)
- Pharmaceutical Unit (Eou) With Formulations, Injectables, Etc.
- Pyridine & Derivatives
- Salt (Iodized Salt)
- Saline & Injection Water
- Saline Water & Dextrose Solution (I.V.Fluid In Plastic Bottles)
- Sorbitol
- Starch (Maize)
- Surgical Adhesive Plaster
- Surgical Bandages
- Surgical Gloves
- Surgical Cotton
- Surgical Cotton And Bandage
- Synthetic Camphor Powder
- Tablets & Capsules
- Tissue Culture
- Tincture From Rectified Spirit
- Trimethopime
- Veterinary College With Hospital
- Veterenary Medicines (Only Formulations)
- Vitamin 'C', Sorbitol' Anhydrous Dextrose, Starch

Market Survey Cum Detailed Techno Economic Feasibility Report on all Projects are available Contact.
"ENGINEERS INDIA RESEARCH INSTITUTE". 4449, Nai Sarak (D), Main Road, Delhi-110006 (India)
Ph. : 09811437895, 91-11-23918117, 23916431, 45120361, 64727385 Fax : 91-11-23916431
E-mail : eiriprojects@gmail.com, eiribooks@yahoo.com • website: www.eiri.in, www.eiriindia.org

ALL FOLLOWING PROJECT REPORTS ARE READILY AVAILABLE

EIRI
We Create Industrialists

- Khandsari Sugar & Imfl
- Lactic Acid From White Sugar By Fermentation Process
- Lactose & By Products Processing From Milk
- Liquid Glucose And Its Bye Products
- Macroni And Vermicilli
- Malt Extraction From Barley
- Mango Processing (Mango Pulp, Juice & Slices)
- Mayur Brand Type Chewing Tobacco
- Mineral Water
- Milk Preservation & Marketing To Whole Sellers (Inpouch Packing By Uht Technology)
- Milk Processing And Packaging Of Milk Products
- Milk Products (Casein, Lactose, Ghee & Whey Powder)
- Milk Toffee
- Mini Flour Mill
- Mini Sugar Plant
- Misri (Pearl Sugar Candies)
- Modern Rice Mill
- Murabba
- Mustard Oil Extraction & Refining
- Mutton Tallow
- Namkeen Industry (Bhujia, Chana Chur Etc.)
- Namkeen (Kurkure Type Snack Food
- Namkeen With Kurkurre Type Snack Food
- Namkeen & Sweets
- Non-Basmati Rice From Paddy
- Oleoresin, Essential Oil, Dyes & Powder Of Spices
- Oleoresin Extraction From Diptero-Carput Turminatus And Pinus Khasyana
- Oleoresin Extraction From Chilli
- Pan Masala With Packing In Pouches And Tin Cans
- Pan Masala, Tobacco, Zarda & Kimam
- Packaged Drinking Water
- Packaged Coconut Water (Coco Jal)
- Paneer From Milk
- Pappad Plant
- Papain From Papaya (Papaya Latex)
- Pectin From Mango Peel Pectin From Apple Pomace
- Phyto Tea (Herbal Tea)
- Pickles And Sauces
- Pickles Murabba Etc. (Veg. & Non. Veg.Pickles)
- Piggery Meat Process
- Pine-Apple Juice Preparation & Packaging
- Potato Chips/Waffers
- Potato Powder
- Pouch Filling & Packaging Of Edible Oil & Ghee
- Poultry Feed
- Processed Foods & Spices (Eou)
- Processed Readymade Food
- Processing Of Fruits & Vegetables
- Puree, Paste, Juice And Ketchup From Khajoor (Dates)
- Rabbit Farming
- Rasgullas Making & Canning In Metal Cans
- Ready To Eat Processed Cooked Food
- Ready To Eat Retort Packed Food
- Ready To Eat Snack Food (Crax, Roll & Ball Type)
- Rice & Corn Flakes
- Rice Noodles
- Roasted/Salted/Masala,Cashew Nuts, Almonds & Peanuts
- Roller Flour Mill (Atta, Suja And Maida)
- Salt Licks For Cattle
- Sattu
- Sausages Food Casing
- Soft Drinks (Cold Drinks)
- Soft Drinks Essences
- Soft Drinks (Non Carbonated) Mango,Licchi, Pineapple Flavours Frooti Type In Tetrapack)
- Softy Ice Cream Cones (Fully Automatic)
- Soft/Cold Drinks (Cola, Orange, Lemon Etc. Flavours)
- Soyabean Products
- Soyabean Bariyan
- Soya Milk & Paneer
- Spices/Masala With Formulae
- Spices And Namkeen (Integrated Unit)
- Snack Food (Kurkure Type)
- Starch & Allied Propduct From Broken Rice
- Strawberry Cultivation & Processing
- Sugarcane Juice Preservation
- Sugar Cubes From Cane Sugar
- Sugar Plant
- Supari (Sweet) – Betel Nut (Synthetic)
- Sweet Aroma Betel Nut
- Synthetic Tallow
- Tamarind Juice Powder
- Tamarind Juice Concentrates
- Tea & Coffee Processing & Packaging
- Toffees, Golies, Candy (Hard Boiled)
- Tomato Products
- Tomato Ketchup, Tomato Puree And Tomato Juice (Tomato Products)
- Trading Business Of Spices & Pan Masala
- Tuity Fruity
- Vermicilli (Including Roasted Vermicilli)
- Virgin Coconut Oil
- Vodka From Potatoes
- Wallnut Processing
- Wine, Brandy, Whisky &Champagne
- Wine From Dates
- Yeast From Molasses
- Zarda, Kimam No. 60,90,120,160,240,300 & 400 (Tobacco)
- Zarda Kimam And Tobacco
- Zarda-Zafrani (Babachhaptype)

GUMS AND ADHESIVES

- Acrylic Adhesive
- Adhesive (Different Types)
- Adhesive (Fevicol Type)
- Adhesive For Stickers
- Adhesive Based On Vinyl Acetate
- Adhesive Based On Polyurethane
- Adhesive For Band Aid (Johnson & Johnson Type)
- Adhesive Industries (Laminated, Sticker,Ddl & Other Types)
- Adhesive For Gasket (Liquid/Paste)
- Araldyte Type Adhesive
- Alkyd Resin
- Bopp Self Adhesive Tapes
- Cyanoacrylate Adhesive
- Ester Gums
- Fevicol Type Adhesive
- Guar Gum
- Gum Bottle (Pvc)
- Gum For Pasting Labels
- Leather To Leather Adhesive
- Liquid Adhesive For Corrugated Boxes
- Office Paste
- Poly Amide Resin
- Pressure Sensitive Adhesive
- Pvc Indulation Tapes
- Printing Gums (Guar Gum Based)
- Rubber Adhesive
- Self Adhesive Labels
- Starch And Dextrin Based Afhesive
- Surgical Adhesive Plaster
- Synthetic Rubber Adhesive
- Synthetic Adhesive For Decorative Laminate Bonding
- Tapioca Starch Adhesive
- Vinyl Ester Adhesive
- Vulcanising Adhesive Formulation Vulcanizing Rubber Solution/Cement For Automobile Tyre
- Urea Formaldehyde Resin
- Water Based Latex Adhesive

Contact EIRI
for required Project report apart from this list.

Market Survey Cum Detailed Techno Economic Feasibility Report on all Projects are available Contact.
"ENGINEERS INDIA RESEARCH INSTITUTE", 4449, Nai Sarak (D), Main Road, Delhi-110006 (India)
Ph. : 09811437895, 91-11-23918117, 23916431, 45120361, 64727385 Fax : 91-11-23916431
E-mail : eiriprojects@gmail.com, eiribooks@yahoo.com • website: www.eiri.in, www.eiriindia.org

ALL FOLLOWING PROJECT REPORTS ARE READILY AVAILABLE

PAINT, ENAMEL, SOLVENTS, THINNERS, INKS & VARNISH
PAINT, ENAMEL, SOLVENTS, THINNERS, INKS & VARNISH

- Acrylic Emulsion Paints
- Acrylic Cement Paint (Dry Powder)
- Aluminium Paint
- Automobile Paints
- Ball Point Pen Refill Ink
- Bituminious Road Emulsion
- Bitumen
- Bituminious Felts For Water & Damp Proofing
- Bituminious Road Emulsion Rapid Medium & Slow Setting
- Buffing & Polishing
- Cement Paint For White & Grey Cement
- Dispersant
- Dry Distemper
- Dry Distemper & Cement Paint
- Duplicating Ink Black For Gestner Duplicator
- Emulsion Paints (Water Based)
- Hammertone Paint
- Insulating Varnish & Wire Enamel
- Iron Oxide Pigments
- Insulating Varnish (Poly Vinyl Butyral Based, Ffc Grade)
- Lime Colour (Cement Colour)
- Synthetic Red Oxide For Floorings
- Solvent & Thinners
- Marking Inks (Water Proof)
- Metal Naphthanate (As Drier For Paints)
- N.C.Putty
- Offset Printing Ink
- Oil Bound Distemper Paint
- Paint Brushes
- Paint Manufacture For Rolling Coating Of Aluminium And Steel Coil
- Paint Removers
- Paint Industry
- Paint & Varnish
- Picture Varnish
- Powder Coating Paint
- Printing Inks (Offset,Flexo & Roto Gravure)
- Primer Paint & Enamel Paint
- Putty & Water Proofing Paint
- Printing Inks (Flexo-Graphic Ink)
- Putty (Metal Casement)
- Red Oxide Primer (Anti Corrosive)
- Refrectory Paint (Graphite Based)
- Screen Printing Inks
- Silk Screen Printing Ink Formulation For Plastic, Paper, Cloth
- Stamp & Pad Ink
- Stoving Paint
- Spirit Soluble Maleic Resin
- Texture Paint
- Thinners And Its Allied Products
- Toner Ink
- Varnish Thinner (Solvent)
- Vacuum Metallizing Lacquers
- Wood Primer

PHARMACEUTICAL, DRUGS, AYURVEDIC/HERBAL COSMETICS & MEDICINES, HOMOEOPATHIC MEDICINES, HOMOEOPATHIC MEDICINES, DISPOSABLE SYRINGE, DENTAL COLLEGE & FINE CHEMICALS ETC. MEDICINES, HOMOEOPATHIC MEDICINES, DISPOSABLE SYRINGE, DENTAL COLLEGE & FINE CHEMICALS ETC.

- Aromatic Pills
- Alumina From Bauxite
- Aspirin
- Ayurvedic Pain Balm Ointments
- Ayurvedic Churan And Tablets
- Ayurvedic Tablets (Hajmola Type)
- Ayurvedic/Herbalpharmacy
- Ayurvedic Sherbats
- Ayurvedic Products
- Bulk Drugs (E.O.U)
- Blood Bags
- Calcium Gluconate
- Capsule, Tablet & Injection With Modern Instruments
- Cashew Feni
- Chloroquinone Phosphate (Bulk Drugs)
- Clinical Thermometer
- Dental Clinic
- Dental College
- Dental Grade Eugenol
- Dextrose Monohydrate, Liquid Glucose
- Dehydrated Onion & Onion Powder
- Dextrose Powder (Anhydrous From Starch)
- Dextrose Saline Solution
- Distillery (I.M.F.L)
- Disposable Needles For Syringes
- Disprin
- Distilled Water
- Empty Hard Gelatine Capsules
- Fairness Cream
- Filling & Packing Of Capsules
- Glucose - D - Powder
- Glycerine
- Hair Colour Mate (Formulations And Process Only)
- Herbal Cosmetics
- Herbal Shampoo
- Herbal Shampoo And Cream
- Herbal Hair Oils (Ayurvedic)
- Homoe & Bio-Medicines With Mother Tincture
- Homoepathic Medicines
- Hypodermic Needles
- I.V. Fluids
- Ibuprofen
- Infusion & Transfusion Sets (I.V. Set)
- Injectable For Pharmaceuticals
- Injection Ampoules Packaging Box
- Integerated Surgical Cotton
- Ice Making Plant
- Ice & Cold Storage
- Lactose & By Products Processing From Milk
- Lichen (Jatamansi Charila)
- Liquid Glucose And Its By-Products
- L-Lysine Monohydro Chloride
- Liquid Glucose From Potatoes
- Medical College
- Methanol (Hpcl Grade)
- Nicotine From Tobacco Waste
- Ointment-Ayurvedic (Yellow & White)
- Pharmaceutical And Food Grade Gelatine
- Pharmaceutical Industry (Tablets, Capsules, Liquid, Gel, Ointment Powder Injectable)
- Pharmaceutical Unit (Eou) With Formulations, Injectables, Etc.
- Pyridine & Derivatives
- Salt (Iodized Salt)
- Saline & Injection Water
- Saline Water & Dextrose Solution (I.V.Fluid In Plastic Bottles)
- Sorbitol
- Starch (Maize)
- Surgical Adhesive Plaster
- Surgical Bandages
- Surgical Gloves
- Surgical Cotton
- Surgical Cotton And Bandage
- Synthetic Camphor Powder
- Tablets & Capsules
- Tissue Culture
- Tincture From Rectified Spirit
- Trimethopime
- Veterinary College With Hospital
- Veterenary Medicines (Only Formulations)
- Vitamin 'C', Sorbitol' Anhydrous Dextrose, Starch

Market Survey Cum Detailed Techno Economic Feasibility Report on all Projects are available Contact.
"ENGINEERS INDIA RESEARCH INSTITUTE". 4449, Nai Sarak (D), Main Road, Delhi-110006 (India)
Ph. : 09811437895, 91-11-23918117, 23916431, 45120361, 64727385 Fax : 91-11-23916431
E-mail : eiriprojects@gmail.com, eiribooks@yahoo.com • website: www.eiri.in, www.eiriindia.org